The Economic Anatomy of a Drug War

The Economic Anatomy of a Drug War
Criminal Justice in the Commons

David W. Rasmussen
and
Bruce L. Benson

Rowman and Littlefield Publishers, Inc.

ROWMAN & LITTLEFIELD PUBLISHERS, INC.

Published in the United States of America
by Rowman & Littlefield Publishers, Inc.
4720 Boston Way, Lanham, Maryland 20706

3 Henrietta Street, London WC2E 8LU, England

British Cataloging in Publication Information Available

Library of Congress Cataloging-in-Publication Data

Rasmussen, David W.
The economic anatomy of a drug war : criminal justice in the commons / David W. Rasmussen and Bruce L. Benson.
p. cm.
Includes bibliographical references and index.
1. Narcotics, Control of—Economic aspects—United States. 2. Drug abuse—Government policy—United States. 3. Drug traffic—United States. 4. Narcotics and crime—United States. I. Benson, Bruce, 1949– . II. Title.
HV5825.R37 1994 338.4'336345'0973—dc20 93–49436 CIP

ISBN 0–8476–7909–8 (cloth : alk. paper)
ISBN 0–8476–7910–1 (pbk. : alk. paper)

Printed in the United States of America

∞™ The paper used in this publication meets the minimum requirements of American National Standard for Information Sciences—Permanence of Paper for Printed Library Materials, ANSI Z39.48–1984.

To

Lacey and Kaitlin

Sarah, Kathryn, and James

Contents

Preface

This research effort began in 1988 when we were given an opportunity to propose an economic research agenda on drug policy to the Florida Legislature. Our early work focused on drug policy per se, but as the project developed we saw that the unintended consequences of the 1984–1989 acceleration of drug enforcement revealed many of the reasons behind the general failings of the criminal justice system. In particular, this war on drugs was conducted as if there were unlimited criminal justice resources. We came to recognize that these resources are used in a common pool environment in which none of the principal players have explicit incentives to use these resources efficiently. The "tragedy of the commons" is reflected in the unintended consequences of rising drug enforcement that are revealed in this book. Although emphasis on drug enforcement in the United States waned after 1989, the adverse effects of the drug war on the criminal justice system are not so easily reversed.

Focusing on the opportunity costs of law enforcement resources, the common pool aspects of the system, and the incentives that influence policymakers in the criminal justice arena, this book uses economics to analyze the efficacy of drug policy during 1984–1989 when it is viewed in the context of the entire criminal justice system. This inquiry reveals excesses of drug policy that are rooted in fundamental problems that plague the criminal justice system. The scope of our study is reflected in the questions we try to answer. What are the consequences of increased drug enforcement in an environment with limited criminal justice resources? How does the "tragedy of the commons" associated with the common-pool criminal justice system lead to the inefficient use of these resources? Why are criminal justice resources allocated in the way that they are? Are there institutional changes that can improve resource allocation in the criminal justice system? What drug policies might be both politically feasible and cost effective from this broader perspective?

Truth in advertising is important. We have limited ourselves to our areas of expertise, which include policy issues involving the responses of drug markets to drug enforcement, policy decisionmaking in a common pool environment, and the opportunity costs of criminal justice resources. These issues, which to date have not received the attention they are due, are crucial to the careful analysis of policies designed to combat drug use. Perhaps more important, they also point to institutional reforms that may be required to achieve safer communities. We argue that such institutional changes can lead to creative policy innovations by state and local governments that are unlikely under the current policy regime that emphasizes national initiatives to combat drug use. We do not discuss what is perhaps the most effective long-term policy that might alleviate the worst concentrations of crime and drugs: increasing legal opportunities for income in our most distressed communities. There is ample evidence supporting the notion that better opportunities for legal income reduces participation in drug dealing and reduces other criminal activity.

To argue, as some have, that an effective drug policy is only possible if the economically disadvantaged get better educational opportunities and higher income is a cop-out. Many things in this society would be better if we could achieve these goals. The immediate problem for the criminal justice system is not to design a drug policy in a world with good and equal opportunity for acquiring income-producing skills; it is to consider drug policy in a society with a large number of children being raised in poverty, that has a high rate of functional illiteracy, and that is plagued by high crime rates in dysfunctional communities. This reality makes it all the more important to develop a rational drug policy which does not abuse the criminal justice commons: the existing policies, which make communities less safe in the attempt to combat drugs, may even diminish the chances for upward mobility for people in these neighborhoods. A drug policy that is rooted in the economic realities associated with the scarcity of criminal justice resources and the unintended consequences of their use is likely to help, not harm, our most vulnerable communities.

Grandiose plans to implement the best policy can be the enemy of good policy. Striving for the "best" drug policy, one that would eliminate illicit drug use, is manifested in the quixotic prohibition crusades that have punctuated U.S. history. Our most recent attempt at achieving this goal, the 1984-1989 "drug war" which proclaimed "zero tolerance," demonstrated the futility of eschewing good policies in favor of what some policy advocates perceive to be the best. Good policy is typically less ambitious than the best, settles for smaller victories, and generally has less appeal in our political environment that nourishes hyperbole. Good policy recognizes the human frailties that the Parke-Davis Pharmaceutical Company implicitly recognized in a late nineteenth century advertisement: it told of a cocaine kit offering a drug that "can supply the place of food, make a coward brave, the silent eloquent and . . . render the suffering insensitive to pain" (Musto, 1991:44). Such goods, whatever the long-term consequences of their use, will always be in demand. In addition, young people will reliably experiment with things condemned by their elders, thereby assuring parents in each generation that their concerns about drug abuse are not in vain. Substance abuse policy is an enduring issue.

A blueprint for a rational drug policy will not be found in these pages. We emphasize the need to discuss all the costs, both direct and indirect, of drug policy alternatives. Any policy (barring those that trammel constitutional rights) which receives broad public support, after the full costs are disclosed, deserves, in our view, careful consideration. Our complaint is that criminal justice policy is sometimes formed behind a veil of legislative and agency self-interest that systematically obscures its true costs. We do not offer many specific suggestions for better drug policy. Instead, we emphasize the questions which must be addressed to rationalize the policy, the questions that are usually glossed over with political rhetoric. When resources are scarce, hard questions must be answered. We provide the questions, many of which are not currently encountered in discussions of drug policy; we argue many of the answers can be found in policy experiments and a public debate that gets beyond the parochial interests of the people who make drug policy.

We hope, in our most optimistic moments, that this book accomplishes two things. One goal is to inform the public debate on drug policy about the unintended consequences that accompanied the rapid rise in drug enforcement during the 1984–1989 period. Our second goal is to stimulate debate about the structure of the criminal justice system itself: how can incentives be changed to prevent the squandering of these common pool resources by the makers and defenders of the law?

Acknowledgments

Our gratitude extends to many people who have helped launch this book. Since it originated in a study done for the State of Florida, we are particularly grateful to Jim Zingale who saw the need for an economic analysis of drug enforcement policy. Ed Montanaro and his staff at the Florida Legislature's Division of Economic and Demographic Research, particularly Wendy Westling, Richard Stephens, and Ken Trager, were especially helpful in the early stages of our research on drug policy. Bob Bradley provided valuable assistance in helping design our early work focusing on Florida. Bill Bales and Linda Dees were helpful on the corrections aspects of these initial technical studies using Florida data.

A special thanks is due Iljoong Kim, Brent Mast, David Sollars, and Tom Zuehlke, co-authors of various technical papers cited in this book. Colleagues who have commented on our technical papers have also contributed greatly to this final product. Among them are Paul Beaumont, Gary Fournier, Henry Glick, Leroy Gould, Barry Hirsch, Randy Holcombe, David Macpherson, and Tim Sass. Joe Bast and Diane Bast of the Heartland Institute gave valuable comments on our monograph investigating the consequences of escalating drug enforcement in Illinois. Charles Barrilleaux, Dan Benjamin, Gary Fournier, and Barbara Morgan read the manuscript and offered many suggestions which improved the final product.

Research related to this book was funded in part by Florida's Institute of Government through its Service through Applied Research Program, the Florida Legislature, the Heartland Institute, the Policy Sciences Center at Florida State University, and a grant from Florida State University's Committee on Faculty Research Support. William E. Laird, chair of the economics department at Florida State, also provided valuable support that was instrumental to the completion of this project. A special thanks goes to Valerie N. Colvin, art publication/production specialist in the Policy Sciences Center, for her efforts in preparing this book for publication.

Chapter 1

The Rhetoric and Reality of Drug Policy

Episodic bursts of activity to combat drug and alcohol use in this century suggest that drugs are an enduring policy issue in America. Perceptions of rising rates of addiction to opium and cocaine during the latter decades of the nineteenth century, partly caused by unrestrained prescription of drugs by physicians, gradually reduced political tolerance of drug use and eventually led to passage of the Harrison Act in 1914. Other episodes of intolerance toward drug use centered on passage of the Volstead Act in 1919, which started thirteen years of alcohol prohibition, and the Marijuana Tax Act of 1937, which was accompanied by outrageous claims about the deleterious effects of this drug. More recently, drug enforcement activities of state and local police agencies rose dramatically during 1965–1970 and 1984–1989. The Office of Drug Control Policy was created in 1989 and with it the "drug czar," a position symbolizing the political commitment against drug use.

Interest in drug policy diminished after 1989, as indicated by a huge decline in the number of survey respondents identifying drug abuse as the nation's most important problem: from 38 percent in November 1989 to 11 percent in March 1991.[1] Drug enforcement issues receded in importance as reduction of the national debt, slow economic growth, medical care reform, and international issues took center stage. This is to be expected. Political issues are constantly emerging and competing for public attention. Most never capture the public imagination; a few are "hot" for a short period, and then settle into the relative oblivion of unsolved problems which are addressed by countless agencies of government, public interest groups, and some private businesses. Only very occasionally an issue emerges that has a major impact on the political landscape.[2]

Anthony Downs (1972:39) argues that domestic "crises" do not result from changes in real conditions but reflect "a systematic cycle of heightening public interest and then increasing boredom with major issues." In his view there is an "issue-attention" cycle, which suggests even a problem of continuing concern cannot continually command the public interest. Since drug policy has regularly emerged during the past century as a winner in the competition among issues, the search for a rational drug control policy is an issue of enduring public concern and not an isolated flare-up on the policy scene. The recurring emergence of drug abuse led Buchanan (1992) to argue that there are long cycles in public tolerance of drugs, the first dating back to rising rates of alcohol use after the Revolution, which are related to deeper institutional and ideological concerns than suggested by Downs' view of an easily bored public. Musto (1991) also sees cycles in U.S. attitudes toward drug use, but attributes them to the consequences of drug use rather than more fundamental social issues. Early in the cycle of increasing drug use there are relatively few casualties, but as the unfortunate effects of excessive drug use mount over time, public tolerance of the abused substance falls.

Whatever the cause of the apparent long cycles in drug use, and despite the vagaries of public opinion and political opportunity that lead to the periodic resurgence of interest in drug policy, a better understanding of drug enforcement policy is important. Even when this issue is in a relatively fallow period in the public consciousness, the absolute impact of drug use and enforcement is large. Alternative uses of scarce state and local government finances is an obvious concern, as are the social costs of crime, health care costs associated with drug abuse, the potential economic costs of lost worker productivity, and the plight of communities devastated by the drug trade.

The successive waves of interest in drug control have done little to improve policy discourse. Throughout this century fear, prejudice, and ignorance have consistently overwhelmed objective appraisals of alternative drug policies in the United States. America's first war on drugs began with the Harrison Act in 1914 and was conceived when the prevailing political view held that opiates and cocaine led to insanity and criminal activity. The conventional wisdom, obviously formulated by white males, held that cocaine degraded "unfortunate women" and created "the wild Negro" while opium was used by the "devious Chinese."[3] Suppression of narcotics increased in the combustible atmosphere created by the "red scare" of 1919, when fears of social disintegration at the hands of socialists, anarchists, radical trade unionists, and foreigners fueled the largely unsubstantiated fears that would become a regular feature of discussions of drug policy.

Contemporary debates over drug policy are not much more rational than these early diatribes, despite increasing medical and social science research that could provide a more informed basis for public action against drugs.[4] Justice William O. Douglas wrote in 1960:

> To be a confirmed addict is to be one of the walking dead. . . . The teeth have rotted out; the appetite is lost and the stomach and intestines don't function properly. . . . Good traits of character disappear and bad ones emerge. . . . Imaginary and fantastic fears blight the mind and sometimes complete insanity results.

Justice Hugo Black joined Douglas in a dissenting opinion in the 1969 case *Turner v. United States* to argue:

> Commercial traffic in deadly mind, soul, and body destroying drugs is beyond a doubt one of the greatest evils of our time. It cripples intellects, dwarfs bodies, paralyzes the progress of a substantial segment of our society, and frequently makes hopeless and sometimes violent and murderous criminals of persons of all ages who become its victims.

In 1982, toughness toward these "heinous" drug crimes was reflected in the Arctic Penitentiary Act, introduced in the U.S. House of Representatives for the purpose of creating "an American Gulag" to punish drug offenders. In 1989, a court argued that any offense for drug sale, no matter how small the amount, was worse than murder.

> Except in rare cases, the murderer's red hand falls on one victim only, however grim the blow; but the foul hand of the drug dealer blights life after life and, like the vampire of fable, creates others in its owner's evil image—others who create others still, across our land and down our generations, sparing not even the unborn.

The Office of National Drug Control Strategy (1989) advocated a drug-free society, declaring "clearly and emphatically that there is no such thing as innocent drug use." In the same year the Supreme Court supported the need to "beat back the drug scourge. . . as much a danger. . . to our country as is an external enemy." The trend in drug policy for much of this century can be characterized by a movement toward implementation of President Reagan's 1982 statement that "Drugs are bad and we are going after them" (Zimring and Hawkins, 1992:47).

Driven by powerful beliefs, drug policy is easily reduced to hyperbole, unrealistic expectations, and denial of the inevitable tradeoffs that accompany public action. Drug policy is often discussed as if the resources available to stop drug use are unlimited: witness the recent policy of zero tolerance in which law enforcement resources were spent trying to find a few marijuana stems and seeds on boats and in cars. Advocating a drug-free society makes good rhetoric, but is not an appropriate basis for drug policy. Perfection in this regard is not possible for two reasons. First, throughout its history, inhabitants of this planet have used mind-altering substances of one sort or another. Whatever human traits are responsible for this behavior, it is far fetched to think that they can be eliminated in contemporary America.[5] Demand for these commodities exists. Second, whatever our commitment to a drug-free society in the abstract, movement toward that goal requires real resources that could be used for something else. Our willingness to reduce our standard of living in order to combat drug use is limited. In an ideal world perhaps no one would ingest dangerous substances; but given finite resources, a rational enforcement strategy must accept some drug use as a matter of policy. Baltimore Mayor Kurt Schmoke was right when in 1988 he testified before the U.S. House of Representatives Select Committee on Narcotics Abuse and Control that "zero use, or zero tolerance, as it is sometimes called, is not a policy at all—it is a fantasy."[6]

At the turn of the century, debate about drug policy was based on relatively little knowledge about the pharmacological aspects of drugs. There was no social science research that could shed light on the connection between drug use and criminal activity. This ignorance could perhaps excuse the hyperbole, paranoia, and prejudice that passed for policy discussion in 1900. This excuse cannot be applied to the political entrepreneurs, interest groups, and public agencies that have supported the acceleration of drug enforcement in the past thirty years and, more particularly, engineered a rapid escalation of the "drug war" during the years 1984–1989. There is now a wealth of solid policy research, which, despite data limitations, provides a firm foundation for a more rational discussion of drug policy. Research now sheds light on the effects of drug use, tendencies toward addiction, connections between drug use and criminality, and lifestyles of persons in the drug culture. This research should be incorporated into a drug policy debate which accepts the reality that there are limited resources available to combat the "scourge" of illicit drugs—

police, social workers, courts, treatment facilities, and prisons will forever be inadequate to achieve anything resembling a drug-free society.

This book brings a new perspective to the debate over drug policy by providing an economic analysis of illicit drug enforcement by the criminal justice system. One widely cited definition of economics is that it is the social science concerned with the way society's scarce resources are allocated among alternative uses. Most people think of the cost of something as the money paid for it. Economists do not; they focus on what is called "opportunity cost," the idea that when scarce resources are used to do one thing, they cannot be used to do something else. Opportunity costs are the alternative uses of resources that must be sacrificed. When costs are viewed in terms of forgone opportunities it is clear that a decision to use resources in a particular way may have consequences, or costs, some of which may not be anticipated by policymakers who tend to focus on a program's impact on the budget rather than on lost opportunities. The economic perspective is particularly relevant to drug policy because America's political process has criminalized the use of many drugs and because criminal justice resources are scarce.

In addition to emphasizing resource allocation and opportunity costs, the economic approach to policy analysis focuses on the incentives that individuals face as they react to constraints. Constraints arise naturally because resources are scarce. They also arise because laws are passed and enforced. Thus, for instance, if participants in the drug trade weigh the expected benefits of this illegal activity against the expected costs, including the costs associated with the probability and severity of punishment, then certain kinds of responses can be predicted as either the costs or benefits of their activities change. Some of those responses may not be anticipated in the absence of an economic analysis, and importantly, these predictions can be tested using statistical or historical data.

Economists have been exploring criminal behavior from this perspective for some time now, but we go beyond much of the economics of crime literature by considering rational responses to incentives, both for those involved in illicit drug markets, and for those involved in decisions about the establishment and enforcement of drug laws. For example, legislators at the federal, state, and local levels, whose own incentives are at least partly tied to reelection, face constraints arising from competing demands for the allocation of tax dollars and simultaneous pressure to hold down taxes. As a consequence, substantially fewer resources are going to be available for law enforcement than would be necessary for solving even a majority of crimes reported or imprisoning most of the criminals caught and successfully prosecuted. The ability of the criminal justice system to police the black markets, such as those in which drugs are traded, is further limited because there rarely is an identifiable "victim" in the form of someone who will report such crimes (Miron, 1991, 1992). Policing will be far from complete or perfect, so participants in illicit drug markets are willing to break the law because they perceive that the benefits from doing so will outweigh the risk of arrest and prosecution. Because law enforcement resources are limited, decisions made within the criminal justice system regarding the control of illicit drug markets are part of a resource allocation problem that is in the domain of economics. As we show in the next section, America has relied on its criminal justice system to escalate the war on drugs.

I. Fighting Drugs

Two "drug wars" have been waged since World War II. Precisely identifying the "outbreak" of these wars is more difficult than in the case of their military counterparts. One method of dating the hostilities is identification of key pieces of legislation or presidential announcements.[7] An alternative and perhaps more satisfying method relies on direct measurement of changes in the allocation of criminal justice resources to drug enforcement. There are several alternative types of data that could be used to measure the extent to which criminal justice system resources are devoted to drug enforcement, including budget allocations, interdiction efforts, prison admissions, and arrest statistics. For now, we focus on the latter.

Using drug arrests per 100,000 population to measure the growth of U.S. drug enforcement, Table 1.1 shows a dramatic increase in this effort since 1960. Drug arrests per 100,000 population reached its peak level of 538 in 1989, a twenty-fold increase from its 1960 level of twenty-six. The drug arrest rate did not increase steadily, however. Most of the increase in drug arrests per 100,000 population occurred in ten of these thirty years of escalating drug enforcement. The first escalation of drug enforcement occurred between 1965 and 1970, when the drug arrest rate rose from thirty-four to 228, a 114 percent average annual rate of increase. Following this burst of anti-drug activity, the drug arrest rate grew slowly between 1970 and 1984, about 2.6 percent per year. Renewed escalation of drug enforcement during the 1984–1989 period saw arrests per 100,000 population rise from 312 to 538, an average annual increase of 14.5 percent. Although the growth rate of drug arrests in this latter period is dwarfed by the 114 percent annual growth of the 1965–1970 period, the absolute increase in drug arrests per capita was largest during the

Table 1.1: Growth of Drug Enforcement in the United States, 1960–1991

Year	Drug Arrests per 100,000 Population	Average Annual Percentage Change
1960	26	
1965	34	6.2
1970	228	114.1
1980	256	2.5
1984	312	4.4
1989	538	14.5
1990	449	–16.5
1991	411	–8.5

Source: U.S. Department of Justice, *Crime in the United States*, (various years).

1984–1989 escalation of drug enforcement. Together the 1965–1970 and 1984–1989 periods account for over 80 percent of the increase in the drug arrest rate from 1960 to 1990. Rapidly escalating drug enforcement during the 1965–1970 period was followed by continued slow growth, whereas the 1984–1989 increase in the drug arrest rate was followed by a period of marked retrenchment. Drug arrests per 100,000 population fell 16.5 percent in 1990 and another 8.5 percent in 1991, from 538 per 100,000 population in 1989 to 411 in 1991. The decline in the drug arrest rate in 1990 alone (i.e., eighty-nine) is larger in absolute terms than its increase in the fourteen years between 1970 and 1984. While the rhetoric of the drug war was unabated during 1990, the reality was a declining drug arrest rate.

Rapidly changing drug enforcement provides an opportunity to explore two themes that are emphasized in this book. First, increasing enforcement efforts against one type of crime relative to others is likely to have significant consequences for the rest of the criminal justice system. Rapidly rising drug enforcement in 1984–1989 provides a unique social experiment in which to observe how the drug war can compromise law enforcement efforts against other crimes by tying up scarce criminal justice resources. Using police, court, and prison resources to combat drug use means they cannot be used to fight other crimes.[8] This cost of drug enforcement is rarely considered in the drug policy debate. The costs of accelerated enforcement can continue long after drug enforcement policy loses its place in the spotlight on the policy stage. Table 1.1 shows the policy cycle since 1960 has had a ratchet effect: a period of increased drug enforcement can permanently push the drug arrest rate above its previous level. A second theme of this book is an exploration of the incentives influencing legislators, police, and the courts in order to understand why the growth of drug enforcement has been so uneven over the 1960–1990 period. More importantly, incentives affecting these key players in drug enforcement policy reveal institutional factors that help explain the rapid growth of drug arrests, a policy which enhances the chances of court delays, early release of prisoners from overcrowded prisons, and a potential misallocation of criminal justice resources.

National data for the United States conceal enormous variation in drug enforcement among state and local jurisdictions. Drug arrests per 100,000 population for the states are shown in Table 1.2. In 1989, they range from a low of eighty-eight (West Virginia) to a high of 1,060 (California). Relatively few states account for a disproportionately large number of the nation's drug arrests. Only eight states have a drug arrest rate higher than the national average of 538, for example. Police in these jurisdictions make over 60 percent of the nation's drug arrests, but these states—Connecticut, Georgia, Maryland, Massachusetts, New York, New Jersey, Florida, and California—account for only 36 percent of the U.S. population. Escalating drug enforcement during the 1984–1989 period was the norm among states, however, with the average increase being 72.4 percent. All but six states increased their drug arrest/population ratio over this period and nine increased it by over 100 percent. Twenty-fifth-ranked Hawaii had a 1989 drug arrest rate of 355, a figure almost 14 percent higher than the national average in 1984. Significantly, populous states like Illinois, Michigan, Ohio, and Pennsylvania, which combined account for about one-sixth of the nation's population, more than doubled their drug arrest rates while remaining below the national average of 538 per 100,000

Table 1.2: Drug Arrests per 100,000 Population, by State, 1984 and 1989

State	Rank	1989	1984	% Change	State	Rank	1989	1984	% Change
Alabama	21	392	190	106.3	Montana	27	332	130	155.4
Alaska	44	162	120	35.0	Nebraska	32	283	150	88.7
Arizona	11	519	380	36.6	Nevada	42	170	110	54.5
Arkansas	30	311	230	35.2	New Hampshire	35	265	138	92.0
California	1	1,060	590	79.7	New Jersey	2	895	460	94.6
Colorado	33	279	230	21.3	New Mexico	13	454	300	51.3
Connecticut	8	647	270	139.6	New York	3	799	510	56.7
Delaware	28	329	230	43.0	North Carolina	20	411	261	57.5
Florida	6	675	360	87.5	North Dakota	49	107	160	–33.1
Georgia	7	661	344	92.1	Ohio	17	426	190	124.2
Hawaii	25	355	420	–15.5	Oklahoma	29	327	270	21.1
Idaho	39	221	140	57.9	Oregon	15	438	240	82.5
Illinois	14	446	120	271.7	Pennsylvania	34	274	130	110.8
Indiana	41	189	130	45.4	Rhode Island	19	422	380	11.1
Iowa	46	119	90	32.2	South Carolina	12	470	300	56.7
Kansas	37	233	140	66.4	South Dakota	47	118	190	–37.9
Kentucky	9	528	300	76.0	Tennessee	36	263	160	64.4
Louisiana	10	526	270	94.8	Texas	16	433	360	20.3
Maine	38	229	130	76.1	Utah	31	291	320	–9.1
Maryland	4	776	420	84.8	Vermont	48	109	n.a.	n.a.
Massachusetts	5	689	310	122.3	Virginia	26	341	200	70.5
Michigan	23	374	170	120.0	Washington	24	369	170	117.1
Minnesota	45	161	130	23.8	West Virginia	50	88	100	–12.0
Mississippi	22	375	190	97.4	Wisconsin	40	207	200	3.5
Missouri	18	422	240	75.8	Wyoming	43	169	180	–6.1
					United States		538	312	72.4

Source: U.S. Department of Justice, Bureau of Justice Statistics (1984/1989).

population in 1989. If the most ardent drug warriors are the states with an above-average drug arrest rate in 1989 plus those with a doubling of this rate from 1984 to 1989, over 50 percent of the nation's population resides in states which have been full participants in the drug war. This is a very stringent definition, however. Many other states' drug policy fit into a national profile of escalating enforcement: consider Arizona with a 1989 arrest rate of 519, up 37 percent from 1984; Kentucky, arrest rate of 528 in 1989, up 76 percent; Mississippi, arrest rate of 375 in 1989, up 97 percent; Missouri, 1989 arrest rate of 422, up 76 percent; and Oregon, with its 1989 arrest rate of 438, up 83 percent from 1984.

Even state-level data may not reveal the extent of variation in drug enforcement. States with large urban populations tend to be among those with the highest drug arrest rates, for instance, a tendency confirmed by the fact that large cities generally have drug arrest rates above the national average and above that of their respective states. As shown in Table 1.3, all cities with a population over 1 million and most with populations between 500,000 and 1 million have relatively high drug arrest rates. Houston has the lowest drug arrest rate among the cities with over 1 million population, but it exceeds the Texas average by over 55 percent and the national average by 3 percent. There is considerable variation among cities with populations between 500,000 and 1 million, as reflected in the relatively low drug arrest rates in Columbus (283), El Paso (349), and Indianapolis (232) compared to Baltimore (2,063), Washington, D.C. (1,738), and Cleveland (1,333). Surprisingly, the drug arrest rate of the notorious District of Columbia is not atypical; when compared to that of other large cities, it is actually lower than the rates in San Diego, Baltimore, San Francisco, Oakland, Fremont, Jersey City, New Haven, Newark, and Springfield. Variation in drug enforcement rates is even more pronounced among jurisdictions with populations between 100,000 and 500,000, ranging from Amherst Town (33) and Madison (57) to Oakland (3,472). The national trend toward increasingly diligent police efforts against drugs between 1984 and 1989 is thus composed of a mosaic reflecting substantial local variation in drug enforcement efforts, a variation that we will attempt to explain through an economic analysis of drug enforcement policy.

II. A Preview

American policies toward mind-altering substances in this century reveal the basic alternatives. Consider the regulatory history of caffeine, tobacco, alcohol, marijuana, and opiates. Laissez-faire, the absence of regulation,

Table 1.3: Drug Related Arrests per 100,000 Population in Selected Cities, 1989

100,000–499,000		500,000–1 million		Over 1 million	
Cities:		Cities:		Cities:	
Oakland, CA	3,472	Baltimore, MD	2,063	Chicago, IL	1,157
Dayton, OH	1,010	Boston, MA	1,253	Dallas, TX	675
Fremont, CA	1,780	Cleveland, OH	1,333	Detroit, MI	1,052
Jersey City, NJ	2,754	Columbus, OH	283	Houston, TX	555
New Haven, CT	2,230	El Paso, TX	349	Los Angeles, CA	1,391
Newark, NJ	1,751	Indianapolis, IN	232	New York, NY	1,255
Peoria, IL	413	Memphis, TX	657	Philadelphia, PA	727
Pittsburgh, PA	723	Milwaukee, WI	359	San Diego, CA	1,836
Amherst Town, NY	33	Phoenix, AZ	530		
Madison, WI	57	San Antonio, TX	475		
Minneapolis, MN	162	San Francisco, CA	1,797		
Rockford, IL	111	San Jose, CA	1,289		
Savannah, GA	707	Washington, DC	1,738		
Springfield, MA	2,718				

Source: U.S. Department of Justice, Bureau of Justice Statistics, *Sourcebook, 1990*, Table 4.35.

has been the policy toward caffeine. Sale of tobacco and alcohol to minors is now prohibited, and alcohol was entirely illegal during the Prohibition era of 1920–1933. Opiates were legal until passage of the Harrison Act in 1914, and marijuana became illegal in 1937, although both of these statutes were actually tax acts rather than criminalization laws per se. All of these regulated products are addictive to some degree and/or perceived to be harmful in some way, and the dominant theme in twentieth-century America is at least partial regulation. Contemporary calls for across-the-board legalization (or decriminalization) of illicit drugs, a radical alternative to the current emphasis on criminal penalties, are not likely to be politically viable in light of this historical tendency to regulate mind-altering substances. The abrupt end to complete alcohol prohibition suggests that partial decriminalization is possible, however.

Once any kind of regulation is adopted, some enforcement mechanism is required to encourage adherence to the rules. The criminal justice system, therefore, is necessarily a potential enforcement tool in *every* regulatory effort, and has been an increasingly important tool in the fight against illicit drug consumption since 1965. Among the most important drug enforcement policy variables are the probability of being arrested, the probability of being convicted, and the severity of penalty. To the extent that the system mandates treatment, the availability and effectiveness of treatment are also part of the enforcement arsenal. Herein lies a major impediment to a coherent drug policy in America: elements of the drug enforcement system are controlled by distinct political or bureaucratic organizations, each operating under perspectives and procedures that are not necessarily governed by a compelling concern for the formulation and execution of an effective drug policy.

Drug policy is rooted in the legislative process which defines the rules governing use of mind-altering substances and determines the penalties for their violation. Funds for subsidized treatment of addicted drug users also come from legislative bodies. Persons wishing to stop their drug use, but requiring treatment assistance to do so, may not encounter the enforcement system if they can afford private treatment, have insurance that will pay for it, or have access to subsidized treatment. For persons who continue drug use, and those providing these illicit substances in black markets, local police agencies largely determine the chances of being arrested and being exposed to the prison system and/or mandatory treatment. The police, however, do not have as their primary mission the creation of a drug policy that is cost effective from a broader social perspective. Legislators give police agencies an incredibly long list of laws to be enforced, but provide budgets which are totally inadequate to the assigned task. Thus the local police play a major role in deciding how to allocate their scarce resources. The probability that criminals of all types, including drug users and sellers, are arrested, is largely determined by police policy. This discretion no doubt explains some of the diversity of drug arrest rates reported in Table 1.2 and Table 1.3. As arrested drug offenders enter the criminal justice system, the prosecutors and judges determine the penalty, which often involves incarceration—the use of prison space that is provided by the state legislature. In effect, the courts can send drug offenders to prisons which do not have space to house them, resulting in prison overcrowding and, in many circumstances, early release of drug and non-drug offenders alike. There is nothing inherent in the incentives and constraints faced in these institutions that necessarily leads them to a desirable drug policy—one that minimizes the social costs of drug abuse while at the same time deters drug use.

This book adopts an economic perspective to explore origins and effects of American drug policy, with specific emphasis on the most recent escalation of drug enforcement, the 1984–1989 period. Our goal is three-fold: (1) to clarify the fundamental scarcity issues that must be at the core of a debate on public policy directed at the control of illicit drugs; (2) to evaluate the consequences of relying on the criminal justice system to conduct the war on drugs; and (3) to understand the process by which a drug policy based on law enforcement and criminal penalties is created. A framework to organize the discussion of drug policy is badly needed. Participants in the drug policy debate often "talk past" each other, partly because the argument dwells on legalization versus the current policy of a law enforcement effort to control drugs.[9] Fundamental differences involving rights to privacy, individual freedom, moral judgments, and the efficacy of government action are among the issues that create a chasm that cannot be bridged in this policy debate. When drug policy advocates do not share any perspectives or assumptions, it is not surprising that the debate flounders. However, sometimes disagreements that appear to be rooted in different values are in fact disputes over the likely cause and effects of policy alternatives. By focusing on the reality of scarce criminal justice resources, alternative uses of these resources, the cost effectiveness of policy alternatives, and the incentives that govern players in the drug policy arena, this book takes a realistic look at what is and is not possible in the area of drug policy. Efficiency in the allocation of scarce criminal justice resources is not the only norm by which drug policy can be judged, of course, but the inevitable fact that resources are scarce means that any policy debate that ignores this issue will fail to recognize real policy consequences. By clarifying the unintended consequences of policy alternatives, we hope this book will lead to a more informed discussion of drug policy.

Law enforcement resources are allocated in an environment which does not emphasize their "highest and best use." These publicly provided services are often allocated on a first-come-first-served basis which reflects the resource allocation problems characteristic of common pool resources. When individuals who allocate resources do not pay the costs associated with their use, the efficient use of the scarce resources is unlikely. Chapter 2 shows that the "tragedy of the commons" aptly describes the resource allocation process of the police, courts, prisons, and other criminal justice resources, and, as a consequence, there are severe institutional barriers to the development of cost-effective drug enforcement practices.

The next three chapters explore some consequences of dedicating an increasing portion of criminal justice resources to combat drug use. Escalating the war on drugs has been justified in part because drug use is generally believed to cause other crime. Most common is the allegation that drug users commit property crimes to support their addiction. Violent behavior is also thought to accompany drug use. If drug users are responsible for many other crimes, a strong law enforcement effort against drugs can potentially lower the property and violent crime rates and discourage drug use simultaneously: that is, drug enforcement may be a positive sum game. Chapter 3 addresses two elements of the proposition that drug enforcement offers a bonus in the form of reduced non-drug crime. First, the reliability of police enforcement as a deterrent to drug use is explored in the context of the standard economics of crime literature. The intuitively plausible assumption that greater police enforcement and more severe penalties necessarily reduce drug use is shown to be incorrect. The bottom line is that tougher enforcement may not yield as much deterrence to drug use as expected. Second, this chapter explores the coincidence of drug use and other crime. Many government reports and academic articles suggest that a large portion of persons who commit violent and property crimes engage in substance abuse. Evidence presented in Chapter 3 suggests that most users of illicit drugs do not commit crimes against persons and property and that increasing enforcement against drug offenders cannot be justified on the grounds that these same offenders are also perpetrators of non-drug crimes.

Escalating drug enforcement can generate consequences other than those anticipated. Efforts to disrupt profitable drug markets, for example, inevitably create incentives for drug entrepreneurs to change their mode of operation in order to reduce the chances of being arrested. Chapter 4 explores how illicit drug markets respond to enhanced enforcement and concludes that buyers and sellers in illicit drug markets may react to these law enforcement efforts in ways that frustrate their intent. The scarcity of criminal justice resources also leads to an unintended consequence of increased drug enforcement: when more police and prison space is devoted to the apprehension and punishment of drug offenders these resources cannot be used to combat other crimes. The opportunity costs of reallocating criminal justice resources to control illicit drugs are explored in Chapter 5.

Chapters 2 through 5 show that unrestrained use of the criminal justice system to combat illicit drugs does not produce the consequences that many of its advocates predict, and that the unanticipated opportunity cost of the drug war may be quite high. Next, we investigate why illicit drug policy developed with such a strong emphasis on law enforcement. Chapters 6 and 7 focus on the institutional structure of the criminal justice system, suggesting that the principal players in illicit drug policy have incentives to pursue this policy while, due to the common access properties of the system, they do not have to pay many of the costs associated with the escalating war on drugs. Chapter 6 discusses the political context of the war on drugs and argues that criminal law in general, and drug enforcement policy in particular, is shaped in part by the bureaucratic interests of criminal justice agencies. The chapter explores the role of legislators and details the incentives that encourage police agencies to increase drug enforcement. Chapter 7 investigates the role the courts have played in formulating this policy. Given the institutional structure of the political and criminal justice systems, it is not surprising that the law-enforcement-effort component of drug policy has become large relative to other policy instruments.

Issues of drug policy are discussed in Chapter 8. American drug policy for the past thirty years has focused on criminal sanctions without recognizing the overall consequences for the criminal justice system. Crucial to the development of a rational drug policy is careful identification of the opportunity costs of criminal justice resources and of the institutional factors that appear to constrain policy options. Drug enforcement policy is viewed in Chapter 8 as an explicit attempt to alter the response of individuals when they encounter a money-price stimulus in a drug market. Thinking of drug enforcement policy in this context reveals many of the unintended consequences that are shown in Chapters 4 and 5. Guidelines for drug policy suggested by the analysis are discussed. These guidelines are highly relevant for the drug policy debate since they emphasize reforms that substantially reduce the opportunity costs of drug enforcement. The conclusion emphasizes that the unintended consequences of escalating drug enforcement during 1984–1989 reflect some fundamental problems of the criminal justice system that transcend the drug policy debate. Thus, this book might best be viewed as a case study which, by focusing on the issues of drug enforcement policy, reveals the fundamental flaws that characterize the criminal justice system in general.

Chapter 2

The Allocation of Law Enforcement Resources: An Overview of the Commons Problem

Congress, state legislatures, and local governments all face tremendous pressure from competing demands as they determine the allocation of tax dollars. Similar pressure to hold total taxes down also is applied. As a result, law enforcement officials (like school officials, highway officials, and officials in virtually every other government bureaucracy) probably never get as large a budget as they think they require. Even the budgets they request may be far from sufficient since bureaucrats probably recognize that their demands have to appear reasonable in order to be credible. Thus, virtually every legislator and law enforcement official recognizes that substantially fewer resources are going to be available for the enforcement of law than would be necessary for solving even a majority of the crimes reported or imprisoning most of the criminals caught and successfully prosecuted. For example, Table 2.1 shows arrests, offenses, and clearance rates for Index I crimes in the United States during 1990. Violent crimes against persons, particularly murder and aggravated assault, have a relatively high clearance rate because the victim frequently knows the offender. Burglary, larceny, and motor vehicle theft, in contrast, are offenses that typically require the police to spend resources to identify the offender. As a result, clearance rates for these offenses are about one-third of the clearance rate for violent offenses. In addition, since only a portion of the crimes committed are reported to the police by victims, the actual clearance rates are considerably lower than those in Table 2.1.[1]

In contrast to Index I crimes with identifiable victims, willing participants in illegal economic exchanges obviously have no incentive to report their offenses. In these illegal markets, principally gambling, prostitution, and drugs, scarce police resources must, therefore, be used to actually search out the offenders. Clearly, the ability of the criminal justice system to police the black markets is even more limited than it is for Index I crimes. Policing will be far from complete and perfect, so both demanders and suppliers are willing to participate in these illicit markets when they perceive that the benefits from doing so outweigh the risk of arrest and prosecution.

Because virtually all resources are limited, including those allocated by the public sector, many public sector decisions are resource allocation problems. Legislators must decide how many resources to allocate to law enforcement (e.g., police and policing capital like patrol cars and jails; courts and prosecutors; prisons, parole systems) given alternative uses of tax revenues (e.g., schooling and highways). Resources purchased for the purpose of law enforcement must be then allocated among competing uses (e.g., control of drug markets; solution of robberies and burglaries; traffic control; crime prevention efforts; solution of rapes, assaults, and murders). In the context of the apparent increasing political incentives during the 1980s to control illicit drug markets, the public sector response can take two forms. First, a legislature may allocate more total expenditures to law enforcement so that more can be allocated to drug control without sacrificing the current police efforts against other crimes. This either requires increased taxes or reduced expenditures for other publicly provided goods and services. It is more likely that competing political demands will have to be taken into account and the resulting compromises will mean that a part of the response will take a second form: the shifting of some law enforcement resources away from other uses (e.g., control of property and/or violent crime) into drug control. Consequently, it seems appropriate to examine, in some detail, the underlying mechanisms that drive the allocation of existing law enforcement resources.

I. Law Enforcement as a Common Pool Problem

When resources are scarce in the sense that the competing demands for their use far exceed their supply, they must be rationed among these competing uses. Many rationing techniques are possible. For instance, in a free market where resources are privately owned, those resources (as well

Table 2.1: Offenses and Arrests in the United States, 1990

Crime	Reported Offenses	Arrests	Percent Cleared by Arrest*
Murder	23,438	18,298	67.2
Forcible Rape	102,555	30,966	52.8
Robbery	639,271	136,300	24.9
Aggravated Assault	1,054,863	376,917	57.3
Burglary	3,073,909	341,192	13.8
Larceny	7,945,670	1,241,236	20.5
Motor Vehicle Theft	1,635,907	168,338	14.6

* An offense is cleared by arrest if at least one person is arrested, charged, and turned over to the court for prosecution. An offense can also be counted as cleared under a number of exceptional circumstances, such as suicide of the offender or if the victim refuses to cooperate in prosecution.

Source: U.S. Department of Justice, Bureau of Justice Statistics, *Sourcebook, 1991*, Tables 3.128, 4.7, and 4.20.

as goods and services) are rationed by price: anyone willing to pay the market-determined price has access to the desired resources. Public law enforcement resources are not rationed by price, of course. Indeed, some would suggest that they are not rationed at all since everyone supposedly has access to them free of charge. But the fact that no money price is charged for common access resources simply means that some other rationing criteria must arise (Stroup, 1964; Benson, 1990; Benson and Wollan, 1989).

The implications of common access, or common pool resources, have been examined extensively in relation to publicly or commonly owned resources such as grazing land and fishing grounds, but relatively little attention has been given to the fact that many law enforcement resources are in common pools.[2] The similarity between the problems which arise in grazing or fisheries commons and in law enforcement are striking, however. In the classic commons problem, for instance, when many individuals have free access to graze cattle on the same land, each has incentives to use up as much grass as possible before others with access do the same. Competition for the use of this limited resource takes the form of trying to use as much as possible before others use it up. Thus, the commons becomes crowded with cattle and the grass land is used up quickly, deteriorating rapidly in quality. This problem has been called the "tragedy of the commons." Users have incentives to overgraze the land because they are not liable for the full cost of their decisions. Others who have access to the commons must share the consequences of these actions. Individuals' incentives to limit the sizes of their herds or to consider other ways of maintaining them (e.g., supplementing the grass with feeds grown on private land) are very weak. Indeed, if an individual were to try to conserve the grazing resource by limiting his or her use or using alternatives, he or she would not reap the benefits, because others would simply increase their use; so incentives are to conserve alternatives and exploit the commons. Thus, all those with access, acting in their own self-interest, crowd and inefficiently use the commons.

"Free access" public law enforcement resources are similarly crowded and inefficiently employed. For example, prosecutors and judges have common access to prison space. They have at best only weak incentives to limit the number of prisoners they "herd into the commons" when making their sentencing recommendations and decisions, or to consider alternatives to imprisonment such as fines, restitution, community service, lesser degrees of constraint like community control, treatment programs, and work release.[3] Many such alternatives are well known to prosecutors and judges, and some are frequently employed; but the incentives to consider them are relatively weak because these decisions are made in a common pool environment. Indeed, in as much as prosecutors have incentives to demonstrate to their local constituencies that they are "tough on crime," imprisonment is a relatively attractive punishment. Even if they recognize that their actions add to the crowding problem, their personal benefits (the political support they get from their "tough" image) may exceed their personal costs (perhaps the anxiety associated with the recognition that they are crowding prisons and raising costs to society at large). Thus, imprisonment is chosen relatively frequently. The effect is that prosecutors and judges as a group crowd the common-access prisons much as cattle owners crowd common access grazing land.

State legislators can also crowd the criminal justice commons since, like judges and prosecutors, they have no incentive to conserve scarce prison resources. When passing laws that increase the penalties for drug crimes, such as mandatory minimum sentences, the legislature's action is equivalent to increasing the number of people who can use the classic grazing commons. Of course, the legislature also has the power to offset the resulting overcrowding since it can increase the number of prison beds, the equivalent of increasing the common land. But the temptation to overcrowd the commons is likely to prevail, since individual legislators are unlikely to suffer any costs from this course of action, particularly in the short run. Legislators can reap political benefits by passing longer sentences for crimes, so they appear to be tough on criminals, while ignoring the fact that the law can undermine other aspects of the criminal justice system. Since expanding criminal justice resources involves the politically unpopular task of either cutting other government functions or raising taxes, the politically astute course of action is to crowd the commons.

Crowded conditions have existed for as long as there have been prisons (Benson, 1990:71–73), but in the United States that fact apparently did not come to the attention of the general population or cause tremendous concern for legislators until a series of federal court rulings in the 1970s and 1980s mandating that crowded prison conditions be alleviated. As of October 1987, forty-five states, the District of Columbia, Puerto Rico, the Virgin Islands, and an undetermined number of county and municipal governments were under court order to remedy jail and/or prison conditions (McDonald, 1989:2). Most of these court orders had to do with conditions arising from crowding. For example, thirty-four of the states were under explicit orders to ease crowded conditions (Hackett et al., 1987:5), while others had orders to improve specific conditions, like medical care, which indicates that at least some components of the prison system had insufficient capacity.[4] Estimates of capacity utilization in 1988 indicate that the federal prison system was operating at somewhere between 133 percent and 172 percent of capacity, depending on how capacity is defined (e.g., original architecturally designed capacity; operating capacity as constrained by staff and services; or some form of official "rated capacity"), while state systems in total were at between 107 percent and 123 percent of capacity (U.S. Department of Justice, Bureau of Justice Statistics, 1989:5). Similarly, a Bureau of Justice Statistics (1988:1) estimate of 1987 jail capacity utilization in the 358 largest local jurisdictions, whose 611 jails housed about 76 percent of all jail prisoners in the country, indicated that the overall occupancy was 111 percent of rated capacity. At the time, 102 of these 358 jurisdictions were under court order to reduce the number of inmates they held.

Parole could be one method of alleviating prison crowding in the absence of sufficient reductions in judicial prison sentencing. However, parole arrangements have not always proved adequate either. California's attempts to control the prison population with parole resulted in rising caseloads for parole officers, who were quick to return technical violators to prison in order to lighten this burden (Phillips, 1992). In Florida, where the parole system had been phased out, the demand for scarce prison space has been growing dramatically. New prisons have been built, but Florida's legislature has been reluctant to build prison capacity at a pace that is sufficient to accommodate increased demand. Florida's prison population rose from 26,170 at the end of the 1981/82 fiscal year (FY) to 38,059 as of June 30, 1989, implying an increase of 45 percent in the supply of prison space, while annual prison admissions rose by 203 percent over the period, from 14,301 in FY 1981/82 to 43,387 in FY 1989/1990. Note that a substantial portion of the increased pressure on the Florida prison system traces directly to the war on drugs. There were 1,620 prison admissions for drug offenses during FY 1983/84, accounting for 12.9 percent of total admissions. By FY 1986/87 this figure had risen to 22.9 percent of total admissions (5,274). The trend continued with 15,802 drug admissions for FY 1989/1990 or 36.4 percent of total admissions. Thus, prison admissions for drugs rose by 875.4 percent between FY 1983/84 and FY 1989/1990, while non-drug admissions rose by only 153 percent (from 10,896 to 27,585).

The increased flow into the prison system in the face of federal court mandates to maintain less crowded conditions forced Florida to implement a program to "facilitate the transition from prison to civilian life" in fiscal year 1986/87 which lowered sentences to be served in FY 1987/88 by thirty-seven days for eligible inmates. Furthermore, overcrowding led to an Administrative Gain Time Program in February 1987, resulting in a 122-day reduction in sentence for almost all prisoners scheduled for release in FY 1987/88. The consequences were dramatic. In January 1987 inmates were serving an average of 52.8 percent of their sentences, but as drug admissions continued to rise during 1987, the prison crowding problem became acute and gain time accelerated. By January 1988 the average portion of sentence served had fallen to 40.6 percent, and by December 1989 it sank to 33 percent. In fact, about 37 percent of the prisoners released in December 1989 had served less than 25 percent of their sentence, and some served less than 15 percent.

Crowding occurs at all levels of the criminal justice system. In fact, one reason for judges' and prosecutors' failure to consider alternatives to imprisonment is that the courts themselves are severely crowded (Neely, 1982; Benson, 1990), implying that judges may not have time to explore alternative punishments at length. The war on drugs contributed to this problem as well. A recent General Accounting Office study emphasized that the federal courts had not been able to keep up with the growing caseload resulting from increases in drug arrests and prosecutions.[5] There was a 1,200-case backlog waiting for federal court action at the end of fiscal year 1989, but one year later the backlog had increased to 7,400 cases. And judges must consider other crowded conditions in their sentencing decisions as well. Probation is the most commonly used alternative sanction to imprisonment, for example, and the typical sanction for first-time offenders. In fact, roughly three times as many convicted offenders are placed on probation each year as are sentenced to prisons and jails combined. But as James Byrne (1988:1) noted, "Although prison crowding draws national attention and increased resources, 'probation crowding' poses a more immediate threat to the criminal justice process and to community protection." The probation population has been increasing at roughly the same rate as the prison population, severely taxing the ability of the system's limited resources to monitor and supervise probationers. All alternatives to imprisonment, other than forgiveness and release, require the use of some scarce resources for monitoring, so the potential for crowding arises even if judges do not herd criminals into the common pool prisons.

But crowding is only one aspect of a commons problem. Indeed, even though crowding may be the most visible consequence of common access, it is not the most significant consequence. When grazing land is overused, its rapid deterioration in quality means that the output of the production process which employs that land similarly deteriorates in quality. The same problem results with common-access law enforcement resources.

Prisons, for instance, are intended to serve several functions (produce several outputs), including punishment of convicted criminals, deterrence of potential criminals, incapacitation of dangerous criminals, and rehabilitation of criminals who can be reformed. All of these outputs of the prison system decline in quality because of the commons problem and crowding. Early release programs mean that criminals are not punished to the degree that judges, victims, and others in society feel justice requires. Potential criminals recognize that prison sentences are rarely fully served and that the portion of sentences served declines with increased admissions after capacity is reached, so deterrence may be diminished. Some unrehabilitated and insufficiently deterred criminals are released early despite the need for continued incapacitation, and commit more crimes. Finally, when prison budgets are consumed by efforts to accommodate overflowing prison populations, resources may not be available for rehabilitation programs; and if they are, early release may mean that criminals are not enrolled in rehabilitation programs long enough to benefit from them. Thus, the tragedy of the commons occurs with all common-access public law enforcement resources.

Individual prosecutors and judges are not liable for the costs of their decisions. Instead, costs are imposed on taxpayers who face the ever increasing cost of building more prison space; on victims who are not satisfied with the level of punishment offenders actually incur; on citizens who are victimized by prematurely released criminals and other criminals who are not sufficiently deterred; on criminals who may have reduced opportunities for rehabilitation and are faced with the increased violence and abuse that may accompany prison crowding; and on corrections officials who must focus their efforts and resources on coping with crowded conditions rather than on other functions, such as rehabilitation and treatment.

The Illinois Department of Corrections (1989a:8–9) has reported some of the consequences of crowding on the prison population, as well as the cost of administering prisons. Four Illinois prisons experienced significant increases in population without increases in design capacity between 1985 and 1988: Centralia, Graham, Sheridan, and Vandalia. These four prisons, crowded through double- and multi-celling, housed roughly 18 percent of the increase in medium and minimum security prisoners over the period (the rest of the increase was housed in new facilities), but they accounted for 48 percent of the increase in attempted suicides by inmates, 23 percent of the increase in adjustment reports, and 31 percent of the increase in inmate deaths for all medium and minimum security prisons in Illinois. Problems with the prison population seem to increase faster than the population itself when crowded conditions set in. Thus, for instance, when the daily populations of Graham and Centralia increased by 33 percent through double-celling, total disciplinary reports increased by 63 percent, revocation of good time rose by 1,552 percent, and assaults on staff increased by 120 percent.

Common access really means that many public law enforcement resources are rationed on a first-come-first-served basis.[6] The first case of a certain type filed gets the first available slot on the court docket, for instance, and the first prisoner of a particular type sentenced gets the first open space of that type in the prison system. But rationing by first-come-first-served generally means rationing by waiting in queues, as backlogs of unmet demands build up. Thus, as noted above, there is a backlog of court cases waiting to be heard and county jails fill with prisoners waiting to be tried or to be placed in state prisons. In fact, 52 percent of the prisoners held in local jails during 1987 were queued up, awaiting arraignment or trials, and a substantial portion of the remaining 48 percent, who were convicted inmates, were being held until they could be transferred to another authority (U.S. Department of Justice, Bureau of Justice Statistics, 1988:1). Among the 358 largest jurisdictions, for example, 26,838 of the 224,811 inmates were being held for other authorities, and 11,257 of those were being held specifically because the state prison was too crowded to accept them, given court mandates (U.S. Department of Justice, Bureau of Justice Statistics, 1988:1). Similarly, backlogs of thousands of supposedly "open" police cases receive little or no attention, waiting forever to be solved.

When rationing by waiting becomes prevalent and the time cost of waiting grows, many potential demanders opt out of the queue and choose not to be served. Consequently, prosecutors and judges feel pressure to expedite waiting cases by plea bargaining, and judges may grant more suspended sentences than they otherwise would. Furthermore, many crime victims choose not to report crimes either because of the low probability of satisfaction (since police facing excess demands for their services will likely be unable to solve the crime; plus the likelihood that even if the police are successful, prosecutors will drop the case or plea bargain it down to a level of punishment that is unsatisfactory from the victim's perspective) or because of the time cost associated with cooperating in prosecution.

Simply increasing the supply of law enforcement resources is not likely to solve the queuing problem. Making more courts and judges means that some who previously would not report crime now do; but with their entry into the queue, the queue gets longer again and the backlog of cases and trial delay remain (Church, Chantry, and Sipes, 1978; Fleming, 1973). Building more prisons may mean prosecutors and judges are even less willing to consider alternative forms of punishment, particularly if resources going into the probation system and other alternatives are not simultaneously expanded, so prison crowding remains a problem. For example, under Illinois law, some drug offenders are given the choice of obtaining treatment, provided that certain statutory requirements are met. If an offender chooses treatment, and if an examination concludes that the offender is an addict who is likely to respond to treatment, then the court can impose a sentence of probation with treatment monitored by TASC (Treatment Alternatives for Special Clients). In FY 1988 there were 1,082 adults so sentenced (Illinois Criminal Justice Information Authority, 1989:129–130). However, insufficient resources had been allocated to treatment facilities, so in February 1988, for example, 275 people sentenced to TASC-monitored treatment were on a waiting list, eight-six of whom were incarcerated while waiting for an opening in a treatment program, while the rest were under community supervision. Thus, the shortage of treatment facilities adds to the crowding of both jails and community supervision facilities. People eligible for treatment continue to exceed those accepted into treatment, those accepted exceed those placed, and the gap between eligible and placed continues to widen.

II. Crowding the System: A Case Study

Understanding the consequences of increasing drug enforcement in a commons environment might be enhanced by a detailed study of one state.[7] Illinois' drug arrest rate in 1989 was below the national average, but the state's drug arrests per 100,000 population over the 1984–1989 period had increased faster than that of any other state. Prison crowding became so significant in Illinois during the late 1970s and early 1980s that the state instituted a forced release program, beginning in June 1980. Multiple ninety-day increments of meritorious gain time were applied to inmates' sentences, on top of the traditional day-for-day good conduct credits. From FY 1980 to FY 1983 there were 10,019 inmates released early (after serving relatively small portions of their sentences) as a consequence of this program. A total of 2.66 million days of gain time was awarded to 63,616 inmates over this period; but in July 1983, the state supreme court ruled that only one ninety-day increment of meritorious gain time per inmate could be awarded under the state's law. Thus, the state's prison population exploded, growing by an average of 234 inmates per month over the next year.[8]

Illinois was faced with moderating its early release program and either finding other mechanisms for allocating scarce prison space or building more prisons. "Ideal capacity" for the Illinois prison system more than doubled between 1978 and 1988 (from 8,150 to 16,310) by building more prisons. "Rated capacity" also increased from 10,944 in 1978 to 19,993 in 1988, in part by double-celling prisoners, while the actual population rose from 11,736 to 20,544. Following the court-ordered change in the forced release program in 1983, double-celling was immediately instituted, and efforts to build new facilities increased. By the end of 1985, four new facilities had opened: Jacksonville with designed capacity for 500 beds, Lincoln with 558, Dixon with 582, and Shawnee with 986. These were followed by new facilities in FY 1986, Danville, and in FY 1987, Hill, both of which were designed to hold 896 prisoners. Existing and recently built facilities were also expanded. Two additional facilities, Mt. Sterling which opened in April 1989, and Canton, have since been added.

While the number of prisoners held increased steadily throughout the 1980s through new construction and double-celling, the cost of holding each prisoner has simultaneously increased. Thus, the percentage increase in Department of Corrections expenditures has been greater than 5 percent every year since 1983 except for 1988, and it exceeded 10 percent each year between 1983 and 1986. These large increases produced a 105.4 percent increase in the state expenditures for corrections from its 1982 level of $268.9 million to its 1988 level of $552.2 million (Council of State Governments, various years). Nonetheless, prison construction and increased expenditures were not sufficient to bring design capacity up to the level of actual use. Double-celling continued, and more meritorious gain time was granted. In fact, meritorious gain time increased steadily after 1984. In 1986, for example, the average number of meritorious gain time days was thirty-six, but by 1988 it had reached seventy (Illinois Department of Correction, 1989a:28). The 1989 Illinois Department of Corrections *Annual Report* notes that the state's prison system held 3,085 more prisoners than it was designed to house at the end of FY 1985, and that, despite building new prisons, the inmate population was expected to exceed designed capacity by 4,566 prisoners at the end of FY 1990 (1989b:8). Illinois prisons were 28 percent over design capacity in 1988, and 47 percent over by the end of 1991.[9] As a result, double- and multi-celling of prisoners increased. Thus, the very substantial prison construction program clearly did not eliminate crowding or early release, although relative to some states, such as Florida, Illinois' early release program is quite modest.

Prison crowding and early release requirements reflect both demand and supply considerations. Illinois prisons are less crowded than Florida's, in part because Illinois has increased the supply of prisons relatively fast compared to increases in demand, and it appears that this is at least partially due to the fact that Illinois' participation in the war on drugs has been more limited than Florida's. A 96 percent increase in drug admissions to prison over a five-year period is not trivial, but compared to Florida's 875 percent it is relatively modest. However, the difference between these states may actually reflect the fact that state prison crowding was alleviated in another way in Illinois as well. A state law was passed in 1983 mandating that all misdemeanants serve their sentences locally rather than in state prisons. This simply shifted part of the demand for prison space from the state level to the local level. Thus, the average daily jail population for the state rose from 6,848 in FY 1982 to 9,121 in FY 1987.

Local jails hold both pretrial detainees and sentenced prisoners. One impact in Illinois of the actions taken at the state level was an increase in the portion of the local jail population that is serving sentences. Consider three different types of local jails in Illinois: (1) jails with capacities of fewer than 100 persons; (2) all jails that have capacities exceeding 100 prisoners except for the Cook County jail (in Chicago); and (3) the Cook County jail. Among jails in group (1), sentenced offenders accounted for 26 percent of jail days in 1981, but this rose to 33 percent by 1987, in large part because the state had shifted the burden of holding misdemeanants to the local level. Similar figures for group (2) are 18 percent and 23 percent, respectively. Furthermore, total jail population for all jails other than Cook County (i.e., groups 1 and 2) increased steadily over this period, so these percentages involve substantial increases in actual numbers of inmates serving sentences in local jails.

Cook County's response to the increased demand for local jail space was somewhat different, however. As a consequence of previously existing crowded conditions (the jail's inmate population had increased by over 32 percent between 1981 and 1983), in 1983 the U.S. district court ordered the county to alleviate crowded conditions, threatening a fine of $1,000 per day for each day the inmate population exceeded the number of beds. To avoid the threatened fines, county officials responded by releasing 80–100 accused felons on their own recognizance on certain days and by expanding capacity (500 beds were added in 1985, for example). In 1988, jail authorities began releasing defendants with bonds of up to $50,000 on their own recognizance. They also experimented with electronic monitoring and home confinement, and the jail's Periodic Imprisonment Unit was moved into a community setting. Even so, the county was fined approximately $55,000 in early 1989 for persistent crowding. Thus, apparent mitigation of prison crowding in Illinois is deceiving because at least part of the crowding problem was simply shifted to another component of the criminal justice system.

Much of the increased pressure on the Illinois prison system that occurred as the state built more prisons traces directly to the war on drugs. Between 1985 and 1988 the average sentence for drug offenders increased by 16.7 percent as the number of drug offenders admitted increased by 96.2 percent (see Table 2.2). The combined effect of these increases in drug sentences and admissions increased the portion of the prison population with drug offenses as their primary conviction from 4.5 percent to 8.2 percent in just four years. These changes reflect both an increase in the level of prison resources through new construction and a reallocation of such resources. However, non-drug prison admissions rose by a modest 1.9 percent between 1984 and 1988, while drug admissions rose by over 96 percent. Thus, drug admissions were clearly the primary source of growing demand for prison space. Indeed, the war on drugs exacerbated the Department of Corrections planning efforts. The department's *Annual Report* noted (1989b:15) that "unprecedented increases in court admissions to the department have resulted in prison population levels far exceeding projected levels. By the end of June 1989, the actual population was 855 above the projected population. The primary reason for this growth has been the increased admissions for drug offenders." The fact that drug admissions as a percentage of total admissions more than doubled over the 1984–1988 period means that crowding exceeded expectations. Consequently, as noted above, more meritorious gain time was granted each year.

III. Will Adding More Resources Solve the Problem?

Increasing expenditures at various levels of the criminal justice system may exacerbate crowding problems at other levels. In general, more police and prosecutors lead to greater pressures on the courts, unless their capacity is also expanded. This point was made with respect to prosecutors in a General Accounting Office study of increasing backlogs in federal courts.[10] The budget for U.S. attorneys increased by more than 95 percent over the 1988–1991 period (from $380 million to $742 million), while the federal court budget increased by just 82 percent ($1.42 billion to $2.59 billion) and the administration lagged in appointing judges to fill new and vacant positions (141 federal judge positions were unfilled as of May 1991).

Table 2.2: Drug Admissions, Drug Sentences, and the Illinois Prison Population

Fiscal Year	Total Drug Offense Admissions	Drug Admissions as a Percent of Total Admissions	Average Drug Sentence in Years	End of Fiscal Year Drug Prison Population	Drug Offenders as a Percent of Total Prison Population
1985	656	5.7	3.6	793	4.5
1986	753	7.1	3.8	1,009	5.2
1987	1,008	8.6	4.0	1,267	6.3
1988	1,287	11.8	4.2	1,692	8.2

Source: Illinois Department of Corrections (1989a:21) and Illinois Criminal Justice Information Authority (1989:153).

Increasing prosecutors relative to judges contributed to the clogging of federal courts.

One example of crowding and queuing for police resources is particularly instructive since it can be directly tied to the war on drugs. As police resources allocated to the control of drug crime have been increased in Illinois, so that the numbers of drug arrests, investigations, and seizures have increased, the demands placed on the state's crime labs have increased dramatically. For example, 9,419 drug cases were submitted to the Illinois State Police crime lab in 1983, but by 1988 the caseload had increased 41 percent to 13,273 (Illinois Criminal Justice Information Authority, 1989:56). Other police labs saw similar increases in caseloads over the same period. The Northern Illinois crime lab's drug case rose by 63 percent (from 1,285 to 2,092), for instance, and the DuPage County Sheriff's Office crime lab saw a 30 percent jump in drug cases (868 to 1,132). The demand on the Chicago Police Department lab increased even more dramatically, rising by almost 108 percent from 17,639 drug cases in 1983 to 36,639 in 1988.

Drug cases increased much faster than other cases for the crime labs over this period, so a substantial reallocation of crime lab resources is indicated. For example, 46 percent of the cases going to the Illinois State Police lab were drug cases in 1985, but by 1988 drug cases accounted for 56 percent of the lab's caseload. Similarly, drugs accounted for 34 percent of the Northern Illinois lab's cases in 1983, and 45 percent in 1988. Increasing numbers and proportions of drug cases do not tell the full story, either. Labs are also being asked to perform complex analyses more frequently. For instance, an increasing portion of the labs' drug cases involved "controlled substances" rather than marijuana, and controlled substances take longer to analyze. At the Chicago lab, for instance, only 43 percent of the drug cases involved controlled substances in 1983, but 73 percent of the cases were of this type in 1988. The result: "At many labs, drug analysis capabilities have been unable to meet the increased demand for services. Consequently, drug analysis backlogs have risen and the ability of some labs to provide timely information to police and prosecutors has been eroded" (Illinois Criminal Justice Information Authority, 1989:56).

The two largest crime labs in the state have been particularly hard hit. The Illinois State Police lab had a thirty-seven drug case backlog at the end of 1983, but there was a 253-case backlog at the end of 1985 and a 1,806-case backlog at the end of 1988. The lab was processing 75 percent of all of its drug cases within one to seven days in 1983, but this fell to 19 percent by 1988 when 53 percent of all drug cases were taking more than four weeks to process. Similarly, an internal audit of the Chicago Police Department crime lab found that a 2,162-case backlog in January 1986 had increased 118 percent by September of that same year. Indeed, in July 1986, eighty-eight drug cases were dismissed by the courts because analysis results were not available from the Chicago Police lab in a timely fashion; and in December of that same year, 776 cases were dismissed for the same reason. Both the Illinois State Police and the Chicago Police Department added staff in an effort to reduce the backlog of drug cases. The State Police lab added twelve new chemists in 1988, for example, but the backlog continued to increase. The Chicago Police lab added twenty chemists in 1987 and 1988, but the effect was simply to reduce the number of cases dismissed by the courts due to the unavailability of crime lab reports. Dismissals were not eliminated, however, nor was the backlog.

Congestion of the criminal justice system may not be relieved even if all criminal justice aspects of the system are simultaneous expanded. If victims believe the system is more effective, they are somewhat more likely to report crimes and to increase the workload of police, prosecutors, and courts.[11] More police and prosecutors are also likely to increase the numbers of arrests and prosecutions of unreported crimes such as drug offenses, so the backlog of unsolved Index I offenses is not necessarily reduced.

IV. The Rationing of Law Enforcement

First-come-first-served is not the only rationing criterion applied in the allocation of public law-enforcement resources. Indeed, initial allocation decisions made by police administrators are not likely to be influenced by first-come-first-served considerations. Police administrators decide how to allocate their limited supply of resources among categories of competing uses such as traffic, vice, homicide, burglary, and general patrol. That decision (examined in more detail in Chapter 7) then determines the dimension of various common pools. For instance, some cities may have investigative officers respond to every burglary call, while some cities simply take the information down on the phone and send no officers to the crime scene. Still other cities may allocate sufficient resources to burglary to respond to a portion of the burglary calls (e.g., 20 percent), which are then largely allocated on a first-come-first-served basis.

Some police resources are allocated to crime categories which are not typically thought of as common pools in the sense that individuals come to the police and demand service. Vice and drugs fit this description, for example. Participants in gambling, prostitution, and drug exchanges enter the transaction voluntarily, unlike the victim of an assault or a burglary. Thus, individuals are not coming to the police and demanding their attention to correct a specific offensive act, and there is no identifiable queue (e.g., a filing cabinet full of unsolved burglary complaints). Nonetheless, since the resources allocated to drug crimes are not allocated on a market price basis, there is still an implicit common-pool allocation system. The source of demand for police services is simply less easily identified. Rather than individuals queuing up to receive services, demand filters through the political process. Some neighborhoods have no drug dealers or prostitutes walking their streets, for instance, while such activities are very visible in other neighborhoods. Police resources are allocated on the basis of the relative political clout of the population in these communities. Indeed, first-come-first-served need not be the primary determinant of the allocation process even when individual victims are queuing up. Police may be able to differentiate among those in the queue on the basis of other considerations and allocate their effort accordingly (Neely, 1982:140).

More generally, those who manage and staff law enforcement bureaucracies have considerable discretion in resource allocation because there is an excess demand for the resources they control. They can often choose how to allocate scarce resources among competing demands, both across and within crime categories. With thousands of statutes to uphold, police officers face an impossible task if they are expected to apply those laws evenly. Theoretically, the huge array of criminal laws might be thought of as an administrative device intended to define precisely what types of illegal behavior officers might encounter, leaving no room for police discretion. In fact, however, the tremendous number of competing demands for police services reflected by these statutes precludes the mechanical application of law. Instead, individual police officers and police departments as a whole must decide which laws to attempt to enforce and how rigorously.

There are many different kinds of criminal activities that demand the attention of police (e.g., traffic violations, property crimes, vice, violent crimes, drug crimes). In essence, each of these types of crime flow into the legal system, forming their own queues. Perfect and complete law enforcement is simply impossible, so police must establish a system of priorities. While this discretion will be constrained due to political factors, police agencies will have some influence over the portion of their resources and effort to be allocated to each type of illegal activity. This allocation decision results in selective enforcement of the law, as some crime categories receive very little consideration, while others receive much more. In other words, some crime queues move through the system fairly quickly with relatively few cases waiting for attention. Others receive virtually no attention, so most cases simply wait, remaining unsolved. Because victims often recognize this, many crimes are not even reported.

The consequences of police discretion in the allocation of resources across crime types can even be seen in terms of response to crimes reported in progress. Victims of some types of crime must wait longer to be served than others. For example, the Police Information Management System (PIMS) of the Illinois Criminal Justice Information Authority reported the thirty-one PIMS agencies' average response time to crimes in progress in 1987. These averages varied from 2.5 minutes and 2.6 minutes for murder and arson respectively to 4.5 minutes and 4.7 minutes for burglary and theft (Illinois Criminal Justice Information Authority, 1989:27). Thus, it took police approximately 81 percent longer to respond to a theft in progress than to an arson. In between these low and high average figures, we see average response times of 3.9 minutes for sexual assault and motor vehicle theft in progress, 3.5 minutes for aggravated assault, and 3.6 minutes for robbery. Such relative rationing of scarce resources may be quite reasonable given the potential costs of arson or murder versus theft or burglary. But it must also be recognized that if fewer police resources were allocated to the control of drug crimes the police response time for burglary, theft, sexual assault, or perhaps even arson could be reduced.

Prosecutors and judges have similar discretion. Court time is rationed to a large extent by waiting; but even with the time cost, demand for a place on the docket significantly exceeds availability. Thus, prosecutors and judges decide which cases to pursue and which to drop, and then which cases to plea bargain and which to try. It is the tremendous excess demand for the services of the common access court system that creates this discretion and the resulting allocation of court time. In Illinois, for instance, the number of felony defendants adjudicated by a guilty plea rose by 64 percent between 1977 and 1987 (from 17,827 to 29,239) while the number of felony cases decided by the courts through bench or jury trials rose by only 42 percent (Illinois Criminal Justice Information Authority, 1989:107–108). Thus, the portion of felony dispositions achieved through plea bargaining increased by roughly 2.4 percent over this period. By 1987 over 84 percent of all felony dispositions in Illinois were obtained through guilty pleas rather than by trial; and if we exclude Cook County, then 91 percent of felony dispositions in the rest of the state were achieved through plea bargaining.

Data on pretrial dismissals in Illinois apparently are not available, so we cannot determine whether increased crowding of courts has led to increased dismissals. The Illinois Criminal Justice Information Authority (1989:106) simply reports that "a large, but statistically unknown, percentage of felony defendants exit the criminal court system during various pretrial stages. Felony charges may be dismissed at the preliminary hearing, defendants may fail to appear in court, or they may be diverted to special programs as an alternative to prosecution." Similar trends are occurring elsewhere as well. Roughly 98 percent of all criminal convictions in Florida in 1990 were obtained through plea (or charge) bargaining. And, as noted above, prosecutors and judges also have considerable discretion in allocating punishment, including prison space. Indeed, some state legislatures have passed sentencing guidelines in an effort to limit judicial discretion. Florida adopted determinant sentencing in October 1983, for example, and the resulting Sentencing Guidelines were fully implemented by October 1984 (Justice Research Associates, 1988). Sentencing discretion was substantially limited as a result, but it was clearly not eliminated: 5,221 offenders in 1990 who had a recommended non-prison sentence under the guidelines were sentenced to prison, accounting for 12.9 percent of all prison admissions for the year (Criminal Justice Estimating Conference, 1991). While extenuating circumstances no doubt justify a prison sentence in some circumstances, it is interesting to note that 1,557 of these offenders had no prior record, and that 47 percent of these exceptions to the guidelines were drug offenders.

Evidence of sentencing discretion also comes from comparisons of sentencing practices across jurisdictions. For instance, Illinois also has a determinant sentencing structure that went into effect in February 1978 "in an effort to reduce disparity in sentencing practices and to increase the certainty and deterrent effect of criminal penalties" (Illinois Criminal Justice Information Authority, 1989:100). Nonetheless, beginning in about 1977, and particularly since 1984, consistently higher percentages of convicted felons have been sentenced to imprisonment (rather than probation or other sentencing options) by Cook County courts than by courts in the rest of the state. In 1987, for example, 44 percent of Cook County's convicted felons were sentenced to prison while 31 percent of the convicted felons in the rest of the state received prison sentences (Illinois Criminal Justice Information Authority, 1989:113). Of course, this may reflect a difference in the types of felons convicted in Cook County (more serious offenders and habitual offenders for whom prison is mandated are in fact convicted in Cook County); but even when we focus on those felony types for which the judge has sentencing options, Cook County courts give sentences of imprisonment more frequently than the rest of the state. The Illinois Criminal Justice Information Authority (1989:114) concluded that "it is not readily apparent why, proportionally, probation is used more frequently for felon offenders outside Cook County than in Cook County," but the difference clearly indicates the existence of judicial discretion.[12]

V. Drug Enforcement in a Common Pool System

The increasing political emphasis on illicit drug laws during the 1980s was accompanied by a substantial shift in the allocation of law enforcement resources over a fairly short period of time. Arrest statistics cited in Chapter 1 illustrate this fact, but there are numerous other indicators as well. For example, the nation's shifting emphasis in its law enforcement efforts is reflected in the fact that drug offenses accounted for 51.6 percent of the increased number of admissions to state prisons between 1981 and 1989.[13] Court commitments to prison for selected serious offenses rose from 93,838 in 1981 to 117,344 in 1989, a 25.1 percent increase.[14] Over the same period, admissions for drug offenses rose 665 percent, from 11,487 to 87,859. Over 90 percent of these increased admissions took place in the 1984–1989 period. Increasing prison commitments for drug offenses came from two sources: increasing drug arrests; and more court commitments per 1,000 drug arrests. Drug arrests in the United States more than doubled during the 1980s, rising from 418,056 in 1981 to 1,247,763 in 1989. Court commitments per 1,000 drug arrests rose from twenty-four in 1981 to seventy in 1989. For serious offenses, the number of court commitments per 1,000 offenses was virtually unchanged, falling from 134 in 1981 to 131 in 1989.

Similar trends can be seen in the use of the nations' local and county jails (Harlow, 1991:2). The portion of inmates in jail with drug charges as their primary offense increased from 9 percent in 1983 to 23 percent in 1989, and the portion of inmates with at least one drug charge rose from 11 percent to 26 percent. These percentage changes tend to mask the drug war's real impact on jails, however, because the change occurred as the total number of inmates held in local jails rose by 77 percent. Perhaps a more revealing fact is that the actual number of jail inmates with a drug charge as their most serious offense rose by 328 percent from 20,479 to 87,551, while the number of persons held for all other offenses rose by only 47 percent (199,094 to 292,649).

These resource shifts have occurred in the context of a common pool system, so there may be many unforeseen consequences. As drug crimes receive more attention from police, along with greater allocations of prison and jail space, the queues for other offenses must move slower as fewer resources are allocated to them. After all, when law enforcement resources are used to perform one type of service, those same resources are not available for other uses. Very little is known about the consequences of this large shift in the focus of law enforcement efforts. For instance, as law enforcement resources are shifted to control illicit drugs, what happens to the incentives facing criminals who commit other types of crimes? Do other crimes increase because they are less effectively deterred? In addition, since resources allocated to illicit drug control will not be adequate to completely control all aspects of the various illicit drug markets, the incentives drug criminals face will be affected, leading them to change their behavior in order to lower the risks created by the policing effort. The effectiveness of drug enforcement policy is the subject of the next two chapters.

Chapter 3

Drugs and Criminality

Illicit drugs are sold in well-organized markets that are much like other markets. Individuals demand drugs because they expect to derive satisfaction or "utility" from consuming them. Furthermore, they expect this utility to exceed the value of the things they must give up to buy drugs, including the risks involved in purchasing and consuming the drug. Drug suppliers are motivated by prospective profits: the expectation that revenues generated by drug production and sales will exceed production costs, which include the risks associated with participation in illegal activity. Thus, entrepreneurs, anticipating a sufficiently large profit, are willing to bear the risk of investing their time, effort, and capital in the illicit drug business. Production of illicit drugs requires the use of scarce resources (capital, labor, land, and entrepreneurship), and those resources must be attracted away from alternative uses. Since drugs are produced and sold in a market environment driven by individual demand and supply decisions, the "drug problem" and drug policy can be analyzed by the standard tools of economics.

Illicit drug markets do have characteristics which distinguish them from many other markets and which must be taken into account when modeling an individual's demand and/or supply decisions in this market. Two primary factors deserve emphasis in this regard: (1) the production, transportation, sale, purchase, and possession of these drugs are all illegal in the United States and other parts of the world; and (2) some illicit drugs are addictive for some people, and addiction may substantially alter behavior. Neither of these considerations is unique to illicit drugs. Alcohol and tobacco are also addictive, but there are well-established legal markets for both goods.[1] Furthermore, there are many activities which individuals choose to undertake that are illegal, including many market activities involving illegal production and/or transactions. In fact, whenever government regulates a market by imposing limits or restrictions on the free exchange of the good or service, incentives arise to avoid the limitations. Illegal means are used and black markets are a typical consequence. Price ceilings, for instance, create tremendous potential for gains from illegal trade, as some individuals are willing to pay more than the legal price but cannot obtain the good legally due to the artificial shortage created by the price ceiling. Some suppliers are willing to provide the good if they can profitably sell it at an illegally high price. In this situation, a limited legal market and an illegal market exist for the same good.

An individual's willingness to buy and sell in illegal black markets reflects the fact that policing is never perfect. If individuals knew that they would be caught and severely punished every time they traded in a black market, then such markets would not exist. On the other hand, when it is obvious that the probability of being caught and punished is relatively low, incentives to participate in such markets may be strong. Increased risks faced by buyers tend to reduce the expected net benefits of consumption, and thus demand may fall—but it will not disappear unless the risks are very high. For suppliers, the risk of being caught makes production more costly as more must be paid to labor that is put at risk, and additional expenses, such as bribes, may be required. Suppliers will, therefore, require a relatively high price for supplying any given quantity.

When the production and sale of a good is always illegal (e.g., prostitution, and alcohol during the Prohibition period)[2], then the result is simply a special case of regulation and the black market problem; in effect, the price ceiling is zero. As long as policing is imperfect, however, the good is likely to be demanded and sold. Illicit drugs clearly fit this situation. This chapter explores the rationale for a war on drugs from an economic perspective. Section I presents the general case for using enforcement to deter criminal activity. "Getting tough on crime" is a popular catchphrase on the political scene, but we show that deterrence efforts have their limitations: just getting tough does not lead everyone to "just say no." Drug consumers and their response to enforcement and other incentives are analyzed in Section II. We show that many drug users, even those who are addicted, can be "rational" in that they are somewhat responsive to the incentives generated by public policy and the drug market. Section III explores the impact of addiction on the choices made by drug consumers, and Section IV shows that the proposition that drug use causes other crime is a much touted but overrated justification for enhanced drug enforcement.

I. Criminal Decisionmaking: The Economics of Enforcement Policy

Economic analysis of crime attempts to identify variables that affect the costs and returns to criminal activity in order to predict the incidence of crime (Becker, 1968). The underlying rationale for this approach is that criminals respond consistently to incentives. Individuals try to maximize their satisfaction—or in economics jargon, "utility"—given their psychological makeup and preferences, by choosing among legal and illegal activities after considering the expected gains and costs associated with the alternatives. Because most economists do not inquire into the psychological and sociological factors that ultimately determine the individual's response to these incentives, the economic approach is best viewed as being complementary to, rather than a substitute for, the disciplines that have generated most of the research on criminal behavior.

A great advantage of the economic approach is that it focuses on the efficacy of enforcement policy, a variable that can be altered to achieve specified goals. Consider the decision to commit a crime. The utility derived from its commission is related to the expected benefit (broadly defined to include psychological satisfaction, however perverse, as well as monetary gain) and the anticipated punishment, which includes lost legal income, broken personal relationships, and other costs associated with being incarcerated. Thus, the decision to commit a crime reflects the potential criminal's assessment of the net benefits to be realized by committing it. Attempts to prevent crime are an integral part of this approach. If the probability of punishment—the chances of arrest and conviction—rises, an individual may be less likely to commit the crime. Policies which increase the severity of punishment, such as longer incarceration or a bigger fine, may have a similar effect. In the economist's view, people are less likely to commit a crime when society raises the expected "price" of committing it. The probability of being caught, the likelihood of conviction, and the severity of sentencing are the components of price that can be directly influenced by public policy.

Consider a policy of tougher enforcement against marijuana consumption—which implicitly raises its price. Consumers of this illicit drug now have three options: (1) cease the use of marijuana and instead substitute legal alternatives such as alcohol; (2) continue to use the drug, though with reduced frequency in order to lower the probability of detection and arrest; and (3) substitute some other illicit drug, such as cocaine, which is now relatively cheaper. In the same way, increased sentences for burglary changes its relative price, leading the burglar to rely more on legal income, to commit fewer burglaries, and/or commit more robberies which now have a relatively less stringent penalty attached to them. In these examples, the first option (complete cessation of illegal activity), and to a lesser extent the second (reduced participation), are the deterrence effect enforcement is supposed to accomplish. The third suggests that deterrence for one kind of illegal activity may simply lead to an increase in another, so that overall crime does not diminish. In fact, it is well established by economic theory that some individuals might actually increase criminal activity when faced with increased enforcement.[3] Theoretically, deterrence is not an inevitable result of enforcement. The only way to determine whether enforcement works is to investigate its deterrent impact empirically.

Empirical analysis of criminal decisionmaking. Two empirical questions have been extensively examined from the perspective provided by the economic model of crime: do crime rates rise with, first, a reduction in the opportunity costs of crime (lower legal income levels; reduced job security; higher unemployment) and, second, a decline in the expected cost of crime due to a reduction in the probability of arrest and/or the severity of punishment? There is a large literature which indicates that a fall in the opportunity costs of crime, either in terms of a reduction of wages or an increase in unemployment, leads to an increase in crime.[4] In fact, a general conclusion of the empirical literature on the economic theory of crime suggests that the best way to reduce crime is to increase legitimate opportunities. Individuals who have the fewest and least appealing legal opportunities are the most apt to participate in criminal activities. These findings are not unique to economics. Virtually all social scientists agree on this point.

There is evidence to support the hypothesis that crime rates rise with reductions in the probability of and severity of punishment as well. Indeed, tests of the "deterrence hypothesis" are not unique to economics either. After reviewing a great number of studies, using different methods and varied data, we conclude that they essentially support the findings of early surveys of empirical literature on the economic theory of crime by Elliot (1977) and Silver (1974).

1. Relatively poor legal income opportunities appear to result in more crime.[5]

2. Potential criminals are apparently deterred by higher probabilities of punishment.
3. The severity of punishment also may deter crime, but the evidence for this effect is not as convincing as that for higher probabilities of punishment or for the impact of such factors as unemployment.

Critics (e.g., Brier and Fienberg, 1980; and Cameron, 1988) who do not agree with these conclusions, argue that the data and at least some of the econometric techniques used to obtain the results have been poor. To a certain extent the economics profession has agreed with this assessment since it has increasingly turned to data sets featuring individual records, rather than the cross-section studies that proliferated in the early work on deterrence.[6] Nevertheless, as Elliot (1977:82, 85) observed, while many people have "very effectively illustrated some serious problems with crime data, these problems do not appear to make existing crime data unsuitable for empirical tests of the economic theory of crime." In fact, when the most widely cited problem with crime data—biases from underreporting—are eliminated, it appears that the deterrent impact of sanctions is greater (Myers, 1980b; Craig, 1987). In addition, "the econometric problems associated with recent studies of crime are not noticeably more serious than in other areas of applied econometrics—especially when one 'seasonally adjusts' for its relatively late development—and, moreover, the findings are in agreement with a priori theoretical expectations and are robust across widely different geographic cross-sections" (Taylor, 1978:81). At the very least, the existing evidence suggests that enforcement policies provide some deterrence effects, although their magnitude is open to debate.

II. Drug Demand and Crime: An Economic Perspective

In order to understand fully the relationship between the price of a drug and a consumer's willingness to buy it, some basic theoretical concepts must be introduced. Demand in economics is defined as the relationship that specifies the quantity of a good a consumer (or group of consumers) is willing to buy at various prices of the good. The quantity of a good demanded at a specific price depends on the consumer's preferences, the level of the consumer's income, and the relative prices of related goods; but economic theory does not predict the precise relationships between these demand determinants and the level of demand.

These factors influence demand in the following ways.

Income. An increase in income normally leads to an increase in demand (hence the term "normal good"), but it can lead to a reduction in demand if the commodity is an "inferior good." If the demand for marijuana rises with income, it is a normal good; but if higher income results in less consumption, marijuana would be an inferior good. To say a good is "inferior" implies no value judgment; it simply means that as income changes, given the individual's preferences, purchases of the good change in the opposite direction.

Prices of related goods. An increase in the price of a good causes an increase in the demand for substitutes. When the price of one brand of beer rises, consumers will increase their purchases of rival brands that are now relatively cheap. Demand for a commodity rises with a fall in the price of complementary goods (i.e., if the goods are consumed together). Taverns frequently give away pretzels (i.e., lower the price to zero) in order to stimulate the demand for beer, a product that is complementary to salty pretzels.

Price of the good. An increase in the price of the good causes a reduction in the quantity demanded under virtually all circumstances. This is because of the "substitution effect" of the price change: people generally substitute relatively low priced goods for a relatively high priced good in an effort to maintain a relatively high level of satisfaction. A price increase has a second effect, however. It reduces the consumer's overall purchasing power, much like a reduction in money income would (hence, this effect is called the "income effect" of a price change). This reduction in purchasing power lowers purchases of most goods, but there is an exception: as purchasing power falls, more of an inferior good will be bought. Therefore, if the good is inferior, the general tendency to substitute relatively low priced goods is partially offset by the tendency to buy more of the good due to the reduction in purchasing power. The substitution effect virtually always dominates this income effect for inferior goods, so generally we observe that quantity demanded falls with higher prices. But it is theoretically possible for the opposite to occur for an inferior good: the quantity demanded could rise with price. Thus, definitive demand relationships for any particular good are not forthcoming from economic theory. This same theoretical reasoning explains why crime is likely to be deterred by increased law enforcement, but that this is not a necessary result.

The responsiveness of quantity demanded to a price change is an important empirical issue in many studies of demand, and in many policy studies. For instance, if many substitutes are available for a good, an increase in its price could result in a very large reduction in the quantity demanded as consumers shift to substitutes. If the percentage change in quantity demanded is greater than the percentage change in price that brings it about, demand is said to be "elastic" (i.e., very responsive). Because the reduction in purchases is relatively large in this circumstance, the consumer's total expenditures on the good will fall as price rises. On the other hand, if no good substitutes are available for the commodity, the consumer may not reduce purchases of the good by very much as its price rises. In this case the percentage change in quantity demanded may be less than the percentage change in price, and the consumer's expenditures on the good rise with a price increase. Demand for such a good is said to be "inelastic" (not very responsive). The elasticity of demand depends on the income and substitution effects. The substitution effect always reduces quantity demanded as price rises; but for instance, if a large share of a person's income is spent on the good, and it is an inferior good for the consumer, demand can be quite inelastic.

The elasticity of demand, defined as the percentage change in quantity demanded divided by the percentage change in price, can often be estimated, at least for a group of consumers. Demand for most goods actually has both elastic and inelastic ranges. When prices are relatively low, demand tends to be inelastic. However, as the price rises, demand generally becomes more elastic. This occurs for several reasons. One is that consumption decisions are made subject to a budget constraint. With limited income, an increase in the price of one good means less of something else must be purchased. Thus, there is a tendency to substitute lower priced goods for the increasingly higher priced good in order to mitigate the sacrifice that must be made. Furthermore, even if such substitution incentives are weak (perhaps because other goods do not satisfy the consumer to the same degree), as the price rises an increasing portion of the consumer's income would have to be devoted to the good in question. At some point, this portion would get so high that the consumer would have no choice but to reduce expenditures on the good. Therefore, demand must become elastic at some relatively high price.

The concept of elasticity of demand has important implications for drug policy. It is theoretically conceivable that over some price range demand could be "perfectly inelastic." That is, quantity demanded may not fall as price rises. This is a highly unlikely phenomenon, however. The good must be inferior for such a non-negatively sloped demand curve, but in addition the income effect must be exactly equal to the substitution effect. In fact, economists have never found a good for which demand is perfectly inelastic, including addictive goods like tobacco and alcohol (Moore, 1990:114).[7] Both alcoholics and chain smokers adjust their consumption as prices change (Nicholson, 1985:184–187). Nonetheless, it frequently can be inferred from claims about drug use and drug-related crime that addicts have a perfectly inelastic demand curve, because drug addicts will supposedly do virtually anything to avoid the disutility of withdrawal pain. This is evident from policymakers' arguments that addicts "need" drugs so badly that they go to tremendous lengths to get them. In particular, it is often argued that addicts commit large numbers of property crimes in order to finance their habits.[8] But as Moore (1990:114) explains, "the equation of physiological dependence with a perfectly inelastic demand reveals a fundamental misunderstanding of addiction and dependence. The physiological mechanisms of addiction and dependence are nowhere near as compelling as this simple equation suggests."

If the idea that drug demand is perfectly inelastic is rejected in favor of a negatively sloped although perhaps quite inelastic demand, then it might seem reasonable for law enforcement to focus on suppliers. Direct interdiction efforts can be made, punishment of suppliers can be made more severe than punishment of users, and so on. As long as there is some elasticity to the demand curve, supply-side efforts which raise the risk to suppliers and therefore raise the price will reduce the size of the drug market. The assumption of inelastic (although not necessarily perfectly inelastic) demand has been made explicitly by most economists who have offered theoretical discussions of heroin markets; but at the same time, the conclusion that supply-side enforcement strategies are desirable has been challenged. It has been suggested that there may be a logical inconsistency in drug enforcement objectives if drug demand is inelastic, and if drugs users commit other crimes in order to finance their habits.[9] When demand is inelastic, consumer's illicit drug expenditures rise as price rises. If demand is very inelastic for the typical drug consumer who is at a subsistence level of income and who faces few substitution possibilities, such as eating less in order to pay the higher price, the only option would be to commit more predatory crimes.

There are at least two potential problems with this rising price/inelastic demand/predatory crime argument. First, there are reasons to suspect that demand for most drugs is not inelastic. Consider heroin, long viewed as the most addictive drug. Kaplan's examination of studies of heroin indicates that there is a striking analogy between alcohol and heroin use (1983:38). Many heroin addicts or "problem" users voluntarily abstain from use for substantial periods for any number of reasons, just as do problem drinkers. Indeed, Moore (1977) and Roumasset and Hadreas (1977) both contend that addicts' behavior exhibits considerable responsiveness to price changes. This is possible because, for instance, average daily consumption often significantly exceeds the amount needed to avoid withdrawal pain, so the argument that a specific amount of heroin is required to avoid withdrawal does not imply that demand is inelastic. Furthermore, the average addict actually goes through "sick outs" several times a year because he or she is unable or unwilling to incur the cost of a purchase. The average addict consumes well above the amount of heroin needed to avoid withdrawals roughly 70 percent of the days in a year and actually suffers withdrawals the other days. Some will go without a drug for several days and actually detoxify themselves. Thus, an addict's demand apparently does not even have a zero elasticity at the level needed to avoid withdrawals. This should not be too surprising since the withdrawal pains for addicts are remarkably mild relative to popular perception (Nyswander, 1956:121–124; Kaplan, 1983:35; Moore, 1990:114). They are not extremely painful for most addicts, in part because of the low quality of many drugs available in the black market, but "even in its classic form, heroin withdrawal is not *that* serious. Pharmacologists compare it to a bad case of one week flu" (Kaplan, 1983:35). In the case of cocaine, withdrawal pain is even less severe than for heroin; cravings for cocaine stem from the drug's euphoric effects rather than from avoidance of withdrawals and, on balance, it is less addictive than heroin (Gould, 1990:11).

The suggestion that an addict's demand may not be so inelastic as generally claimed is reinforced by the fact that there are obvious substitutes for drug consumption. For the most severely addicted persons, treatment programs and drugs that block withdrawal are available and are used when heroin prices rise.[10] In addition, research suggests that most drug users stop drug consumption eventually, whether they use a treatment program or not to facilitate the change in behavior.[11]

There is an even more fundamental reason to suggest that most consumers of drugs will have an elastic demand for these products. Although the argument that drugs cause crime generally involves an explicit statement to the effect that drug addicts are driven to commit crimes to finance their habits, the fact is that not all drug users are addicts. Indeed, there is a large population of regular heroin users who are not addicted, just as there is a large population of non-addicted drinkers and "these users bear the same relation to heroin addicts as normal drinkers do to problem drinkers or alcoholics" (Kaplan, 1983:33). Variation in the pattern and intensity of use is also found among consumers of cocaine. The NIDA *National Household Survey of Drug Abuse* (*National Institute on Drug Abuse*, 1988) indicates that most cocaine users are not regular consumers of the drug. Among young adults (ages eighteen to twenty-five), fewer than one in four "lifetime" users—that is, individuals who indicate that they have ever consumed the drug—report use in the previous month. More strikingly, among adults over the age of twenty-five, only one in eleven "lifetime" users reported use of cocaine in the previous month. This implies either that a large number of long-time users are not addicts or that a tremendous portion of the long-time cocaine-consuming population managed to withdraw for at least a month prior to being surveyed. The first of these explanations seems more reasonable and is consistent with findings on heroin.

Some consumers are apparently susceptible to addiction while others are not. Even for addicts, the severity of addiction probably varies across individuals depending on how long they have been consuming and how much they have consumed in the past (Moore, 1973; Becker and Murphy, 1988). Various physiological and psychological characteristics shape an individual's preferences and influence his susceptibility to addiction. Research suggests that while "heavy use" may occur within a few months after first consuming a narcotic (Winick, 1961), actual addiction can take a year or even longer. For instance, McGlothlin, Anglin, and Wilson (1978) report that the mean age between first narcotics use and first daily use for males in two samples from the California Civil Addict Program was approximately two years. Similarly, Gerstein, Judd, and Rovner (1979) find a one-and-a-half-year mean lag between first use and daily use for a sample of women from the City of San Diego/University of California Narcotic Treatment Program. Drawing on this distinction, Moore (1973) focuses on the differences in elasticity of demand between long-time users and short-time users. He suggests that supply-side enforcement policies that push the price up are likely to be relatively effective against new users, because new users have the most elastic demand, a finding also supported by Becker, Grossman, and Murphy (1991).

Even if the inelastic demand argument holds for addicts, the market demand of the total drug-using population will not be inelastic. Indeed, White and Luksetich (1983) contend that the demand for heroin, like most other goods, probably has both elastic and inelastic ranges. Thus, the structure of an illicit drug market may be an important determinant of the elasticity of market demand. If a market is monopolized, the seller has a strong incentive to raise price as long as demand is inelastic. After all, as price rises, consumers spend more on the good as long as demand is in the inelastic range.[12] Moore (1977) argued that the retail market for heroin in New York was fairly (although not perfectly) competitive at the time of his study. However, he also contended that there was sufficient tacit coordination among the relatively small number of importers to keep price in the elastic range of market demand. Roumasset and Hadreas (1977) argued that the Oakland heroin market was quite competitive, but they also contended that price was in the unitary elasticity range of market demand (i.e., the percentage change in quantity demanded by all consumers in the market was roughly equal to the percentage change in price, so that total consumer expenditures on heroin remained fairly constant as price changed). On the other hand, Silverman and Spruill (1977) estimated that elasticity of demand for heroin in the highly competitive Detroit market was inelastic at –0.22, and other estimates have been even lower (Koch and Grupp, 1971:340). Indeed, Silverman and Spruill (1977) and Brown and Silverman (1974) both found small but significant relationships between predatory crime and the price of heroin in Detroit.[13] Of course, even if the Detroit results were to hold consistently across all markets for heroin users, it does not follow that they must hold for consumers of other illicit drugs which may be more or less addictive. Misket and Vakil (1972) estimated the elasticity of demand for marijuana to be elastic at –1.5 for UCLA students, for example.

The second problem with the price increase/inelastic demand/rising crime argument is that it implies that heavy drug users' labor supply decisions are different from those of other people. The claim is that drug users must commit predatory crimes in order to finance their consumption.[14] However, as drug prices rise, the purchasing power of a dollar obtained through illegal actions declines. The implicit real wage from crime falls. If low-income addicts commit more crime under these circumstances, this would be inconsistent with much evidence on labor supply and on the economics of crime. The empirical evidence from the economics of crime literature suggests that criminals tend to commit fewer crimes when the relative returns to crime fall. These results suggest that criminal activity is dominated by people who are not drug addicts, or that the argument that rising drug prices lead to more property crimes is either not very generalizable or otherwise flawed.[15]

III. The Impact of Addiction on Drug Demand and Non-drug Crime

Arguing that an individual's demand for drugs is inelastic does not necessarily imply that drug consumption is a primary cause of crime. Given a drug user with low income relative to the price of drugs in illicit markets, drug addicts face a choice: "either quit the drug and go through withdrawal, or turn to criminal methods of acquiring the necessary money"

(Canadian Government's Commission of Inquiry, 1973:321). Indeed, this same report pointed out that affluent persons with low-risk access to drugs, like physicians, pharmacists, and perhaps police, generally do not turn to property crime as a consequence of drug consumption, reinforcing the idea that drug consumption and decisions to commit crime involve economic choices.[16]

Addiction. When economists attempt to model addiction, they move into the realms of psychologists and pharmacologists.[17] As a general rule, economists take preferences as given and focus on incentives and constraints. However, it is clear that addiction can affect preferences directly, so we must draw upon these other disciplines to understand how it changes individuals' reactions to incentives and constraints. Of course, one might simply contend that addicts are not rational, so an attempt to consider addiction in the context of an economic model of decisionmaking is of little use. Such an argument could be based on the assumption that "certain kinds of people who want to use drugs . . . cannot be dissuaded by laws, social disappropriation, or inconvenience" (Moore, 1990:113). That is, such people simply do not respond to incentives, as Fernandez (1969:487) suggested when he wrote that "for heroin users, jail sentences cease to be a deterrent." However, as Moore (1990:115) argues in contradicting the assumption of irrationality, the fluidity of drug use patterns over time and across demographic groups "seems inconsistent with the hypothesis that there are some people who by virtue of their biology, upbringing, or character are simply destined to use drugs. Those patterns seem much more consistent with the hypothesis that patterns of drug use, like the patterns of consumption for many other things, are vulnerable to changes in tastes, prices and availability."[18] Furthermore, Becker and Murphy (1988) have demonstrated that a model of decisionmaking can incorporate addiction and still explain many aspects of the addict's behavior in terms of rational responses to incentives and constraints (recall that by rational, we do not mean "sensible" as defined by other peoples' norms; rather, rational simply refers to the idea that people respond to changes in incentives—e.g., costs and benefits—in predictable ways). Becker and Murphy did not address the potential link between addiction and crime, however.[19]

When modeling the effect of addiction on the decision to commit a crime, several characteristics of addiction must be considered. First, addicts may experience withdrawal pain. That is, when too little of the drug is consumed, utility associated with drug consumption may become negative. For a non-addictive good, zero consumption means that total utility is a function of other goods consumed. But for an addict, zero consumption—or even relatively small levels of consumption—of the addictive good adds a negative value to total utility; utility is a function of the addictive good even when the good is not consumed. This does not imply that demand is perfectly inelastic for an addict at the level of consumption needed to avoid withdrawal, however. Recall evidence cited above which implies that withdrawals resulting from heroin or cocaine addiction occur regularly and that they may not be extremely painful for most addicts.

As a person becomes addicted (i.e., consumes a drug over a longer period of time), a tolerance for the drug is developed (Donegan et al., 1983). This frequently observed characteristic of addiction suggests that more of the drug is required to achieve a particular high (level of utility) as the period of drug use is prolonged. Thus total utility for any given level of drug consumption falls as addiction increases. This is consistent with the idea that addicts are often relatively discontented or depressed (Winston, 1980). As a person becomes addicted, his or her consumption of the drug must increase, ceteris paribus, due to increased tolerance, or utility will fall. But since increasing amounts of other goods must be sacrificed in order to achieve the same "high", total utility falls.

Demand for an addictive drug therefore depends on price, income, the prices of related goods, and preferences as influenced by the level of addiction. Increased addiction implies an increase in demand for the drug, but the relationships between demand and the other factors are still indeterminate. There clearly is a tendency for demand to become less elastic with addiction, however. If the drug is an inferior good, then demand must become less elastic as addiction rises. If the drug is a normal good, the outcome is indeterminate: although there is a reduced propensity to substitute, this is offset by the tendency for an increase in elasticity as price rises due to the income effect. Demand may nevertheless become less elastic with addiction to a normal good, because addiction could have a greater impact on the substitution effect than on the income effect.

Some might contend our model of addiction is incorrect because it predicts neither inelastic demand nor even a reduction in elasticity with increasing addiction. A reduction in the elasticity of demand for addicting drugs is likely, but it is not inevitable. However, addiction as modeled here has the following attributes: (1) rising demand for a drug as the level of addiction increases; (2) withdrawal pain (disutility) as consumption of the drug falls below some threshold for an addict; (3) increased tolerance, and therefore, increased levels of consumption to achieve any specific level of utility as addiction increases; and (4) the possibility that the severity of addiction can vary across individuals or for one individual over time.

These four characteristics are commonly associated with addiction. A low price elasticity of demand for an addict, on the other hand, is a hypothesized characteristic that still requires general empirical verification. Indeed, even if an addict was observed over time to hold his or her purchases relatively constant as the drug price rose, it does not follow that the addict has inelastic demand, because the ceteris paribus assumption may not hold: the addict's level of addiction could be rising over the same period, implying that his or her demand has been shifting up. Thus, the primary theoretical implications of adding addiction to the consumer choice model are these two: (1) as the level of addiction rises, demand for the addictive drug increases; and (2) other impacts of addiction on the effectiveness of deterrence policy cannot be predicted a priori.

Illicit drugs. The preceding discussion of addiction could be about tobacco or alcohol. Heroin and cocaine differ because possession is illegal. Simply making the sale and/or possession of a drug illegal is not likely to make much difference, of course, unless an effort is made to enforce the law. The potential for arrest and punishment make sale and/or possession of drugs risky, and that is what creates incentives for a change in behavior. If law enforcement efforts are focused exclusively on suppliers, then the impact of illegality on the consumer's decision is easily determined. Such an effort will raise the market price of the drug as risk increases for sellers, ceteris paribus. If consumers respond to relative prices, they should buy less of the drug. How much less will depend on each consumer's demand elasticity, which in turn depends on the person's level of addiction.

If possession is illegal and there is a threat of arrest and punishment for the drug consumer, the impact may be slightly different. However, the consequence of such a law enforcement effort can be analyzed as a price change. Moore (1973) suggests that the buyer's "full price" of illicit drugs includes not only the money price, but also the value of time spent searching for drugs, as well as risk factors associated with unknown purity of drugs, toxicity of adulterants, threat of victimization, and threat of arrest. To Moore's argument we can add the severity of punishment (e.g., expectations regarding the portion of arrests that actually lead to conviction, and the resulting sanction, such as a fine, probation, or incarceration). Such risks affect demand decisions in ways that are very similar to the drug's money price, since they represent costs above the money price associated with the purchase and consumption of the drug. Thus, if the risk of arrest rises, or the severity of the expected punishment increases, the impact should be similar to the impact of an increase in the money price of the drug. This increase in full price should normally lead to a reduction in the quantity demanded of the drug. However, addiction can affect the response to changes in the probability of arrest and severity of punishment since addiction clearly reduces the willingness to reduce drug consumption. Thus, an individual will tend to be less effectively deterred from drug consumption as his or her addiction increases.

If drug addicts are substantially different from other people, including non-drug criminals, then it may be that increases in the probability and/or severity of punishment will not have any deterrent impact. Perhaps the claim that "for heroin users, jail sentences cease to be a deterrent" (Fernandez, 1969:487) is correct, for example. Kim and his co-authors (1993) report the results of empirical studies of recidivism among drug offenders, using data from the Sentencing Guidelines/Florida Department of Corrections Matching Data Base. The researchers identified 4,298 persons who had been incarcerated for a drug offense after 1985 and released prior to April 2, 1990 (these data are discussed in Section IV below), and an econometric analysis of the determinants of recidivism was performed. After controlling for individual and socio-economic factors, it was found that an increase in the number of police in a jurisdiction reduced the probability of recidivating, supporting the hypothesis that an increase in the probability of arrest reduces drug crime. Furthermore, drug criminals sentenced to probation were more likely to recidivate than drug criminals sentenced to prison. Assuming that prison is a "more severe" punishment than probation, this result also suggests that drug criminals respond to the severity of punishment. However, it was also found that, given a prison sentence, an increase in the length of that sentence did not impact the likelihood of recidivating. This implies that increasing the length of prison sentences for drug offenders may not be an effective deterrent. While this is a limited sample—and apparently the only sample of drug offenders that has been used to study the deterrent hypothesis—the results are strikingly consistent with the much larger economics-of-crime empirical literature summarized above. The probability of arrest appears to be a significant factor in the decision to commit drug crimes, just as it is for other crimes, while evidence on the severity of punishment is inconclusive.

Other risks, such as potential impurities and toxicity of the drug, can be treated in a similar fashion. Note that the risks of victimization, toxicity, and impurities are also a function of illegality, at least in part. The illegality of drug use makes users themselves very attractive targets for predatory crime. Barnett (1984:53), a former criminal prosecutor, wrote:

> I would estimate that close to half of the murders I prosecuted were drug-related, but not in the sense that drug addicts committed the crimes. On the

> contrary, drug users and particularly sellers are typically the victim of violent crimes . . . they (and those close to them) are . . . routinely robbed and murdered. If they are robbed, their robbers know that the offense will rarely be reported to the police. And if they are murdered, and the police, prosecutor, judge, or jury conclude that this was a "drug-related" killing, the seriousness with which the case will be treated is greatly reduced.

In other words, the offender's risk of being caught or prosecuted is considerably reduced when a drug user is chosen as a crime target. A recent study of drug dealers in Washington, D.C., most of whom are also drug consumers, indicates that these individuals are indeed subject to very high probabilities of injury or death relative to virtually any imaginable legal profession (Reuter, MacCoun, and Murphy 1990). Similarly, the relatively high price of heroin due to its illegality has led to adoption of intravenous injection of the drug because this is a more efficient means of generating the drug's effect than smoking or snorting. However, it is also more dangerous: the risk of overdose and infection is much higher and it is a major factor in the transmission of the AIDS virus. Thus, illegality may raise the full or effective price of drugs whether or not it has an impact on the money price or the probability of arrest.

IV. Financing Drug Consumption

The study of drug sellers in Washington, D.C., mentioned above also found that the vast majority of dealers were also drug consumers. Importantly, however, the majority also had legitimate jobs which, on average, earned them about twice the minimum wage. Other studies report that use of illicit drugs is associated with higher wages among young adults.[20] Drug consumers need not specialize in one method of income generation, and it is apparent that many have legal jobs. Thus, the theoretical possibility that there is a tradeoff between legal and illegal work effort appears to be quite significant. Many drug users have multiple sources of legal income including jobs, parental assistance, and welfare payments. And contrary to the claims of some drug warriors, it is apparent that not all drug purchases require criminal activity.

The National Commission on Marijuana and Drug Abuse (1973) examined a large number of studies of drug use and crime, and reported that between 41 percent and 66 percent of the various populations of people arrested, incarcerated, or entering treatment for drug use were employed immediately prior to arrest or treatment. Similarly, a New York State Narcotic Addiction Control Commission (1971) study estimated that

53 percent of regular heroin users were employed, 34 percent were in school, and only 13 percent were unemployed. Lukoff (1974) noted that "typical" patients (i.e., black with less than a high school education) in a treatment program he studied, which was limited to those who were at least twenty-one years old and had been addicted to heroin for at least two years, listed the following as their primary sources of income: legitimate jobs (18 percent); welfare (19 percent); support from spouse, kin, or other individual (14 percent); and crime (48 percent). In a 1986 survey of state prison inmates, almost 50 percent of those who reported daily drug use prior to their offense had been employed full-time in the year prior to their offense. Another 10 percent reported they were employed part-time. These incarcerated regular users of drugs also reported income from other sources: 22.8 percent had income from welfare; 30.5 percent from family and friends; and 47.6 percent from illegal sources.[21]

Similar findings come from a 1989 Bureau of Justice Statistics survey of 395,554 jail inmates from 3,312 city and county jails (Harlow, 1991). This report compared jailed inmates of six types: those who reported (1) never having used any illicit drug; (2) never having used any "major drug" (heroin, crack, cocaine, PCP, LSD, and methadone), but having consumed some illicit drug (marijuana, hashish, amphetamines, barbiturates, methaqualone); (3) consuming a major drug daily for the month prior to the offense for which they were arrested; (4) using a major drug at least once in the month before the offense for which they were arrested (this therefore includes all those who used daily); (5) using a major drug at some time in their life (this therefore includes all who used in the previous month, including daily users); and (6) using some illicit drug at some point in their life (this therefore includes all those who had consumed a major drug). The results of this survey are detailed in Table 3.1. In some ways, the findings for these categories were strikingly similar. For example, while 77.8 percent of those who reported never having consumed a major drug listed wages or salaries as one of their sources of income, 65.6 percent of the daily major drug users also had wages or salaries as a source of income. On the other hand, while 69.1 percent of the non-major drug users were employed at the time of their incarceration, only 49.8 percent of the daily major drug users were employed. Furthermore, while 4.7 percent of the non-major drug users report illegal sources of income, 29.4 percent of the daily major drug users do so. Naturally, such survey results may be suspect, because inmates may underreport both illegal drug use and illegal income. However, the trends revealed by the survey are suggestive. In particular, these results indicate that as the frequency of drug consumption rises, the likelihood that an individual can maintain legitimate employment falls and the probability that the individual will turn to criminal activities

Table 3.1: Employment Status, Sources of Income, and Monthly Income of Jail Inmates by Drug Use History, 1989

	Never Used		Used Illicit Drug in Lifetime	Used Major Drug		
	Illicit Drug	Major Drug		In Lifetime	In Past Month[a]	Daily/Past Month[a]
Employment Status[b]						
Employed	69.1%	69.1%	63.5%	61.1%	54.1%	49.8%
Full time	57.3	59.6	51.9	49.9	43.4	39.5
Part time	10.5	9.5	11.6	11.2	10.7	10.3
Source of Income						
Wages or Salary	77.3%	77.8%	75.8%	74.7%	69.2%	65.6%
Benefits	18.5	18.2	18.4	19.5	21.0	21.0
Family/Friends	13.7	14.2	21.9	19.9	21.4	21.8
Illegal Activity	4.3	4.7	13.1	16.9	24.7	29.4
Other	2.7	2.8	3.1	3.3	2.0	1.9
Number of Inmates	46,878	87,826	306,427	122,228	60,289	37,607

[a] These columns apply to the month before the offense.
[b] At the time of arrest or admission to jail.

Source: Harlow (1991:6).

as a source of income increases. However, they also illustrate that illegal sources of income are by no means the only source from which drug consumers obtain funds.

While some drug addicts clearly appear to be involved in illegal activity, property crime does not seem to account for most of the illegal income generated by these addicts. They probably raise almost as much money through such crimes as prostitution, pimping, and drug sales as they do from property crimes (Kaplan, 1983:54; Reuter, MacCoun, and Murphy, 1990). Moore (1977) estimated that heroin addicts obtained about 45 percent of their funds for purchasing heroin from working within the drug distribution system, with more than a third of the remaining funds coming from legitimate income or victimless crimes. Similarly, Gould and his co-authors (1974) reported that profit margins for drug sales exceeded 100 percent, and suggested that half or more of the money spent on heroin at the time could have been generated through the sale of that drug. In one study (Waldorf, 1973:50), one-third of the addicts in the sample supported their habits exclusively by selling drugs, and 48 percent partially supported themselves in this fashion. In this instance over 80 percent of the addicts were involved in the drug trade. Among another sample of addicts (Baridon, 1976:45), more than 60 percent sold drugs and most also worked at legitimate jobs. So the implication is that the impact of a change in the price of the drug on the level of any particular crime (e.g., burglary, robbery, drug sales) is not theoretically predictable. Addiction tends to enhance the possibility that as the price of the drug rises, more effort will be devoted to income generation; but it still does not follow that the addict will commit more property crimes in the face of higher drug prices.

There is another issue that deserves attention. What happens to drug demand as illegally obtained income rises? In other words, instead of asking, "Does drug use lead to crime?" we might ask, "Does crime lead to drug use?" If the expected return to illegal activities rises (e.g., because the probability of being arrested falls), then under most circumstances we should see an increase in the illegal activity. The resulting increase in income can be spent on goods, including illicit drugs; and if a drug is a normal good, increasing income will produce an increase in demand. There appears to be little attention given by policymakers and criminal justice officials to the potential causal relationship running from crime to drug use, in sharp contrast to the frequent claim that drug use causes crime. A recent study of Washington, D.C., drug dealers suggests that there could be an important connection of this type, however (Reuter, MacCoun, and Murphy, 1990). In particular, the Rand Corporation researchers found that when juveniles start dealing drugs they are typically not drug users. Thus, they are not committing the crime of drug dealing in order to finance a drug habit. The explanations for this behavior include the fact that these juveniles perceive drug dealing to provide an attractive economic opportunity relative to their legal opportunities. However, the longer someone stays in the drug supply business, the more likely it becomes that he or she will become a user and ultimately an addict. Indeed, most adult dealers in Washington, D.C., apparently are addicts.

Studies of the temporal sequencing of drug abuse and crime also suggest that criminal activities generally precede drug use.[22] For example, a Bureau of Justice Statistics survey of prison inmates found that approximately half of the inmates who had ever used a major drug, and roughly three-fifths of those who used a major drug regularly, did not do so until after their first arrest for some non-drug crime, that is, "after their criminal career had begun" (Innes, 1988:1–2). Similarly, the survey of jail inmates discussed above found that more than half of local jail inmates who reported that they were regular drug users said that their first arrest for a crime occurred an average of two years before their first use of drugs (Harlow, 1991:7). Indeed, Chein and co-authors (1965:64–65) conclude that delinquency is not caused by drug abuse, but rather, "the varieties of delinquency tend to change to those most functional for drug use; the total amount of delinquency is independent of drug use." Once an individual has decided to turn to crime as a source of income, he or she may discover that drugs are more easily obtained within the criminal subculture and perhaps that the risks posed by the criminal justice system are not as great as initially anticipated. Furthermore, criminal activity generates the income with which to buy goods that previously were not affordable, including drugs. Thus, under this scenario, crime leads to drug use, not vice versa. Of course, if the individual later becomes addicted, his or her preferences change; and at that point the "drugs cause crime" relationship might well come into play.

Criminality among drug offenders. The fact that many criminals are also drug users is well documented. During 1988, 72.2 percent of male arrestees in twenty U.S. cities tested positive in a urinalysis for the use of an illicit drug (National Institute of Justice, 1990). A Bureau of Justice survey of 12,000 inmates indicated that over 75 percent had used drugs, 56 percent had used drugs in the month prior to their incarceration, and one-third admitted to being under the influence of drugs at the time of their offense (Wexler, Galkin, and Lipton, 1989). Similarly, the survey of jail inmates from which Table 3.1 is drawn found that 77.7 percent of the inmates admitted using some illicit drug and that 55.4 percent had used a major drug (Harlow, 1991:4). Furthermore, 43.9 percent had used some drug in the month prior to the offense for which they were admitted, and 27.7 percent had used a major drug during that period. Twenty-seven percent admitted being under the influence of a drug at the time of the offense, and 17.3 percent said that they were under the influence of a major drug. Since the crime for which 23 percent of this jail inmate population were charged was a drug offense, that could account for a large portion of those under the influence when charged. Indeed, a disproportionate number of the drug offenders in the jail survey were under the influence, but substantial percentages of the non-drug offenders were, as well: 24.9 percent of the violent offenders admitted to being under the influence of an illicit drug at the time of the offense, as did 31 percent of the property offenders, as compared to 40.9 percent of the drug offenders (Harlow, 1991:10). Furthermore, research has established a correlation between daily drug use and criminal activities (NASDAD, 1990) and documents that drug offenders are responsible for a great deal of the crime committed in American cities (Gropper, 1985; Johnson et al., 1985; and Ball and Nurco, 1983). Confirming this connection are research findings that criminal activity increases with the intensity of drug use, as suggested by Table 3.1. A decline in drug use by some drug offenders may result in a reduction in non-drug criminal activity, particularly income-generating crimes such as robbery, burglary, and theft.[23]

These research findings have contributed to the claim that drug use is a primary cause of property crime, which in turn has led to increasing emphasis on the control of illicit drugs as a means of general crime prevention. Reallocating police and prison resources to combat drug use would appear justified if drugs truly are the root cause of most other crime and if most drug offenders are engaged in property crime. Indeed, if this were true, a crime control policy that focuses on drugs would be a positive sum game in the sense that incarceration of drug offenders would reduce both drug offenses and crimes against property.

Drug enforcement, unfortunately, is not a positive sum policy. Despite the high rate of drug use among persons arrested for other criminal activity, most research suggests only a loose connection between drug use and criminal activity. Chaiken and Chaiken (1990:210) summarize recent research and conclude that "there appears to be no simple general relation between high rates of drug use and high rates of crime." Nurco, Hanlon, and Kinlock (1991:222) review this literature and conclude that "while addicts, as a group, commit a great deal of crime, they cannot be regarded as a homogeneous class because of the extent of individual variability in the type, amount, and severity of crime committed." Fagan (1990) also questions the link between substance abuse and violent crime.

The arrest history of persons having at least one misdemeanor or felony drug arrest in Florida provides more evidence of only a modest link between drugs and other crime, suggesting that most drug offenders have no violent criminal record and many have few previous arrests for non-violent crimes. Table 3.2 shows the arrest history of persons arrested for drug offenses in 1987. Consider the distribution of violent crime arrests among drug arrestees. The 45,906 persons reported in Table 3.2 who had been arrested for at least one drug possession offense in 1987 have a history of 19,436 violent crime arrests, an average of 0.42 violent crimes per arrestee. But of those 45,906 persons, 76 percent had no prior arrest for a violent crime. Among the seven drug crimes enumerated in the table, the percentage of persons never having been arrested for a violent crime ranges from 65.5 percent (sale) to 86.5 percent (production). Column three in Table 3.2 reports a "concentration index" which is the share of all violent arrests, by drug crime category, accounted for by the most criminal 2.3 percent of the drug arrestees.[24] In the case of drug possession, this small portion of the arrested population accounted for 6,687 violent felony arrests—34.4 percent of the total. This group included 1,066 offenders who averaged 6.27 violent arrests in their past. The concentration index is substantial in each category, ranging from a low figure of 26.2 percent for drug sale to a high of 41.9 for drug production.

Table 3.2 also provides information regarding the non-violent arrest history of persons arrested for drug offenses in 1987. Since most of these persons were arrested for a drug felony (the exception being a few possession misdemeanors), column four reports the percentage of drug arrestees with the minimum possible number of non-violent felony arrests, including drug felonies (zero or one). The proportions with no non-violent felony arrest history, beyond the felony drug arrest that put them in the sample, are again substantial, ranging from 27.8 percent for the drug sale category to 63.3 percent for drug production. A small proportion of the arrested population also accounts for many non-violent arrests, as indicated by the concentration index that varies between 18 percent (drug sale) and 34.1 percent (possession).

Many of the non-violent felony arrests, of course, are for drug offenses which do not contribute to the Index I crime rate consisting of reported crimes against persons and property. Persons arrested for possession, for example, had a history of 84,588 non-violent felony arrests. This group was apparently much more heavily involved in drug activity than in non-drug felonies. The misdemeanor and felony arrest history of these offenders records over 75,500 possession arrests and 6,784 arrests for drug sale, leaving 2,304 possible property crime arrests. Table 3.3 shows that the vast majority of persons arrested for sale or possession of drugs had no

Table 3.2: Florida Drug Offenders: A Profile of Offenders with at Least One Misdemeanor and/or Felony Drug Arrest in 1987

		Arrest History			
		Violent Felony Crime*		Non-violent Felony Crimes	
Drug Offense	Offenders	Percent None	Concentration Index[a]	Percent Zero or One	Concentration Index[a]
Possession	45,906	76.0	34.4	42.2	34.1
Sale	8,472	65.5	26.2	27.8	18.0
Smuggling	384	69.5	29.6	40.4	19.8
Production	452	86.5	41.9	63.3	23.7
Trafficking	3,308	82.6	40.3	53.3	22.0
Delivery and Distribution	1,997	69.4	28.5	31.9	20.4
Possession of Drug Equipment	6,256	68.2	30.1	31.0	18.8

* Violent crimes include homicide, sexual assaults, robbery, aggravated assault, kidnapping and arson (zero or one). Non-violent offenses include burglary, larceny, and automobile theft, and drug felonies.

[a] The proportion of arrests in each category accounted for by the 2.3 percent of the population that is most frequently arrested. These offenders exceed the mean number of arrests by two standard deviations.

Source: Trager and Clark (1989).

Table 3.3: The Property Arrest History of Florida Offenders with at Least One Misdemeanor and/or Felony Drug Arrest in 1987

	Percentage with No Property Arrest History	
	Arrested for Possession	Arrested for Trafficking
Burglary Arrests	80.4	74.3
Stolen Vehicle Arrests	92.3	90.5
Grand Larceny	89.9	85.0
Stolen Property Arrests	98.2	97.0
None of the Above	70.9	61.9

Source: Trager and Clark (1989).

prior arrests for property crimes. Among persons arrested for sale of drugs, a group more inclined to property crime than persons arrested for possession, 61.9 percent had no previous arrest for a property crime. Among the 45,906 persons arrested in 1987 for possession, over 80 percent had never been arrested for burglary and almost 71 percent had never been arrested for any property offenses. Thus, these data suggest that many drug offenders are not active participants in non-drug crime. And surprisingly, given popular and political perceptions, drug consumers appear to be relatively less likely to be involved in property crime than drug sellers; that is, people willing to commit property crime to obtain income appear to be relatively likely to sell drugs to obtain income.

Analysis of recidivism patterns among drug offenders in Florida reveals a picture similar to that of incarcerated drug offenders. A statistical portrait of the 4,298 persons who had been incarcerated for a drug offense after 1985 and released prior to April 2, 1990, is shown in Table 3.4. This population is disproportionately black, male, and not employed at the time of arrest. Forty percent claim to have had twelve or more years of education, a figure that is comparable to the entire prison population in

Table 3.4: A Statistical Portrait of Incarcerated Drug Offenders in Florida	
Median Age at Admission	28.3
Percent Black	78.6
Percent White	21.4
Percent Male	90.6
Percent Female	9.4
Median Years of Education	11.0
Percent with 12 or more years	40.1
Percent with a Prior Conviction	83.4
Number in Sample	4,298.0

Source: See Kim et al. (1993).

1988.[25] Most offenders have had a previous conviction. This is expected since in Florida most first-time offenders are not incarcerated.

Of the 4,298 offenders in the sample, 734 were first-time drug offenders with no prior convictions. Table 3.5 shows the return to Department of Corrections (DOC) control among this population. By April 2, 1990, 48.6 percent had returned to DOC custody via probation or incarceration. The offenses for which these returning offenders were convicted are also shown in the table. Over 75 percent of the returnees (36.7 percent of the total population) were convicted for another drug offense. Only 11.9 percent of the total population were convicted for non-drug offenses; less than half (49 percent) of the identifiable non-drug offenses were burglary and theft.

Returns to DOC control among drug offenders with a prior conviction are also shown in Table 3.5. Slightly more than 51 percent of the 3,564 offenders in this group returned to DOC control prior to April 2, 1990. As in the case of offenders without a prior record, the overwhelming majority

Table 3.5: Reconviction among Drug Offenders Released from Florida's Prisons

	Drug Offenders			
	First-time Without Prior Convictions		With Prior Conviction(s)	
	Number	Percent	Number	Percent
Total Population				
Not returning to DOC custody	375	51.4	1,739	48.8
Returning to DOC custody	359	48.6	1,825	51.2
Total	734	100.0	3,564	100.0
Returning Population				
Return for Drug Offense	268	36.7	1,236	34.7
Return for Non-drug Offenders	87	11.9	589	16.5
Total	355	48.6	1,825	51.2
Returning Non-drug Offenders				
Murder, Manslaughter	1	0.1	8	0.2
Sexual Offenses	1	0.1	1	0.0
Robbery	14	1.9	87	2.5
Violent Personal Crimes	14	1.9	69	1.9
Burglary	16	2.2	161	4.5
Theft, Forgery, Fraud	23	3.2	139	3.9
Weapons	10	1.4	86	2.4
Other	5	0.7	27	0.8
Unknown	3	0.4	11	0.3
Total	87	11.9	589	16.5

Source: See Kim et al. (1993).

Table 3.6: Felony Probationers Who Were Arrested for a Felony Offense While on Probation

Most Serious Felony Conviction Offense	Percent of Probationers Arrested for:			
	Total[a]	Violent Offense	Property Offense	Drug Offense
All Offenses	43.0%	8.5%	14.8%	14.1%
Violent Offenses	41.0	17.9	9.4	8.9
Property Offenses	43.4	7.4	23.7	7.3
Drug Offenses	48.9	7.4	10.3	26.7

[a] The violent plus property plus drug percentages do not add up to the total because there are two other small categories in the original study: weapons offenses and "other offenses."

Source: Langan and Cunniff (1992, Table 4.6).

of these returnees were again convicted for a drug offense. Burglary and theft account for half of the offenses committed by the 589 returnees who were convicted for non-drug offenses, but these convictions account for only 8.4 percent of the total population.

Recently released data suggest that the characteristics of the Florida drug-using criminal population just described also apply to the nation as a whole. A 1992 Bureau of Justice Statistics report on recidivism of felons on probation between 1986 and 1989 found that drug offenders are far more likely to recidivate for a drug offense than for a violent or property offense. Furthermore, violent offenders who are rearrested tend to recidivate most often for a new violent crime, and property offenders are most likely to recidivate for another property crime (Langan and Cunniff, 1992). Table 3.6 summarizes some of the key results from this study. Consider the property offense line across, for instance. It suggests that 43.4 percent

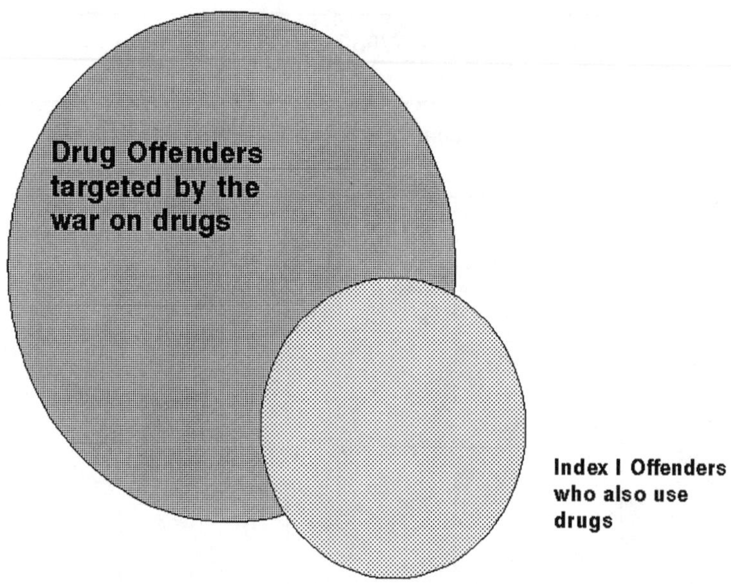

Figure 3.1

of the probationers in the sample who had committed property offenses had recidivated at the time of the study; furthermore, 7.4 percent were re-arrested for a violent crime, 23.7 percent for another property crime, and 7.3 percent for a drug crime, suggesting that property criminals were over three times as likely to commit another property crime as to commit a drug crime. Similarly, drug criminals apparently were more than two and a half times as likely to commit another drug crime as a property crime.

These statistics, combined with survey data on drug use among persons arrested and convicted of Index I crimes, suggest that the set of people who are drug offenders only partially overlaps with the set of people who commit Index I crimes. The simple diagram in Figure 3.1 helps visualize the implications. Two distinct types of drug users apparently exist. First, a substantial portion of drug offenders apparently do not commit property or violent crimes. Second, many offenders arrested for violent and property crimes also use drugs. The Florida data presented above suggests there are relatively few habitual offenders who are heavily involved in both drugs and other crime, so the overall population of arrested and convicted drug offenders is probably not a population of hardened criminals that is unresponsive to incentives due to immersion in a life of crime.

Chapter 4

The Impact of Enforcement on Drug Markets

Drug enforcement policies are implicitly based on the proposition that buyers and sellers in drug markets respond to incentives. This is a firm foundation for the war on drugs. Greater enforcement against suppliers presumably will reduce the amount of drugs supplied at any given price; efforts against drug users similarly are expected to lower the net benefits of drug use so the quantity of drugs purchased at any price will be lower. Furthermore, evidence discussed in Chapter 3 suggests that drug offenders do in fact respond to incentives. Therefore, the expectation of lower demand and smaller supply appear appropriate and this suggests enforcement policy should be the formula for a successful effort against drugs. In obvious contradiction to these expected benefits of increased enforcement, the "drug problem" is not demonstrably smaller as a result of the 1984—1989 drug war.

It is not the foundation of the war that is flawed. The mistaken root of drug policy is the belief that people can respond to increasing enforcement in only one way: curtailing sale and use. Motives of people in drug markets—the desire for short-term pleasure and profit—are so powerful that many try to continue their drug activity while still reacting to the constraints imposed by drug laws and enforcement efforts. Rather than passively accepting the effects of increasing enforcement as inevitable, drug entrepreneurs will attempt to "beat" the police by adopting new production techniques, offering new products, and developing innovative marketing strategies. Users can change their buying habits and use different drugs to maintain their pleasures in the face of rising police interference.

The reactions of buyers and sellers of drugs which reduce the effectiveness of enforcement efforts are the focus of this chapter. Section I analyzes alternative market outcomes that result from a war on drugs and considers alternative measures of drug enforcement success. The reactions of drug users and sellers to increasing enforcement are discussed in Sections II and III. Strategies to avoid rising risks of arrest in drug markets sometimes lead to outcomes that are contrary to the goals of drug policy. Section IV summarizes some of the unintended consequences of enforcement policy that arise from the defensive strategies adopted by users and sellers.

I. Market Effects of the Drug War

Drug policy can have an impact on the market for various illicit substances by affecting market prices and reducing the volume of drugs traded. This reality is captured by rudimentary market analysis. The market demand for a specific drug will be downward sloping, reflecting the fact that the quantity demanded will fall when the price rises. Market supply will be upward sloping, indicating that a greater quantity of the drug will be offered for sale as its price increases. In Figure 4.1, demand (D_1) intersects with the supply curve (S_1) at an equilibrium price P_1 and quantity Q_1.

Enforcement works because it changes the cost, or full price, of buying and selling drugs. Increasing efforts to arrest drug dealers and tougher penalties for those convicted increase the cost of selling a drug, and will be reflected in the market by a shift in the supply curve from S_1 to S_2. Because the market demand for a drug is somewhat elastic (i.e., not perfectly inelastic), this results in a higher price and a decline in the equilibrium quantity sold at the intersection of D_1 and S_2. Direct efforts to reduce drug demand may also affect the market. A "just say no" campaign, better information about the deleterious effects of drugs, and/or enforcement against users should cause a decline in demand, from D_1 to D_2. This further reduces the amount of drugs sold in the market. Rising enforcement, when other factors are held constant, will unambiguously lower the volume of drugs sold. Anti-drug policies will have a greater effect on the quantity sold when demand and supply are more elastic. Drug prices may fall, rise, or be unchanged as a result of a *change* in enforcement policy, depending on the magnitudes of the shifts of demand and supply and the responsiveness of buyers and sellers to changes in

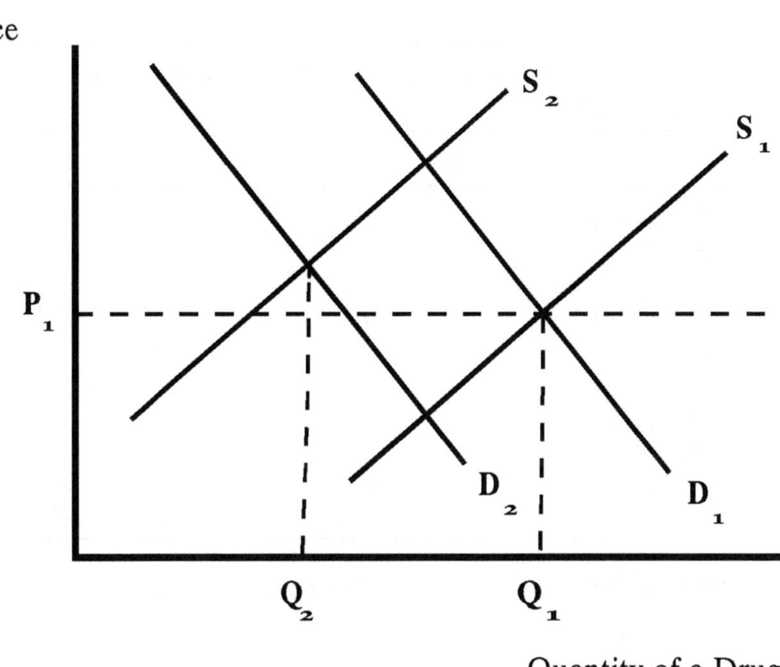

Figure 4.1

price. But in aggregate there is no question that illicit drug prices are much higher than they would be if these commodities were legalized. Moore (1990:124) estimated that heroin was selling at seventy times its price under legalization, cocaine eight times the legal price, and marijuana fifteen times the legal price.[1]

Market effects of the 1984–1989 anti-drug offensive are best measured by changes in the quantity of drug sales; but for obvious reasons, sales data for these illicit markets are not available. Limited evidence regarding the size of drug markets can be pieced together, however. The 1990 *National Household Survey on Drug Abuse* (National Institute on Drug Abuse, 1991) provides information on the two principal components of the demand for drugs at current prices for at least a portion of the drug market: estimates of the number of drug users and the frequency of use among members of households. Table 4.1 shows, for various years, the percentage of the surveyed population between twelve and seventeen and between eighteen and twenty-five using marijuana or hashish and cocaine during the past year. These data show a marked decline in use of both drugs. Almost

Table 4.1: Estimate Prevalence of Drug Use during the Past Year, 1979–1990

	1979	1982	1985	1988	1990
Age Group					
12–17:					
marijuana and hashish	24.1	20.6	19.7	12.6	11.3
cocaine	4.2	4.1	4.0	2.9	2.2
18–25:					
marijuana and hashish	46.9	40.4	36.9	27.9	24.6
cocaine	19.6	18.8	16.3	12.1	7.5

Source: National Institute on Drug Abuse, (1991).

25 percent of persons between eighteen and twenty-five used marijuana or hashish in 1990, a prevalence rate that declined over 47 percent from its 1979 level of 46.9 percent. Cocaine use among this age group also fell, from 19.6 percent in 1979 to 7.5 percent in 1990. Survey data also show use during the previous month declined substantially during the 1980s. These results are consistent with expectations of the effects of rising drug enforcement. Those least committed to drug use are most likely to stop when faced with a higher full price resulting from more information about the harmful effects of drug use and greater legal risks. Casual drug use among members of households fell sharply between 1985 and 1990. Estimates of persons using cocaine during the past year fell from an estimated 12 million to 6 million; current users, defined as those consuming the drug in the previous month, fell from 5.8 million to 1.6 million.

Showing that a smaller percentage of persons in households are using marijuana and cocaine does not necessarily mean that these drug markets are getting smaller, however. Persons not included in a survey of households, particularly those incarcerated in jails and prisons and the homeless, may use drugs more intensively than those who live more conventional lives. Furthermore, most illicit drugs are probably consumed by relatively few users.[2] Over 60 percent of all cocaine use in households may be consumed by about 11 percent of the user population, according to estimates based on the 1990 NIDA survey.[3] In fact, despite the declining number of drug users reported by NIDA's survey, it is possible that the 1984–1989 escalation of the drug war had relatively little impact on drug markets because the number of frequent drug users increased. The 1990 household survey revealed that the number of people using cocaine once a week or more rose slightly between the 1985 and 1990 surveys, from 647,000 to 662,000.[4] Furthermore, if persons not in households are among the heavier users of drugs, the household survey is likely to exaggerate the decline in casual use while underestimating the rise in the number of regular drug users. Hospital emergency room cases in which cocaine use is mentioned rose fourfold from 1985 to 1988, for instance, a trend consistent with an increasing intensity of drug use.[5] Thus, the evidence does not support a conclusion of substantial reductions in the demand for drugs during the drug war period, at least among heavy users.

If increasing drug enforcement had the predicted effect of reducing supply, we might expect a reduction in the availability of marijuana and cocaine. Surveys of high school seniors indicate no decline in their access to these drugs, however. Perceptions of the availability of marijuana among high schoolers was virtually unchanged from 1984 to 1990, while the proportion of students saying it was "fairly easy" or "very easy" to get cocaine increased by about 20 percent. It appears that the drug war did not have much impact on reducing drug supplies, either.

Effective enforcement against a particular drug, other things unchanged, will always lead to a decline in the quantity sold. Although definitive data are not available, what information we can get suggests the market for cocaine did not appreciably shrink as a result of the 1984–1989 drug war. Other things did change, of course, in that the reactions of drug buyers and sellers to rising enforcement were designed to offset the effect of enforcement. We now turn to the ways in which drug trade entrepreneurs and consumers of these illicit goods respond to a drug war in an effort to protect their profits and short-term pleasures.

II. The War on Drugs and Drug Demand

Demand for a drug is a relationship between price per unit and the quantity purchased during a particular time period. This relationship will change (i.e., shift upward or downward) when income, tastes and preferences, and prices of related products change. The notion of a "full price" of drug use, introduced in Chapter 3, includes the dollar price, time spent shopping for drugs, risks of being robbed or otherwise victimized in this illegal market, threats of toxic adulterants, and the possibility of being arrested and punished for drug possession. While full price accurately captures what drug users may pay for drugs, it is not appropriate to use this concept for the relationship between the price per unit and quantity demanded that a demand curve represents. Price per unit in the context of a demand curve is limited to the money price. An increasing money price of drugs causes a decline in the quantity demanded, a move along the demand curve shown in Figure 4.1. Most other changes in "full price" represent shifts in the demand curve. Increasing risks to consumers of drug toxicity, criminal victimization in the drug market, and legal sanction will shift the demand curve downward, putting downward pressure on drug prices and reducing the amount purchased.

Search cost requires special attention, in part because some analysts of drug policy place particular emphasis on the advantages of increasing search costs to reduce drug use. Kleiman (1992:138) treats rising search costs as a downward shift in demand, arguing "raising search time . . . reduces consumption without raising prices: it thus leaves consumers both less drug involved and better off financially (and thus less prone to become sick, deprive their families, or turn to crime), while depressing the earnings of drug dealers." This promises more than rising search costs can deliver, for there is no guarantee that dealers will not profit from higher drug prices.

To clarify the impact on prices of policies that increase search costs, it is important to recognize that drug markets can be segmented by experience (Cave and Reuter, 1988). Inexperienced and casual drug consumers constitute the market segment to which Kleiman's view is most applicable. Increased search costs do lower demand, but the higher search costs are the product of increasing enforcement against suppliers, who reduce supply due to the increased risk of doing business. When both the demand and supply curves shift in this way, the quantity sold will unambiguously decline but the price may rise, fall, or stay unchanged depending on the shifts and elasticities of demand and supply. Nevertheless, rising search costs for the casual user segment of the market will result in fewer users, in part because of a shift in demand.

Regular users, who probably account for most drug demand, are in a different circumstance. Unlike more casual and experimental users, regular users are likely to have steady sources of supply which are less likely to be disrupted by law enforcement activity aimed at increasing search costs.[6] These regular suppliers now have increased market power to raise prices, because their customers' alternative sources of supply are now more risky.[7] Since relatively few users demand most of the drugs used in the market, it is possible that suppliers on average are enriched by rising search costs that effectively discourage use among casual users.

Law enforcement efforts may be relatively more effective against some kinds of drugs compared to others. For example, marijuana is much bulkier and harder to conceal than cocaine and heroin. Furthermore, consumers of marijuana are probably much more responsive to price changes than consumers of cocaine or heroin (i.e., the elasticity of demand for marijuana is greater in absolute value than the elasticity of demand for "harder" more addictive drugs, as noted in Chapter 3). Thus, it is actually inappropriate to speak of "the drug market." Instead, there are several distinct but interrelated markets for illicit drugs, which may be differentially affected by drug enforcement and/or education efforts. They are interrelated on the supply side because drug entrepreneurs apparently can often supply more than one drug and substitute among them depending on availability. They are interrelated on the demand side to the degree that consumers find different drugs to be substitutes or complements. Let us briefly consider the evidence regarding changes in the two largest illicit drug markets.

Marijuana. Increasing drug enforcement can affect the demand for drugs in two ways. First, the added risk of arrest and punishment for possessing drugs directly discourages consumption. Second, if prices rise as a result of efforts to limit drug supply, the amount of illicit substances consumed will fall. In the case of marijuana these two effects have worked together to reduce consumption. The price of marijuana rose continuously from 1974 to 1984, although a simultaneous eightfold increase in potency may have actually caused price per unit of THC to fall over this period.[8] During the 1984–1989 war on drugs, however, marijuana prices rose sharply with very little change in potency.[9] These data, coupled with Reuter's (1991) estimate that the severity of punishment per marijuana transaction rose between 1979 and 1988, suggests that the war on drugs may have played a significant role in reducing the demand for marijuana while also raising its price.

Cocaine. The story for cocaine is quite different. Estimated use of this drug started rising in 1979, and growth of consumption accelerated after the onset of rising enforcement efforts in 1984. Prices did not rise as a consequence of enforcement and there is no discernable trend in purity.[10] In fact, 1989 cocaine prices in nominal terms were less than half their 1979 level. Nor did enforcement increase effective punishment for cocaine. Admittedly rough estimates of the user and seller populations led Reuter (1991) to speculate that the risk of arrest for cocaine users declined between 1979 and 1988, while the change in expected punishment of sellers was less certain.

Perhaps an even more important explanation of the increasing use of cocaine, however, was the relative success that law enforcement has had against marijuana (Thornton, 1991). Much of the law enforcement success against marijuana has been due to interdiction efforts, which have been considerably more successful than similar efforts against cocaine and heroin. In 1990, for example, 86 percent of local police departments and 94 percent of the sheriffs' departments in the country made marijuana seizures, as compared to 70 percent and 78 percent respectively for cocaine and 17 percent and 16 percent for heroin (Reaves, 1992a:3, Table 2). Furthermore, it has been estimated that as much as a third of the marijuana shipped into the United States was being intercepted (Kleiman, 1985:Ch. 3). This is not surprising since marijuana is much bulkier and harder to conceal than other drugs. Thus, the transportation alternatives available to smugglers of this drug are relatively limited.[11] The success of interdiction efforts with regard to marijuana means that its price is considerably higher in the United States than in source countries (Reuter and Kleiman, 1986).[12] This has created incentives for consumers to substitute other drugs for marijuana.

One drug that is being substituted for marijuana is alcohol. Recent and as yet unpublished statistical studies by DiNardo and Lemieux (1992) and Chaloupka and Laixuthai (1992), and a paper by Model (1993), have confirmed previous perceptions that alcohol and marijuana are substitutes.[13] But alcohol is not likely to be the only drug which is substituted for marijuana. The falling price of cocaine, which has occurred simultaneously with the relatively successful interdiction of marijuana, suggests that it has become a relatively attractive substitute. Indeed, while alcohol is an obvious alternative to marijuana as the price of pot rises, there is evidence that marijuana users sometimes use more lethal drugs when their drug of choice becomes less available. In Oahu, Hawaii, there was a precipitous increase in the use of crystal methamphetamine during 1985–1986 after a crop destruction program reduced the supply of marijuana (Chaiken, 1993). Thus, the increased use of cocaine appears to be at least partly a result of relatively successful law enforcement efforts directed against marijuana (Nadelmann, 1993:45). In other words, the allocation of law enforcement resources *within* the broad category of drug control makes a difference too. More resources effectively allocated to the control of one drug, say marijuana, leads to increased demands for other drugs. The opposite is also expected: reducing the probability of arrest and/or severity of punishment for marijuana should lead to reductions in the use of other drugs.[14] Indeed, Model (1993) found that decriminalization of marijuana, which had occurred in some states, was associated with lower numbers of emergency room episodes related to other kinds of illegal drugs.

Note that the money price of a commodity rises as demand increases when the supply is unchanged. Therefore, an outward shift in demand alone does not explain the changes in the cocaine market, where the quantity sold has apparently increased while price has fallen. Increasing supply is required to have greater quantity at lower prices. Apparently the effect of law enforcement on cocaine supply was not sufficient to offset other forces working to increase the supply of this drug.

III. The War on Drugs and Market Supply

Increasing drug enforcement against suppliers of drugs, which raises the probability of arrest and the severity of expected punishment, generates higher costs of production and a decrease in supply. The expected severity of punishment is determined by the probability of arrest, the probability of conviction, and the severity of punishment. Higher arrest rates generally imply a greater expected punishment, since the drug seller has a greater probability of receiving the proscribed sentence. Experience during the 1984–1989 war on drugs suggests that a higher arrest rate does not necessarily increase the expected severity of punishment. Consider an increase in police efforts against drug sellers that raises the probability of arrest, with a constant probability of conviction, when the prison system is not increased accordingly. The result is prison overcrowding. Aggregate state prison populations exceeded the design capacity of correctional facilities by 22 percent in 1990, up from 11 percent in 1984. More than one in five state prisons in 1990 were under a court order to limit population. About 35 percent of jail inmates were in facilities similarly ordered to reduce population.[15]

Florida's Department of Corrections response to a court order to reduce overcrowding resulted in a decline in the percentage of sentences served by prisoners—from 52 percent in January 1987 to 33 percent by the end of 1989. This was the result of a rapid rise in the number of drug crime arrests and convictions. States not under court order also expanded the use of early release programs to deal with the rising number of prisoners.[16] Thus, it is possible that as the probability of arrest rises for drug suppliers, the severity of punishment falls. The net effect of these two changes may mean that the supply does not shift to the left as in Figure 4.1 or at least that such a shift is very short lived. Indeed, supply could shift to the right. The initial increase in the probability of arrest raises the expected cost of punishment; but as prison overcrowding leads to an observed reduction in the actual time served, the expected cost of punishment may actually decline. Thus the net effect of the war on drugs could be either an increase or a reduction in the cost of supplying drugs. If supply shifts out instead of back in Figure 4.1, the price of drugs could fall as a result of increasing police efforts.

Court crowding and the necessity for plea bargaining may have a similar impact. Plea bargaining is generally used to relieve some of the pressure on the prosecutorial and judicial systems arising from non-price allocation and the resulting commons problems. Court delays are the typical justification for the widespread use of plea bargaining (Benson, 1990:Ch. 6). Thus, as increasing drug arrests place greater demands on prosecutorial and/or court resources, more cases will be plea bargained with the result being guilty pleas for lesser crimes than were actually committed. The accused offender must expect a better deal under the plea than he or she would anticipate in trial, since trial by jury is a right that cannot be taken away; that right would not be given up if the offender thought that he or she would be worse off as a result. If increasing drug arrests and growing pressure for drug convictions force prosecutors and judges to plea bargain even more, then the increasingly crowded court docket could put offenders in even stronger bargaining positions, and reduce their expected punishment.[17] When arrests rise faster than the resources used to prosecute and punish criminals, the resulting reduction in the expected severity of punishment reduces the potential deterrent impact of rising arrests. Thus, the expected reduction in the supply of a drug will be diminished and supply could actually increase.

Supply may not fall for another reason as well. Entry into the drug market will occur if the drug market becomes increasingly attractive, *or* if other alternatives become less attractive. For instance, people whose usual way of making a living is disrupted are also a potential source of new supply and distribution. Some suppliers of marijuana, for example—primarily farmers whose livelihood can no longer be sustained by legal crops—feel they are forced to enter the business. In a survey of marijuana growers in Illinois, Weisheit (1992:43) identifies one class of new suppliers of marijuana as "the pragmatist who enters the marijuana business out of economic necessity . . . . This individual would rather not be in the marijuana business but feels there are few options available to relieve his or her distress." This motivation has also been reported among growers in California and Kentucky.[18] Thus new suppliers of drugs can emerge as a result of a response to the incentive of rising prices of drugs or a decline in opportunity costs that make drug production relatively more attractive. In the latter circumstance, suppliers can be attracted to the industry even if drug prices are falling, so long as the opportunity costs fall more than drug prices.

Changing opportunities in other countries can also lead to the development of new international sources of drugs. The collapse of industry in the former Soviet Union, which left many workers without a job or with reduced incomes, has apparently led some Russians to turn to drug production for sale in Western Europe. As one U.S. Drug Enforcement Administration (DEA) officer put it, "Here's a state-owned factory taking orders from drug traffickers to deliver illegal drugs . . . [because] . . . they just needed the business."[19]

The supply of drugs can also be reduced by creating alternatives for current suppliers. For example, the Institute for Liberty and Democracy in Lima, Peru, has interviewed the leaders of the groups who grow cocaine in Peru.[20] These groups reportedly grow roughly 70 percent of the world's cocaine. The surveys found that these growers made approximately $600 per capita, less than farmers who grow and sell several other crops, including coffee. When asked why they did not switch to other crops, they reported two reasons: (1) the fact that the government of Peru does not recognize their property rights to land, which reduces the incentive to invest in improvements necessary for most kinds of agricultural production; and (2) the state's economic regulations grant exclusive production and/or exporting rights to limited numbers of politically powerful individuals so that there is no potential for producing exportable cash crops. These cocaine producers have all signed agreements to stop cocaine production if the government of Peru recognizes their property rights and gives them some regulatory relief so they can enter a legitimate line of agricultural production and export their products.

Input substitution effects. Drug suppliers will also react to increased drug enforcement in order to reduce its impact on their activity. By changing combinations of inputs and supplying different drugs, these entrepreneurs can mitigate the effects of law enforcement on their profits and the supply of drugs. Production and distribution of a drug may require the combination of several inputs, each of which must be rewarded with an acceptable return. These include raw materials or agricultural products like marijuana plants, opium poppies, and coca shrubs, capital equipment and labor for growing the plants and processing the drug, as well as labor and capital for distribution. To maximize profits from selling a particular quantity of drugs, the producer must use the most cost effective combination of inputs. The key is substituting cheaper inputs for more expensive ones. For example, a drug smuggler using many individuals to carry drugs across a border can choose a more capital intensive alternative such as making fewer large-volume shipments in planes or boats. The lowest cost method of transportation will be chosen, and these relative costs depend in part on the relative success of law enforcement interdiction efforts against each mode of drug transportation.

The price that owners of inputs require to supply their inputs partially depends on the risks involved. Rising law enforcement efforts, and/or more severe punishment of a particular input, makes supplying that input more risky and raises its price. The quantity supplied of that input to drug suppliers is reduced. However, all entrepreneurs have an incentive to respond to changes in input prices. Changes in enforcement policy that affect one input price more than others will change the relative prices of various inputs used in the production or distribution of drugs. Profit-seeking drug suppliers will replace the relatively high priced inputs, and in the process ameliorate the impact of enforcement. For instance, if a change in enforcement policy makes punishment of adult dealers more severe while leaving punishment of juvenile dealers unchanged, then risk-averse adult dealers will want higher compensation, and juvenile dealers may be substituted for adults.

Drug entrepreneurs diffuse the risks they face by employing others to make street sales, and the relative wages that must be paid to potential employees determines the makeup of the group. There are other ways to diffuse risk besides employing intermediaries. For instance, punishment is almost always a function of the weight of drugs held by a dealer, so the entrepreneur can employ larger numbers of low volume pushers as the probability of apprehension rises. Indeed, even if punishment is not a function of the size of drug holdings, as the risk of arrest increases there are incentives to reduce the number of direct transactions made. Therefore, the entrepreneur has incentives to lengthen the distribution chain, thereby personally dealing directly with a smaller number of individuals. Thus, risk-averse drug entrepreneurs will be willing to pay relatively more for a few intermediary brokers who in turn set up their own network of pushers, rather than deal directly with a large number of users. Law enforcement policy may actually make production of drug distribution more labor intensive and encourage the use of juvenile pushers who face relatively less risk, at least in terms of the severity of punishment. Thus even if drug enforcement pushes the price of drugs up and the quantity traded falls, the number of people involved on the supply side of the drug trade could rise. This suggests that enforcement can cause one measure of the drug problem—the pool of people to be arrested—to rise even as another measure—the quantity sold—falls.

Another group which could be increasingly employed in drug trafficking as enforcement increases is that of drug addicts. If addicts are less deterred by the threat of punishment, then as risk rises, addicts will become relatively low cost pushers because they will not demand so high a wage as more risk-averse individuals would. Thus, we might expect to see a growing portion of drug supplier arrests falling in the juvenile and/or addict categories as law enforcement efforts increase.[21] Indeed, large numbers of arrests of this type may be made with very little impact on the supply of drugs, especially if drug addicts are relatively risk neutral and/or juveniles face very little risk since the modest punishment and increasing numbers of people involved in supply effectively neutralize the increasing number of arrests. This suggests that the supply of potential pushers may be extremely elastic and new pushers can be found to replace those who are arrested without raising the wage for dealing.[22] Indeed, as Moore (1990:137–138) emphasized, "there is no scarcity of human capital prepared to enter the [drug] business. . . . The supply is not limited to those with prior criminal records or with a taste for violence and corruption. Laborers and specialists are easily recruited."

Other substitution effects are also likely. As drug enforcement efforts become effective in one area (e.g., South Florida) drug shipments will be shipped to another destination where the risks are lower (e.g., California or perhaps North Florida). Similarly, as enforcement efforts become more effective against one source of a drug, incentives to increase production or processing elsewhere arise.

One way to avoid the risks of shipping a drug across national borders is to increase domestic production. The success of interdiction efforts with regard to marijuana has created strong incentives to develop domestic supplies. As a result, it is now estimated that marijuana is the largest cash crop in California, the largest agricultural state in the United States in terms of the value of output. Substantial marijuana crops are grown in many other parts of the country as well. The increase in domestic sources may not have completely offset the impact of interdicted international supplies, given the price trends already noted, but it did reduce the effectiveness of law enforcement efforts by diversifying the sources of supply.

California's effort to thwart marijuana growers with aerial surveillance shows how the industry can respond to changing constraints. As the risks of outdoor cultivation increased, growers started indoor cultivation using marijuana strains that are particularly well suited for high performance under artificial light. Automated hydroponics are used to feed plants, diesel generators are required to conceal high energy use, and thick concrete walls mask the heat buildup that might be detected by infrared sensors on aircraft. The capital-intensive production techniques are placed beneath structures that look like ordinary houses and produce four crops a year that are more potent than the strains previously grown outdoors. Despite the higher costs of production, it was estimated in 1990 that a $1 million investment could generate $75 million in profits when the wholesale price is $3,000 per pound.[23] A long history of drug enforcement efforts suggests that elimination of supplies coming from one area will soon lead to increased cultivation elsewhere (Reuter, 1985:13–16).[24] The fact is that the total U.S. demand for drugs can be supplied by crops grown on a very small amount of the total world acreage that is suitable for growing opium poppies, coca shrubs, and marijuana plants (Reuter and Kleiman, 1986:306–315).

Successful control of Turkish heroin in 1973–1974, the famous "French connection" case, resulted in a significant reduction in the flow of heroin into the United States. Heroin prices rose sharply in this country, reducing use but also giving other suppliers an incentive to enter the market. The benefits of breaking the French connection lasted for two to three years before there was an expansion in heroin supplies from Mexico and Southeast Asia (Moore, 1990:136). This is an instructive example because it demonstrates that the effect of law enforcement efforts focused in one direction can be completely mitigated by drug market entrepreneurs within a relatively short period of time. Indeed, the very successful attack on Turkish heroin actually resulted in a more diversified supply system that made future control even more difficult (Moore, 1990:136). Other consequences may have been substantial, however. For instance, Moore also argues this disruption of the heroin market may have led to a reduction of heroin use relative to what might have existed, because a cohort of teenagers found it harder to get the drug. On the other hand, it is also likely that some would-be heroin users turned to other drugs. The point is, however, that the benefits of even major successes in drug enforcement are likely to be significantly offset over time as drug market entrepreneurs react to the new situation and make various input substitutions. Drug entrepreneurs have substantial incentives to frustrate police innovations in drug enforcement.

The French connection effect on diversifying heroin production has recently been repeated with cocaine. At one time, most of the cocaine coming into the United States went through Colombia, including cocaine grown in Peru and Bolivia. The massive effort directed against the Medellin cartel in Colombia has clearly done some damage to this group, but it has also led to a much more dispersed processing and shipping network for cocaine. A 1992 report of the staff of the House Judiciary Crime Subcommittee pointed out that now there are labs processing cocaine in at least nine Latin American countries, and perhaps thirteen.[25] Furthermore, the number of countries serving as transshipment points for cocaine has increased from eleven to twenty-five. Thus, the efforts directed against Colombia have resulted in the expansion of the cocaine trade into most countries of South and Central America, making interdiction efforts increasingly costly and ineffective.

The impact of increased law enforcement on the supply side of the drug market could be quite modest, given that drug entrepreneurs can substitute some inputs which are subject to relatively modest risk for other inputs which bear greater risks. Thus, the short-run supply shifts for any one drug, as shown in Figure 4.1, may significantly exaggerate the long-run impact of increased law enforcement in that market. Unfortunately, if enforcement has a significant long-run effect on one illicit drug market, these entrepreneurs may respond by increasing the supply of another drug.

Output substitution: increasing the supply of one drug in the face of effective control of another. Drug suppliers do not have to specialize in one kind of drug. They can shift from one drug to another, often using in the second market the skills and contacts that they developed while supplying in the first. Indeed, some dealers may supply several different drugs. Thus, successful enforcement efforts that raise the risks of dealing in one particular drug can lead to an output substitution. Such a substitution occurred in 1984 when a drug task force dramatically increased its efforts to intercept drugs in the Miami area and virtually eliminated the incoming supply of marijuana.[26] The marijuana smugglers responded to the threat by converting to cocaine smuggling because it was much more difficult to detect; so the local supply of cocaine increased, pushing the price down (Thornton, 1991:109). Thus, while the supply of one drug declined, the supply of another increased. In fact, this was probably occurring generally throughout the 1980s. Given the relative success of interdiction efforts against marijuana, drug suppliers had incentives to shift into other markets where the risks were not as great. The cocaine market seems to have been the most attractive alternative.[27]

Another reason to expect an increase in supply of a drug is the potential increase in demand as consumers substitute among drugs, which tends to push price *and* profits up in the short run. This induces entry of new suppliers. Thus, for instance, as law enforcement efforts drove up the price of heroin in the 1970s and marijuana in the 1980s, the substitution effect that led to increases in demand for cocaine created incentives to develop more sources of cocaine supply even in the absence of any change in the relative costs of producing cocaine. This has two impacts. First, the existence of more individual suppliers means that market supply increases. Second, since the number of transactions should increase with output substitution and new entry, for a given level of enforcement the probability of arrest during any one transaction will fall, at least partially offsetting the deterrent impact of any increased law enforcement effort against suppliers. Thus, each supplier may be willing to supply more, due to a decline in the risk of doing business.

As noted above, in drug policy analysis it is inappropriate to speak of "the drug market," as if all drugs are identical. The allocation of law enforcement within the drug control arena influences the relative prices of drugs for consumers and the relative costs of providing drugs for suppliers. Successful efforts against one particular drug mean that both demand and supply are likely to increase in another drug market. Indeed, given the reality of scarce law enforcement resources and the inevitable reactions of drug entrepreneurs to increased enforcement, drug enforcement efforts might best be aimed at the drugs which are most objectionable. Zero tolerance may be appealing politically, but it is an unattainable goal under any conceivable conditions. Trends in price and use suggest that law enforcement has had considerable effect on the marijuana market over the past decade, but this very success probably led to increases in both the demand for and supply of cocaine (and alcohol). Other sources of increased supply also exist.

Increasing supply: technological change. Entrepreneurs always face strong incentives to find ways to produce or distribute existing products at lower costs and to offer new products which will attract consumer demand. The result of such developments are broadly described as technological change, and virtually all legal markets regularly exhibit at least some technological advances. The pace of technological advancement in some markets like computers and communications has been phenomenal and the impact has been widely recognized. Supply shifts out rapidly in markets undergoing substantial technological change, and price falls.

There is no reason to believe that entrepreneurs in drug markets differ from entrepreneurs in legal markets in this regard. In fact, drug entrepreneurs should have even stronger incentives to look for technological change than entrepreneurs in legal markets because they have an added cost to consider and try to avoid: the arrest and punishment cost associated with illegal activity. If a drug entrepreneur can find a way to lower either production or distribution costs or to lower the probability of arrest, the business will be more profitable. Since reduced costs, including reduced risks of arrest and punishment, lead to an increase in output for a firm, a technological advance on any front will lead to an increase in market supply. Drug markets, like all others, spawn technological change.

Perhaps the most dramatic change in recent years was the introduction of crack cocaine, which allowed drug suppliers to produce and sell cocaine at a much lower price than before the innovation.[28] The increase in supply and drop in the price of a "high" from consuming cocaine that resulted from this technological change may even be comparable with some of the more remarkable technological advances in computer or communications technology. Since the crack technology can be adopted fairly easily by new entrants into the cocaine market, the profitability of crack (due both to falling costs and perhaps to increasing demand, for reasons suggested above) apparently has attracted considerable entry and led to the development of substantial production capacity in South and Central America. Improved methods of transporting and marketing cocaine greatly increased supply in the United States. The impact of this single source of increasing supply could easily be swamping all the increased law enforcement efforts against cocaine, so that even if those efforts had the anticipated results, the market for this drug could still be expanding and price falling.

Crack is not the only technological change that has occurred in drug markets. We have seen the development of synthetic drugs like LSD, for instance, which avoids the risk associated with importing drugs derived from cultivated crops in Asia and South America. In addition, new varieties of drugs have been introduced that are considerably stronger than previous ones. Indeed the tendency for potency to increase with increased enforcement efforts is virtually inevitable, given current laws and law enforcement efforts (Thornton, 1991).

Increasing potency: technological change arising because of consumer and producer substitution effects.[29] Drug statutes generally consist of three parts. First, the commodities which are declared to be illegal are described in terms of minimum potency levels. For example, a product containing any detectable amount of heroin is generally illegal. Similarly, during Prohibition a product containing more than 0.5 percent alcohol was illegal. Second, given that a product contains at least the minimum statutorily defined potency, penalties are generally levied on the basis of weight. For example, maximum Indiana penalties for possession of up to thirty grams of marijuana, regardless of potency, are one year in prison and a $5,000 fine, but the penalties double for amounts over thirty grams. Third, different penalties are set for production, distribution, and possession, all based on weight, not potency. Smugglers caught with relatively heavy shipments face stiffer penalties, for example. Thus, punishment is clearly a function of the weight of the commodity possessed, sold, or transported.

The probability of being caught is also likely to be a function of the physical volume that an individual is trying to conceal. This is clearly a factor in smuggling, where larger bundles are more difficult to conceal and therefore more likely to be detected.[30] Size is clearly related to weight, so both the probability and the severity of punishment are functions of the weight of the illegal commodity. This law enforcement focus on weight creates incentives to avoid holding heavy bundles of a drug, but it also creates incentives to increase the potency of illicit drugs.

Consider a simple example. Assume that two types of marijuana are available in a particular market. Type A is not very potent (1 percent THC) but type B is more potent (3 percent THC). Suppose that the money prices of types A and B are $30 and $90 respectively for thirty-gram packages. Thus, the $30 price of a unit of THC in B is identical to that of A in the absence of any other non-monetary price effects. However, possession of marijuana is illegal and the risk of arrest and punishment will affect the full price of both types of marijuana. Assume that in a particular jurisdiction, the expected probability of being caught with thirty grams of marijuana is .01 and the expected punishment for possession of this weight of marijuana is a $5,000 fine no matter what the potency is. Then the expected full price of thirty grams of marijuana is the money price paid to the pusher plus the expected value of punishment (i.e., $50, which is .01 × $5,000). The full price of types A and B would be $80 and $140 respectively. However, the full price *per unit* of THC in type A marijuana is $80, while the corresponding price for one unit of THC in type B is just under $47. The per unit price of THC is now relatively cheaper in its more potent form. Illegality and punishment based on weight lowers the relative expected price of the most potent drug. Since consumers have an incentive to substitute the high-potency drug for the low-potency drug, the demand for type B rises while the demand for type A falls.

Now suppose that the police increase their efforts against marijuana, and the probability of being caught rises to .02 (alternatively, the legislature could mandate a stiffer penalty or judges could give stiffer sentences). Expected full prices for thirty grams of marijuana now rise to $130 and $190 for types A and B respectively. The price of a unit of THC in type A rises to $130 while in the more potent type B it rises to $63. The relative price of the more potent drug has fallen even further. When the probability of arrest was 1 percent, the price per unit of THC in the weaker form was 71 percent higher than in the more potent variety. Increasing enforcement efforts which increase the probability of arrest to 2 percent will make the weaker form still more expensive in relative terms: a unit of THC in type A is now 106 percent higher than a unit in the more potent type B. Increasing the expected punishment leads to a substitution effect and even stronger demand for the more potent drug relative to demand for the less potent drug. In addition, since smaller quantities of high-potency marijuana should be required to achieve desired effects, it should be easier to conceal than the larger quantities of lower potency marijuana, implying that the probabilities of arrest could be lower for the high-potency drug as well.

An analogous argument applies to drug suppliers and drug smugglers. If we consider the cost of producing or transporting a particular weight of types A and B, for example, then illegality lowers the expected costs of producing type B relative to the cost of producing type A, and increased enforcement efforts lower type B's relative costs even further. Furthermore, inasmuch as greater potency means that consumers will require smaller weights, sellers and smugglers can reduce the size of their holdings and reduce their expected costs even more. Thus, as law enforcement efforts against the drug market increase, the production and transportation of a relatively potent variety of a drug becomes increasingly attractive at the same time as the demand for it tends to increase.

Now the question becomes, as law enforcement efforts against a drug increase, are drug entrepreneurs able to increase potency in order to lower their relative costs and respond to relatively strong demands for a more potent drug variant? The answer clearly is yes. One way is simply not to "cut" the drug at as early a stage in the distribution. Pure heroin and cocaine are both cut by adding other non-drug substances to reduce potency before consumption. Cutting may be done at virtually any stage in the distribution chain, and several different "cuts" may actually be made (Thornton, 1991:96); so incentives to reduce weight and increase potency may simply mean that the drugs are not cut as early in the chain, or perhaps they are not cut as much, leaving the task to the final consumer. But beyond this, considerably more potent uncut drugs can also be produced. A 1967 Report to the President's Commission on Law Enforcement and Administration of Justice warned, for example,

> If U.S. law enforcement policies become so efficient as to prevent altogether the smuggling of heroin, the black market can readily convert to narcotic concentrates that are a thousand or even ten thousand times more potent, milligram for milligram. A few pounds of these concentrates might supply the entire United States addict market for a year. The skills required are not beyond those possessed by the clandestine chemists who now extract morphine from opium and convert the morphine to heroin or of better chemists who might be recruited. (Arthur D. Little, 1967, as quoted in Brecher, 1972:96)

The synthetic opiates referred to in this 1967 report can easily be produced today. Similarly, the average potency of marijuana increased by a factor of eight between 1974 and 1984, and methods currently exist which can increase the present average potency of marijuana by at least another five times (Thornton, 1991:108). Indeed, the active ingredient in marijuana, THC, can be chemically produced in pure form, although it currently is not economically feasible to do so. If the law enforcement efforts were to become sufficiently effective, however, it could become an attractive alternative to drug entrepreneurs since it takes upward of 100 pounds of marijuana, depending on its THC content, to equal the potency of about sixteen ounces of chemically produced THC.

Do producers in fact increase potency in the face of increasing law enforcement efforts? Again, the answer appears to be yes. Thornton (1991:105–108) regressed marijuana potency data, which has been collected since 1973 by NIDA, on federal drug law-enforcement expenditures and found that a $1 million (1972 dollars) increase in expenditures results in an estimated 0.01 percent increase in potency. While this simple regression is certainly not conclusive evidence of the law enforcement-potency relationship, it is consistent with the expectation that drug dealers increase potency to reduce the expected severity of punishment.[31]

Reliable data on cocaine and heroin potency are not available, although there is some evidence that the retail purity of both drugs have increased during the 1980s (Nadelmann, 1993:45), and the introduction of highly potent crack cocaine suggests that this drug was made available at a lower price per dose. Furthermore, there is another piece of supporting evidence for the "law enforcement causes increased potency" hypothesis: the "well known fact that Prohibition has been more effective at suppressing the drinking of beer, than of whiskey" (Fisher, 1927b:29).[32] During the period of alcohol prohibition, consumption of high-alcohol-content spirits rose sharply relative to the consumption of low-alcohol-content beer. Spirits were relatively easy to conceal and transport so they were relatively more attractive to consumers and producers alike. As a consequence of the increased supply of spirits relative to beer, the price of beer rose sharply relative to the price of spirits.[33] For example, beer prices rose by about 700 percent between 1920 and 1928 while the price of rye whiskey rose by about 312 percent. Total consumer expenditures on spirits rose over this period both absolutely and relative to expenditures on beer. Prior to Prohibition the ratio of expenditures on spirits to expenditures on beer was fairly stable at about .82 (from 1911 to 1916), but there was a dramatic shift in expenditure patterns with Prohibition (Warburton, 1932:114–115). Initial law enforcement successes resulted in fewer expenditures on both beer and spirits; but beer expenditures fell much more rapidly, so that consumers were spending an estimated 14.4 times more on spirits than on beer in 1922. As entrepreneurs began to learn about operating under Prohibition and to innovate around law enforcement efforts, expenditures on both beer and spirits began to rise. In fact, expenditures on spirits exceeded what they would have been in a non-prohibition environment by 1922 (although total consumption of all types of alcohol probably was lowered by almost 20 percent from the long-run trend [Warburton, 1932] as many casual users of alcohol apparently chose to abstain during the period). However, it is estimated that consumers spent somewhere between four and fourteen times as much on spirits throughout the 1920s as they did on beer (Warburton, 1932:170).

Prohibition did more than simply create incentives to shift from low-potency beer to high-potency spirits, however. The spirits available also increased in average potency. Several new products were introduced that contained 50 percent to 100 percent more alcohol than the average potency of pre-Prohibition whiskey. Fisher (1927b:28–29) argued that because of increased potency, "it requires only a tenth as much bootleg liquor as pre-Prohibition liquor to produce a given degree of drunkenness."

The evidence about increasing THC in marijuana and the consequences of liquor prohibition, coupled with the fact that most increases in potency simply involve implementation of known technology, led Thornton (1991:110) to conclude that the availability of increasingly potent illicit drugs is primarily the result of their illegality and increasing law enforcement efforts rather than the discovery of new technology. Supporting this interpretation is the fact that trends in potency are in the opposite direction in legal markets, where consumers do not have incentives to demand increased potency: tar and nicotine content of cigarettes, the caffeine content of coffee and soft drinks, and the alcohol content of liquor consumed since the repeal of Prohibition have all tended to decline over time.

Producers react to consumer demands by minimizing the cost of producing a good that achieves what consumers want. Illicit drugs have many characteristics that can be varied, including weight and potency. When law enforcement efforts increase with risks and penalties closely tied to weight, as they are under U.S. drug laws, the cost of producing relatively heavy low-potency drugs rise relative to the cost of producing relatively light high-potency drugs. Simultaneously, consumers reacting to the increased law enforcement threat increase the demand for lighter high-potency drugs relative to their demand for heavier low-potency drugs. Thus, drug entrepreneurs introduce technological change by adapting known techniques that alter the potency and weight characteristics of their products. Increasing drug potency is clearly a consequence of law enforcement efforts and entrepreneurial adjustments to avoid their consequences. Furthermore, even if the amount of drugs supplied as measured by weight does not increase due to law enforcement efforts, the quantity of drug highs supplied could still increase with rising potency.

The effectiveness of entrepreneurial responses to law enforcement procedures is illustrated by the trends in law enforcement expenditures on liquor control efforts and in punishment through the 1920s. Total federal expenditures directed toward prohibition rose steadily from $3.59 million in 1920 to $44.03 million in 1930 (a 1,134 percent increase). Fines and penalties levied as a consequence of Prohibition enforcement efforts rose from $1.15 million in 1920 to $6.54 million in 1924 but then began to fall; $5.36 million was collected in 1930, for example (Warburton, 1932:46). These fines and penalties are only one measure of law enforcement effectiveness; but, in general, Thornton (1991:101) concluded that "the effectiveness of law enforcement appears to be weakened by the development of specialists in illegal production" (and because of the development of rigidities within the enforcement bureaucracies, and corruption of law enforcement officials—issues examined in subsequent chapters). The interaction between law enforcement and entrepreneurial behavior has even more implications which undermine the effectiveness of drug enforcement policy.

Increasing supply: learning by doing. Technological change is not the only reason to expect increasing supply due to falling production/distribution costs or a falling probability of being caught and punished. Work done at the Rand Corporation focused on the point just made: the possibility that drug entrepreneurs may learn how to reduce their risks and costs as they spend longer time in their chosen occupation.[34] The idea that "learning by doing" can improve the efficiency of an individual or group has been widely recognized in economics. Individuals who enter a market first and survive will often develop a cost advantage because they learn from their experience. Those who enter later will frequently face relatively high costs because they have less experience to draw upon. The key point is that as experience is gained, costs shift down and supply increases. However, Reuter, Crawford, and Cave (1988) and Cave and Reuter (1988) use this notion to explore the possibility that experience also tends to reduce the risk that a supplier in an illegal drug market faces. Thus, the longer individuals are in the drug market, ceteris paribus, the more they will tend to supply. Even though increasing law enforcement efforts may tend to increase the probability of arrest for an individual drug offender, those who learn by observing the police effort, and survive, have added experience that tends to lower their probability of arrest. The net effect may be an increase or decrease in individual supply.

"Experience," or perhaps simply time spent conducting business, may be even more important than Reuter, Crawford, and Cave contend. Moore (1990:138–139) stresses that success in the drug business requires "connections."

> As analysts have considered which factor of production or distribution is in short supply, they have tended to come to the conclusion that what is consistently difficult about drug trafficking is the process of reliably executing large financial transactions in a crooked world with no police or courts to enforce contracts. The importance of this problem is signaled by the importance of a "connection" in the parlance and operations of the trade. Dealers at all levels of the system constantly talk in terms of "making connections." When they have a "connection" things go well. When they do not, they are essentially out of business.

There clearly is a time element associated with making reliable connections. Contacts must be made and individuals must be persuaded that the dealer can be trusted. Thus, not only do individuals learn how to deal with risks as they spend more time in the industry, but they also tend to face much higher risks in the early stages of their entry into the market when they must search for connections. Connections must be established both downstream with customers who can be trusted to pay cash and not inform, and upstream where regular access to a supply of drugs must be established. Once a dealer has an established network of connections, the cost of establishing additional connections is probably relatively low. An established dealer with a reputation for paying the suppliers and providing a quality product to the buyers will have less difficulty persuading new connections that he or she is reliable. To the extent that reputation travels from one connection to another, the costs of establishing new connections should tend to fall, over time.[35]

The "learning by doing" argument and the role of connections are actually complementary to one another. In fact, the second could be phrased in terms of the first. In essence, establishing connections can be characterized as learning to protect transactions from risk. Protecting transactions requires resources and time: it is costly. An entrepreneur who "learns how to solve the problem of making transactions secure by building confidence through repeated deals" (Moore, 1990:139) lowers his or her transaction costs, and gains a competitive advantage in the drug market. The result is an increase in market supply.

Police may find it easiest to arrest less experienced suppliers, who get caught because they do not have good connections. Market supply will be reduced by the exit of these relatively novice suppliers. The net effect might seem to favor a shrinking supply and rising price. However, this is not necessarily the case. Indeed there is a strong possibility of increasing supply and falling prices over time because of the accumulated experience of dealers as a group, despite the fact that an increasing proportion of the supply is seized and increasing numbers of suppliers are arrested. Note that a relatively high drug price, which presumably is the goal of law enforcement efforts against suppliers, is also the goal of experienced drug dealers, provided that the price increases enough to offset any increased risk. As their experience increases and their costs and risks fall, their profits rise sharply if law enforcement efforts tend to keep drug prices relatively high (i.e., higher than they would be in the absence of the law enforcement effort). This high profit demonstrates to others that there is a very high return available to successfully investing time in developing experience and establishing connections. The profitability of investing in experience attracts entry by novices. Entry pushes price down but not below the shutdown point of novices (i.e., a price sufficiently low as to cause immediate exit from the market). Note here that the novices actually can operate expecting a loss in the short run because if they are successful and gain sufficient experience they can expect relatively large profits in the long run. Their entry dilutes the risk to experienced sellers, so the impact of increasing the number of arrests is relatively modest.

Entry by inexperienced novices facing relatively high risk of failure (arrest) and relatively high costs is not an irrational form of behavior. If it were, there would be virtually no entry in any market. New firms entering legitimate markets almost always anticipate losses for some initial period of operation, until they can attract a sufficient customer base and get the business in smooth running order. Even though initially the costs of production exceed the revenues from sales, the *expected* reductions in future costs and expected growth in the firm's sales make entry into the market a rational decision. Furthermore, high failure rates of new entrants in most markets imply that novices generally face relatively high risks. The difference between entry into the drug market and entry into, say, the restaurant business is that in the first, risk of failure is in the form of arrest and punishment, while in the second risk it is in the form of bankruptcy. The high potential return on an investment in experience implies that as some novices are arrested (tending to push price up slightly and raise profits for experience), others, waiting in the wings, eagerly take their place (Moore, 1990:137–138). Thus, arresting novices rarely produces more than a modest reduction in market supply for a very short period of time. Police face a steady stream of novices to arrest, but experienced dealers with well-established connections remain in place. Experience increases for those who avoid arrest, and their costs and risks tend to fall, so that profits available from successfully investing in experience tend to rise even more. This increase in long-run expected profitability tends to increase the risk that novices are willing to bear and lower their shutdown price, so entry continues and price may continue to fall.[36]

Statistics on the arrest of drug dealers and quantities of drugs seized tend to be very poor indicators of the effectiveness of law enforcement efforts. Increased police activity may simply mean that profits for experienced suppliers are rising while the turnover of inexperienced novices is increasing. Law enforcement does constrain the size of the market somewhat, because the probability of arrest is not likely to completely disappear for experienced dealers and it can become quite high for novices, thus raising their shutdown price. However, raising the probability of arrest to reduce supply is offset by raising the price and profits for experienced suppliers, thereby making entry relatively more attractive. Changes in law enforcement efforts which produce more arrests and seizures therefore may have virtually no noticeable impact on the long-term trends in price and quantity available in some drug markets.

Gains from experience are not likely to accumulate indefinitely, of course. At some point the prices and profits in a drug market tend to stabilize. Relatively established markets, such as marijuana and heroin, should not witness falling prices and rising profits the way a relatively new market (e.g., crack cocaine) does. Notice the incentives this creates for new product innovation, however. If a new product can be introduced by an entrepreneur (obvious examples are crack in the mid-1980s, LSD in the 1960s, and new more powerful strains of marijuana), the potential for rising profits for the innovator in the market are very high over a substantial time period. The implication is that drug markets as a whole will tend to go through cycles.[37] Markets for existing drugs will tend to stabilize after some period of time, but entrepreneurial incentives to innovate will generally lead to the introduction of a new drug once existing markets approach maturity. As the new drug catches on, profits will be very large for the innovator, and the market for the new drug will expand. Police efforts will be attracted to the market, and eventually it will stabilize. However, stability occurs when the gains from experience reach their maximum, rather than because the police have shifted sufficient resources into the market to stop its growth.

IV. Conclusions

It should not be surprising to find that the overall results of drug enforcement policy are far different from results policymakers expect. These expectations are formed in a political environment and are based on a less than complete understanding of the consequences of the allocation of scarce criminal justice resources on the incentives affecting individual choice and entrepreneurial behavior. Enterprising drug offenders have apparently effectively mitigated a substantial portion of the increased law enforcement efforts associated with the war on drugs. As Moore and Kleiman (1989:1) put it, police are often "simply overmatched by the resilience of drug commerce." Furthermore, in some very important respects, the efforts to circumvent law enforcement activities have made the drug problem worse. Relative successes in interdicting marijuana, for example, have apparently led to these unintended consequences: (1) increasing potency of marijuana, (2) increased domestic production of marijuana, and (3) a substitution of cocaine for marijuana by some drug consumers and drug suppliers. Indeed, the success of the war on drugs against marijuana appears to be a major cause of the growing cocaine problem of the 1980s. Similarly, increased efforts to control drug markets in some geographic areas or among some populations induce suppliers to seek out new markets in other geographic areas and among other populations. Illicit drugs once were primarily urban phenomena, but rural America must now face them as well. There are many other unintended consequences. In an effort to avoid detection, major suppliers tend to involve more people in the distribution chain in the face of increased enforcement efforts. Juveniles are probably especially attractive in this regard because they are not punished as severely as adults and they are generally less risk averse. Thus, the war on drugs has probably increased the number of people involved in drug trafficking, including the young people the policy is supposed to protect. Unintended consequences of drug enforcement policy also spill over into other criminal activities and further undermine its effectiveness. To these aspects we now turn.

Chapter 5

Indirect Costs of Drug Enforcement

Unintended consequences of drug enforcement policy are ubiquitous. Some are generated because participants in these illegal markets react in unanticipated ways when their pursuit of pleasure or profit is disrupted by police, as indicated in the previous chapter. Others emerge because opportunity costs, the alternative uses of scarce drug—enforcement resources, are not adequately considered when drug policy is formulated in a highly politicized atmosphere. When forgone opportunities are ignored, criminal justice resources may be inefficiently allocated, and we will see that the likely outcome is more non-drug crime. In this chapter we show that enhanced drug enforcement can have effects far different from those expected by the citizenry: problem drug use may not be significantly reduced, while the community may experience rising property crime, more violent crimes, and increasing police corruption.

Our focus in this chapter is on the unintended consequences of the 1984–1989 drug war that emanate from changes in the allocation of criminal justice resources. There are other important consequences of rising drug enforcement during the 1980s which, in the minds of some observers, may be more important than those examined in this chapter. These involve constitutional issues relating to the relaxation of the standards for reasonable search and seizure and invasions of individual privacy.[1] Legal scholars, who have a comparative advantage in examining these issues, have done so in detail. The importance they attach to the drug war's intrusion in these areas is captured in the titles of their articles—for example, "The Incredible Shrinking Fourth Amendment" (Wassertrom, 1983); "Another Victim of Illegal Narcotics: The Fourth Amendment" (Saltzburg, 1986); and "Crackdown: The Emerging 'Drug Exception' to the Bill of Rights" (Wisotsky, 1987). While these are important issues, we focus on other issues to which the tools of economics can be fruitfully applied. However, there are important areas of overlap between these constitutional issues and the allocation of criminal justice resources, notable examples being provisions for asset forfeiture and issues of excessive punishment. These are discussed in Chapters 6 and 7 in the context of their impact on the allocation of criminal justice resources. Broader constitutional issues are left to legal scholars.

During the 1984–1989 war on drugs, police resources were reallocated to combat drug market activities. The effort against drug crime is reflected in drug arrests as a proportion of all arrests, which is shown for each of the states in Table 5.1. Drug arrests on average accounted for 5.8 percent of all arrests in 1984 and 9.7 percent in 1989, an increase of 67 percent. A cursory glance at the data suggests great variability, however. If the states are ranked in order of their increase in relative drug enforcement effort, the range is from a decline of 45 percent in South Dakota to a 268 percent increase in Montana. Most relevant for the national picture, however, is the relative ranking of the most populous states. The states with relatively large increases in drug enforcement efforts, such as New Jersey (55 percent), New York and California (66 percent), Florida and Ohio (67 percent), Michigan (72 percent), Pennsylvania (95 percent), and Illinois (156 percent), account for more than half the nation's population. The 1984–1989 period saw increasing emphasis on drug enforcement in most states, a tendency that was most pronounced in the biggest states.

I. Does Increased Drug Enforcement Increase Crime?

Reallocating police resources toward drug enforcement can affect the number of non-drug crimes in two ways. First, if the population of drug users is a subset of the people who commit crimes against people and property, the arrest of a drug offender simultaneously removes a non-drug offender from the street. This view was a primary political justification for the 1984–1989 war on drugs. High rates of drug use among persons arrested for crimes against persons and property are to a large extent responsible for the widespread belief that drug use causes other crime, because it is assumed that people must rob, burgle, and commit other crimes to finance their habit. The basic premise is unfortunately flawed, for the population of drug users only partially overlaps with that of Index I offenders, as shown in Chapter 3.

Table 5.1: Drug Arrests as a Percentage of Total Arrests, by State, 1984 and 1989

	1984	1989	% Change		1984	1989	% Change
Alabama	3.9	6.4	64.1	Montana	3.1	11.4	267.7
Alaska	3.5	2.5	–28.6	Nebraska	4.2	5.9	40.5
Arizona	7.1	8.2	15.5	Nevada	1.3	1.9	46.2
Arkansas	4.5	5.2	15.6	New Hampshire	n.a	7.1	n.a
California	9.7	16.1	66.0	New Jersey	10.3	16.0	55.3
Colorado	3.2	3.9	21.9	New Mexico	4.9	6.3	28.6
Connecticut	5.1	9.1	78.4	New York	7.6	12.6	65.8
Delaware	5.0	5.8	16.0	North Carolina	n.a	8.9	n.a
D. Columbia	19.6	20.9	6.6	North Dakota	4.1	3.4	–17.1
Florida	7.5	12.5	66.7	Ohio	4.9	8.2	67.4
Georgia	n.a	11.4	n.a.	Oklahoma	5.8	7.3	25.9
Hawaii	10.2	6.2	–39.2	Oregon	5.3	8.4	58.5
Idaho	3.8	4.7	23.7	Pennsylvania	3.9	7.6	94.9
Illinois	3.4	8.7	155.9	Rhode Island	9.5	8.6	–9.5
Indiana	3.6	4.3	19.4	South Carolina	7.1	9.3	31.0
Iowa	3.1	3.1	0.0	South Dakota	4.0	2.2	–45.0
Kansas	7.0	5.5	–21.4	Tennessee	3.0	4.9	63.3
Kentucky	4.8	10.6	120.8	Texas	6.3	8.1	28.6
Louisiana	6.0	9.6	60.0	Utah	6.0	5.0	–16.7
Maine	3.8	5.1	34.2	Vermont	n.a	5.5	n.a
Maryland	8.5	13.6	60.0	Virginia	3.6	5.2	44.4
Massachusetts	10.7	18.1	69.2	Washington	4.4	6.6	50.0
Michigan	4.6	7.9	71.7	West Virginia	2.6	2.6	0.0
Minnesota	4.0	4.0	0.0	Wisconsin	3.7	2.8	–24.3
Mississippi	2.9	5.4	86.2	Wyoming	3.7	3.5	–5.4
Missouri	4.0	6.1	52.5	United States	5.8	9.7	67.2

Source: U.S. Department of Justice, Bureau of Justice Statistics (1984 and 1989).

Second, drug enforcement can also affect other crime rates because law enforcement resources are scarce. Indeed, as emphasized in Chapter 2, law enforcement can be viewed as a resource allocation problem. Legislators must decide how many resources to allocate to the criminal justice system given the alternative uses of tax revenue. The opportunity cost of allocating a larger portion of the budget to law enforcement is forgone expenditures for other purposes, such as schooling, parks, welfare, and highways. Police departments must similarly allocate their resources among competing uses, ranging from "Officer Friendly" programs and traffic control to the solution of robberies and murders. One thing is clear: when police resources are used for one purpose, they are not available for another. Increased efforts to combat speeding, for example, involves a reallocation of police resources that may deter traffic offenses. It also assures that fewer resources are available to combat other crimes, thereby affecting the incentive to commit such crimes. Several studies have examined how offenders respond to changes in enforcement efforts; it appears that a relatively strong policing effort against one crime type (or in one police jurisdiction) induces some existing criminals to shift to a different criminal activity (or to commit crimes in another jurisdiction).[2]

We take this proposition one step further. If criminal justice resources are limited and some are shifted away from the control of crime type B in order to combat crime type A, crime B is less effectively deterred in an absolute sense. Some criminals will substitute crime B for crime A in response to the change in relative deterrence, as suggested above, but the lower deterrence level for crime B will result in a greater number of offenses by both existing criminals and new entrants attracted by a higher expected payoff from crime B. We might say that the law enforcement policy to emphasize enforcement against crime A "causes" crime B. Increasing efforts against drugs can be accomplished by new police resources, but inevitably some of the required resources will at least partly come from a reallocation of existing police resources. Kleiman (1992:153) writes that "much of the increase in local drug enforcement during the 1980s came at the expense of other law enforcement efforts. . . . As a result, certain kinds of property crimes are treated as unworthy of investigation or prosecution."

Empirical studies using Florida data reveal the expected tradeoff: increasing police effort against drug crimes relative to the effort against Index I crime results in a lower probability of arrest for property crimes.[3] The estimated responsiveness of the probability of arrest for property crime to changes in drug enforcement varies; the elasticity ranges from –.20 to –.34. That is, a 1 percent increase in drug enforcement relative to Index

I enforcement, as measured by arrests, leads to an approximately 0.20 percent to 0.34 percent decrease in the probability of arrest for property crime. Shifting police resources to drug enforcement will result in more property crime for two reasons: (1) the lower probability of arrest means that the existing stock of property criminals will commit more offenses before being apprehended; and (2) the lower probability of arrest is a decline in deterrence which may stimulate property crime among individuals who were not previously engaged in this activity.

Estimating the increase in property crime among the existing group of criminals when enforcement falls is straightforward. Suppose, for example, that 100 criminals continue to commit property crimes until they are arrested. If the probability of arrest per offense is .15, these criminals would commit about 562 successful crimes before being apprehended.[4] However, as the probability of arrest for property crime falls due to the reallocation of resources toward drug offenses, fewer of these criminals are apprehended. Under a scenario in which the drug arrest/Index I arrest ratio rises by 41 percent, Benson and Rasmussen (1991) use the lowest of the elasticity estimates noted above (–.20) and estimate that the probability of arrest for property crimes falls to .138.[5] Facing this reduced risk of apprehension, the same 100 criminals would successfully complete over 620 offenses before being arrested, a 10 percent increase in the number of property crimes. These data provide a glimpse of only one of the possible opportunity costs of increasing drug enforcement. They do not, for example, take account of reduced deterrence, which might result in additions to the number of people committing property crimes.

Increasing drug arrests do not necessarily come at the expense of property crime enforcement, of course. The decision as to what to sacrifice is at least partly up to police officials. A different tradeoff apparently emerged in Illinois' war on drugs. Drug arrests in Illinois accounted for 4.77 percent of all arrests in 1984, and rose to 7.01 percent in 1989, an increase of 47 percent. Increasing drug enforcement also resulted in a rise in drug arrests relative to arrests for crimes against persons and property. In 1984, one drug arrest was made in Illinois for every four Index I arrests—a ratio of .25. By 1989 the ratio had risen by 40 percent to .35, a substantial increase although somewhat smaller than the 48 percent increase in the drug arrest/Index I ratio for the nation. By 1989, approximately one drug arrest was made in Illinois for every 2.9 Index I arrests, while for the nation it was one drug arrest for every 2.2 Index I arrests.

The arrest/property offense ratio—an estimate of the likelihood an offender will be arrested—partly reflects the commitment of police resources to solving property crimes. A ratio of 1.0 indicates that an offender will be arrested for each offense; the lower the ratio the less likely it is that an offender will be arrested. Between 1984 and 1989 the arrest/offense ratio in Florida fell from .177 to .155, suggesting a relative decline in enforcement of property crime that could result in a somewhat higher crime rate. Illinois reveals a different pattern during this period. Arrests for property crime accounted for 16.2 percent of all arrests in 1984 and fell to 15.1 percent in 1989. However, Illinois experienced a relatively small increase in the number of property crime offenses during this period of rising drug enforcement effort; as a result, the ratio of arrests to known offenses actually increased in Illinois, from .214 to .224.

The fact that Illinois did not sacrifice the control of property crime relative to what was being done prior to the drug war means that some other enforcement category was sacrificed. Examination of arrest statistics suggests that the most dramatic reallocation of resources for increasing drug enforcement came from traffic control, as reflected by the DUI (drunk driving) arrest category. DUI arrests in Illinois fell from 53,038 in 1984 to 41,093 arrests in 1989—a decrease of 22.5 percent. DUI arrests in the United States fell much less during the same period—from 1.347 million to 1.333 million in 1989, a decline of less than 1 percent.

Declining alcohol abuse is not likely to be responsible for a decline in arrests of such a magnitude, especially if national statistics reflect drinking patterns in Illinois. The fall of DUI arrests in Illinois appears to represent a decline in general traffic enforcement relative to the nation. This may be a cause of the relatively faster growth of traffic fatalities in the state compared to the rest of the country.[6] Nationally, traffic fatalities rose 0.8 percent between 1984 and 1989. Traffic fatalities in Illinois rose over 10.4 percent over the same period. Since the number of motor vehicle registrations and licensed drivers rose more slowly in Illinois than in the nation as a whole, this comparison probably understates the relative growth of fatalities in Illinois.

Reallocating police resources to combat drugs led to unintended consequences in both Florida and Illinois. The experience of these states during the war on drugs reflects the fundamental economic concept of opportunity cost: resources used for one purpose cannot be used for another. What is sacrificed by the reallocation of police time will vary among jurisdictions. Police departments engage in a wide variety of activities; almost every department has responsibility for traffic enforcement, accident investigation, patrol, call for service response, crime and death investigation, and vice and narcotics enforcement. In addition, some departments also have responsibility for animal control, search and rescue, civil defense, emergency medical service, civil process serving, and court security. With limited resources it is obvious that tradeoffs will be a normal part of police operation. Some activities are more likely to be sacrificed than others. Response to most violent crimes is probably less likely to be sacrificed for other activities, because violence crimes usually represent a pressing claim on police time; and since many offenders are known by the victim, subsequent investigation is often successful.

Burglary and larceny are the most common Index I crimes, accounting for over 75 percent of all reported crime in the United States. Since police are usually called long after the crime has been committed (Pate et al., 1976), both the initial response and the subsequent investigation are relatively unsuccessful in finding the offender. Changing police priorities that reduce time spent in investigation of property crime will not be readily observed by the public, even though it may result in a reduction in the probability of arrest for these crimes. Thus, property crimes might be an area for reduced policing efforts in order to increase drug enforcement—an expectation borne out in Florida.

Index II offenses as a group are hard to analyze, in that a large portion are in the "miscellaneous" category. Among those that are specifically recorded, simple assault is similar to other violent crimes and its enforcement is not likely to be compromised by other claims on police resources. Offenders whose activities do not yield a complaint—such as traffic and liquor law violations, which are the largest identifiable Index II offenses—are usually apprehended when observed by officers on patrol. But general patrol is easily reduced when police administrators have an alternative use for the resources. Thus, the tradeoffs from increasing drug enforcement in Florida and Illinois are in the expected categories, those in which the police have relatively more discretion.[7]

Prison crowding, court crowding, and non-drug crime. The expected punishment for a crime is the product of the probability of arrest, the probability of conviction once arrested, and the severity of punishment. Reallocating police resources lowers the prospects of apprehension, but the unintended consequences of increasing drug enforcement may also affect the other components of punishment. Given scarce court and prison resources, we might expect that getting tough on drugs also lowers the severity of punishment for most non-drug crimes. This has been observed in the states which were most active in the 1984–1989 drug war. Indeed, a rising tide of drug convictions swamped state prison and probation systems, which caused the adoption of early release and other programs and diminished the severity of punishment.

Overcrowding of Florida prisons provides one of most dramatic examples of how rising drug enforcement can compromise the punishment of other criminals. Incarceration of drug offenders rose rapidly during the 1984–1989 war on drugs. Recall from Chapter 2 that during fiscal year 1983/1984 there were 1,620 admissions to Florida's prisons for drug offenses, accounting for 12.9 percent of all admissions. By 1989/1990 this figure had risen to 15,802 admissions, or 36.4 percent of the total.[8] Getting tough on drug offenders has resulted in leniency for others. Prior to 1984, prisoners in Florida typically served about 50 percent of their sentences. In 1987 Florida began addressing acute prison overcrowding by increasing gain time awards. At the end of 1989 the average prisoner served only 33 percent of his or her sentence; in fact, about 37 percent of the prisoners released in December 1989 had served less than 25 percent of their sentences, and some served less than 15 percent.

The situation in Illinois was similar to that of Florida.[9] Drug arrests rose almost 70 percent during 1984–1989, a pressure on prison space that was exacerbated by sentencing policies that put increasing numbers of drug offenders in prison for longer periods of time. Most of the enhancements to criminal justice statutes during this period called for tougher sentences for drug offenders. Of the seven major enhancements to the Illinois criminal statutes between 1986 and 1988, six focused on drug offenders.[10] These involved lengthening sentences for some offenses, redefining the severity of possessing five cannabis plants from a misdemeanor to a felony, and reducing the amount of cocaine required to be subject to specific penalties.

Between 1985 and 1988 the number of drug offenders admitted to Illinois' prisons increased 96.2 percent, while non-drug admissions rose by a modest 1.9 percent. During this period, the average sentence for drug offenders increased by 16.7 percent. By the end of 1988, Illinois prisons were 28 percent over capacity; only Ohio, with 42 percent, and California, with 65 percent, had greater overcrowding among the seven largest prison systems in the nation.[11] Despite adding nine new prisons in seven years, the inmate population exceeded capacity by 47 percent at the end of 1991. Like Florida, Illinois turned to early release to ease overcrowding. In 1986 the average number of days of meritorious gain time granted per prisoner was thirty-six, and by 1988 it had reached seventy.[12] In 1990, then Governor James Thompson signed legislation raising from ninety to 180 days the amount of meritorious gain time that inmates could receive for good behavior while incarcerated. Using more prison space for drug offenders, like the reallocation of police resources for the same purpose, results in a relative easing of actual and expected penalties for other offenses and reduces the deterrence effect of the criminal justice system.

California had the highest drug arrest rate among the states in 1989: 1,060 per 100,000 population, a rate almost twice the U.S. average. Drug-related cases overwhelmed the courts, swamped the prisons, and, according to the state's chief justice, compromised adjudication of civilian cases (Phillips, 1992:91). The increasing prison population also caused the number of parolees to rise, resulting in an increase in the caseload for parole agents. The bureaucratic response of the parole staff to technical violations and/or positive drug tests was to lighten their caseload by simply returning the offending parolees to the prison system rather than continue to supervise them in the community. Phillips (1992:100) argues that this has had the unintended consequence of reducing the probability of discharge from parole, which provides the actual outflow from the correctional system, thereby causing the total correctional population, and especially parolees, to expand even more rapidly. Overcrowding of penal systems reduces the severity of punishment and the effectiveness of parole and probation programs, with the inevitable consequence of a decline in the system's deterrence effect.

II. Drug Enforcement and Violent Crime

Increasing violence is often cited as a consequence of increasing drug enforcement.[13] Kleiman (1992:20) argues that enforcement takes its greatest toll on relatively benign drug dealers, leaving the trade with better armed and more violent organizations. Independent of this potential selective enforcement effect on violence, the connection between drug enforcement and violent crime rate is best understood in the context of spatial competition in illicit drug markets. Viewing drug market competition in its spatial context suggests that the drug war may generate unintended consequences with respect to violent crime just as these effects have been shown for property crime and other offenses.

In legal markets, consumers' decisions to shop at a particular location depend on the price differential between that location and others in the vicinity and on transportation costs to the various locations. Producers' location decisions are governed by spatial differences in demand and cost of sales in these alternative market areas. Spatial competition among producers, like the orthodox models of market behavior, is based on differentials in price, quality, and service. Predatory actions in spatial markets that might be "unfair" can be challenged in the courts under federal or state anti-trust laws or under common law precedent (Greenhut and Benson, 1989). Contract and other disputes arising in legal markets are also adjudicated through the legal system, with financial compensation or other relief being offered to plaintiffs when they prevail. The availability of legal redress means that violent forms of conflict or dispute resolution need not arise.

Drug markets are more geographically concentrated than many legal markets. Preliminary results from the National Institute of Justice's Drug Market Analysis Program in Jersey City (New Jersey) show that drug activity is concentrated in a relatively small area (Hebert, 1993). Further, drug dealers have a strong sense of territoriality, as evidenced by the fact that only fifteen of 448 persons arrested more than once for selling drugs during 1990 traveled through an area with no drug activity to sell drugs in another drug market. Competition in these illicit markets, like their legal counterparts, is based on price, quality, and service. These markets differ from legal ones in that when they are disrupted by new competitors, the competitive response is not likely to be limited to the benign forms of lowering price, improving quality, or giving better service. When a new dealer enters a neighborhood drug market, the fight for market share might be conducted on the basis of price, but it might simply involve pushing the competition out by the threat or exercise of violence. Existing drug suppliers may respond in kind to threats of violence and, in any event, will view physical intimidation as an appropriate way to protect their market share. Violence therefore plays a relatively important role in the utility and profit maximizing calculations of drug market entrepreneurs, because non-violent sources of conflict resolution are not available (Miron, 1992). As noted in a U.S. Department of Justice's Office of the Attorney General (1989:16) report on drug trafficking, "the normal commercial concept of contracts, in which disputes are adjudicated by an impartial judiciary and restitution is almost always of a financial nature, is twisted, in the world of drug trafficking, into a system where the rule of law is replaced by the threat of violence"[14]

Here we focus on the consequences of a jurisdiction-specific change in the policing effort against drug market activity.[15] Thus, assume that a spatially competitive equilibrium has been established: drug sellers are dispersed over the market, and marketing territories have been marked out such that each seller is "satisfied" (opportunity costs are covered and potential costs of market expansion, such as violent confrontation with other established sellers, are perceived to exceed the potential benefits). Similarly, each buyer has an established relationship with a specific seller and cannot get the product at a lower full price (money price plus transport costs from a more distant seller). A spatial equilibrium in this context implies that neither buyers nor sellers of drugs have an incentive to change the location of their activity in this market. Now assume that one jurisdiction disrupts this spatial equilibrium by increasing drug enforcement. First consider the effects of this enforcement differential on drug suppliers. The change in police behavior, ceteris paribus, translates into a higher probability of arrest and greater expected costs in the form of legal defense fees and time served in prison for drug sales. Suppliers within this jurisdiction—facing higher costs of production have, on the margin—an incentive to shift their operations toward the adjacent lower cost jurisdiction.

That drug dealers actually relocate some of their operations in response to differential policing is borne out by a study of drug enforcement efforts in Tampa, Florida (Kennedy, 1993:4). The Tampa Police Department, like most large city departments, formed a special drug task force to shut down street dealing locations. The result, according to Kennedy (1993:4), was as follows:

> The task force would typically shut down one spot, only to find the same dealers in business around the corner shortly afterward or dispersed to several new locations. . . . "It was all short term," [Police Captain] Sollazzo says, "the problem in fact escalated and spread throughout the community." The task force apparently made things hot enough in predominantly black neighborhoods that dealers, for the first time, moved heavily into more affluent white parts of town.

But not all of the movement was into previously untapped markets. Tampa also experienced "violent battles over turf" (Kennedy 1993:8).[16] Such results are commonplace. Indeed, along with "pushing the drug problem from one neighborhood to another" and producing violent confrontations among drug dealers, these battles also increase the number of dead and wounded police officers (Stutmann and Esposito, 1992:70).

Relocation—and the resulting entry into an established market in a neighboring jurisdiction—disrupts the spatial equilibrium.[17] In order to establish a niche in this geographic area, the new entrants must necessarily tread on the turf of existing sellers. In legal markets, price and location adjustments follow, as competition intensifies.[18] Some spatially competitive actions may be illegal under anti-trust and fair-trade laws (Greenhut and Benson, 1989), so conflicts may also find their way into the courts. However, in an illegal market, sellers' options are different. In this case, existing sellers and new entrants can choose between price, location, and quality competition, as well as the use of violence, to secure (or protect) a share of the market. Thus violence is a potential cost of relocating or expanding. With the increased cost of producing in the now more aggressive policing jurisdiction, however, some sellers are likely to relocate at least part of their operation. As these sellers move, revenues for those remaining in the jurisdiction rise, thereby compensating for the higher expected costs generated by the police.

The risk of violence is a cost that ameliorates the prospective gains from shifting operations away from the jurisdiction with relatively greater drug enforcement, particularly for those sellers with a relatively secure position in their existing marketing area and rising revenues that occur as rivals relocate. Furthermore, to the extent that the demand for drugs is elastic, the costs of rising enforcement can be shared with consumers, thereby ameliorating the pressure to change locations.[19] This suggests that marginal suppliers are the most likely to move, because their costs of market entry—particularly the likelihood of encountering violent competition—do not vary much between jurisdictions. The net effect on the location of more secure drug enterprises is uncertain, and depends on their response to changes in expected profit, subjective risks of incarceration and physical victimization, the number of marginal firms which move, and other factors. In aggregate, however, rising drug enforcement in one jurisdiction will raise competitive pressures in the other as some illicit drug sellers move. As competition intensifies and predatory practices are employed to establish market share, the probability of violent confrontations increases. Therefore, violent crime will increase in one jurisdiction as a consequence of more intense drug enforcement in neighboring jurisdictions.

Consumers also face a higher risk of arrest and conviction in the jurisdiction that is getting tougher on drugs. They have an incentive to buy their drugs in locations with relatively less diligent enforcement. The result is an increase in demand in nearby areas that reinforces the rising supply of drugs, increasing the size of the drug market in the jurisdiction which allocates relatively few police resources to drug enforcement. If demand increases as fast as supply, then the potential for violent confrontation between rival sellers may be mitigated; but the larger drug market also leads to other sources of violence. A larger market means there will be more street dealers, who usually sell drugs on consignment. Goldstein (1989:34) reports that a common "norm violation" in the drug trade is "messing with the money" which the dealer owes to superiors. Since violence is used to enforce these intrafirm arrangements, a larger drug market is likely to generate more violent crime. Further, neighborhoods in which drugs are regularly sold—particularly low-income areas—experience a relatively high rate of violent robbery because drug users and sellers are carrying either cash or drugs, and when victimized they are not prone to report the theft to the police (Goldstein, 1989:35). This makes drug market participants attractive targets for robbery. These robberies are likely to become crime statistics only if they involve sufficient violence to require medical treatment, in which case the incident will probably be characterized as an assault.[20] Thus, a growing drug market is likely to generate an increase in violent crime independent of that caused by competitors fighting over market share.

Spatial competition in an illicit drug market will necessarily involve tradeoffs involving geographic variations in cost of sales, market price, and risks of violence. Market adjustments to greater enforcement in one jurisdiction are likely to offset some of the ex-ante advantages of the alternative locations, but these competitive effects indicate a jurisdiction will experience more violent crime when neighboring jurisdictions become relatively more diligent in their drug enforcement efforts. The interseller violence may be relatively short lived, as some sellers are eliminated or truces are made. After all, violence is a very costly form of dispute resolution, so cooperation (cartelization) is relatively attractive (Benson, 1990). However, the violence associated with enforcing discipline within drug supply organizations and a larger population of drug market participants who are attractive robbery targets can persist in the long run. Thus, spatial variation in drug enforcement that tends to make some market segments larger than others in terms of demand (and number of suppliers) implies that the high demand areas will be high violent crime areas in the long run.

A higher drug arrest rate is associated with a higher level of violent crime among states. This is consistent with the hypothesis that greater drug enforcement generates increased violence, although there is an alternative interpretation. Jurisdictions with large and highly competitive drug markets should have relatively more violent crime, the existence of which could lead to increased drug enforcement. Thus the positive correlation between drug enforcement and violent crime is of uncertain origin. The competing explanations of the positive relationship between drug enforcement and violent crime can be clarified when a measure of differential drug enforcement among communities is incorporated into an econometric study. As increasing drug enforcement in one jurisdiction disrupts the spatial equilibrium of drug markets, some sellers will attempt to find a market niche in adjacent jurisdictions which are now relatively less hostile to drug market activity. Using data from 279 jurisdictions in Florida, Rasmussen, Benson, and Sollars (1992) found, after controlling for other factors, that the violent crime rate in a community is significantly and positively correlated with the drug arrest rate in adjacent jurisdictions. Furthermore, the elasticity of violent crime with respect to these enforcement differentials is much larger than the spillover effects commonly reported in studies of property crime.[21] Police no doubt respond with greater enforcement when faced with a large violent drug market; but in Florida at least, greater police enforcement appears to generate increased competition in nearby drug markets, which in turn results in a higher violent crime rate.

Increased violent crime as an unintended consequence of increased drug enforcement is the product of drug entrepreneurs' responding to the market disruption caused by the police effort. Its origins are different from the increases in illegal activity that are caused by a reallocation of scarce police resources toward drug enforcement. Examples of the consequences of redirecting scarce resources toward drug enforcement during the war on drugs are increasing property crime in Florida and reduced traffic enforcement in Illinois. The evidence presented in support of the rising violent crime hypothesis suggests another source of unplanned effects of the war on drugs: increasing drug enforcement in one area can cause rising drug activity and violence in neighboring areas.

There is yet another source of violence that is linked to drug enforcement efforts. As noted in Chapter 4, alcohol is a substitute for marijuana. In addition, violence is clearly more highly correlated with alcohol consumption than with the consumption of most drugs, including marijuana. For instance, in the 1989 survey of 395,554 jail inmates discussed in Chapter 3, 8.8 percent of the 34,188 convicted violent offenders reported being under the influence of drugs at the time of their offense, while 30.7 percent were under the influence of alcohol, and 16.1 percent were under the influence of both alcohol and drugs (Harlow, 1991:10). Table 5.2 reports more complete results of this survey and suggests that alcohol use is more prevalent among all types of violent and public-disorder criminals than drug use is.[22] Even if drugs do "cause" some violent behavior (an assumption which is not supported by the evidence),[23] if alcohol has the same effect, then to the degree that drug enforcement induces a substitution of alcohol for drugs, violence need not fall. Furthermore, if alcohol is more likely to lead to violence than drugs such as marijuana, violence could rise with drug enforcement. Indeed, Model (1991) found that the substitution of marijuana for alcohol that accompanied decriminalization of marijuana in a number of states was associated with reduced violent crime rates. This result can be explained by the fact that violent crime and alcohol are much more highly correlated than violent crime and marijuana use. Correlation does not prove causation, of course, as emphasized in the discussion of the relationship between drugs and non-drug crime. However, even if there is no causal link relating alcohol and intentional violence, there is a significant

Table 5.2: Convicted Jail Inmates Who Committed Current Offense under the Influence of Drugs or Alcohol, by Most Serious Offense, 1989

		Percent under the influence of drugs or alcohol at the time of offense			
Most Serious Offense	Convicted Jail Inmates	Total	Drugs only	Alcohol only	Both
All Offenses	205,254	56.6	15.4	29.2	12.1
Violent Offenses	34,188	55.6	8.8	30.7	16.1
Robbery	10,208	53.1	17.7	18.1	17.3
Assault	10,569	58.7	4.5	44.3	9.8
Public-order Offense	64,084	70.1	6.4	54.1	9.6
DUI	29,791	94.6	1.8	82.7	10.1
Other	34,293	48.8	10.5	29.2	9.1

Source: Harlow (1991, Table 16).

relationship between alcohol and accidental violence in the form of traffic accidents. Chaloupka and Laixuthai (1992) examined the effect on traffic accidents of substitution of marijuana for alcohol following decriminalization, and found that non-fatal and fatal accidents were reduced. Similarly, increases in the price of beer and in the legal drinking age led to an increase in marijuana use and a reduction in traffic accidents. This is consistent with the results of the jail inmate survey reported in Table 5.2, which shows the vast majority of driving-under-the-influence arrests are due to alcohol rather than drugs.

III. Corruption

Corruption is a direct consequence of discretionary authority by government officials.[24] When common pool congestion arises and monitoring is imperfect, public law enforcement bureaucrats have considerable discretion in allocating limited bureau resources among competing demands. For example, police are in a position to choose which laws to enforce and which to ignore. Similarly, court time is to a large extent rationed by waiting time, but prosecutors can also ration court time by deciding which cases to prosecute, which to plea bargain, and which to drop; judges similarly decide which cases deserve consideration and which do not. These discretionary powers make corruption possible.

Government can be viewed as an entity which assigns and enforces property rights. In this light, one avenue for political corruption is the illegal (or black market) sale of property rights (Benson, 1981). For instance, where government has modified a rights structure to prevent a competitive market and has, consequently, created *incentives* for an illegal market to arise, the potential illegal transaction can often be easily detected (Benson, 1981). As a result, successful underground markets require illegal transactions that have the appearance of legality or have agreements with officials that the law will not be enforced. That is, individuals must have the right to break the law. Corruption need not go so far as outright changes in statutes or regulations. Public officials may simply ignore violations or make it easy for individuals to find their way through the red tape quickly. The Knapp Commission to Investigate Alleged Police Corruption in New York City (Knapp, 1972:68) discovered that the second largest source of police corruption was

> legitimate business seeking to ease its way through the maze of City ordinances and regulations. Major offenders are construction contractors and subcontractors, liquor licensees, and managers of businesses like trucking firms and parking lots, which are likely to park large numbers of vehicles illegally. If the police were completely honest, it is likely that members of these groups would seek to corrupt them, since most seem to feel that paying off the police is easier and cheaper than obeying the laws or paying fines and answering summonses when they do violate the laws.

There is a closely related opportunity for corruption that has clear and direct applications to drug enforcement. In instances where illegal activities can be disrupted and perhaps even severely hampered through relatively inexpensive enforcement efforts (e.g., gambling, prostitution, drugs), public officials have a valuable "asset" that may be sold. They can allow certain individuals or groups to operate illegally while harassing other potential market participants and discouraging them from entering the market. In effect they can sell monopoly rights to a private-sector underground market and then enforce that rights allocation. Thus, organized crime and corruption tend to go hand in hand. Indeed, Schelling (1971) argued that organized crime is really monopolized crime, and both Rubin (1979) and Anderson (1979) contended that such criminal firms possess monopoly power because there are economies of scale in buying corruption from police and other governmental officials. Demsetz (1968), however, explained that economies of scale are not sufficient for such monopoly pricing. Exploiting a monopoly position requires entry restrictions, typically arising from governmental policy. In the case of underground markets, all entry is illegal; but if enforcement is effective, corrupt public officials can sell to selected illegal firms the right to produce. It should not be surprising, then, that the Knapp Commission (1972:68) discovered that "organized crime is the single biggest source of police corruption" in New York City. Similarly, Charles Ashman (1973:11) reported that "organized crime cannot function without organized justice."

The incentives for corruption. People make decisions on the basis of their values, available information, and incentives. Economics is predicated on the idea that people respond to incentives, on the margin at least, and predicts that public officials will react to incentives just as private individuals do. Thus, relatively strong incentives to become corrupt are likely to result in relatively more corruption. The relevant incentives are those that are delineated in the economic theory of crime: the size of expected payoffs relative to a public official's alternatives; the likelihood of being detected and punished; and the severity of the potential punishment.

The attractiveness to a public official of the expected payoff from corruption depends on a number of factors, not the least of which are preferences (or values) regarding illegal behavior.[25] In general, the potential returns to corruption will be weighed against returns to other activities that may have to be forgone if the official chooses to participate in an illegal market. Of course, law enforcement officials cannot capture profits when they abstain from corruption and concentrate on enhancing efficiency in the production of law enforcement services. They may be able to move to a better paying public-sector job, but few public officials receive large salaries. Officials may also gain satisfaction from the prestige and discretionary power (as well as discretionary budget, as discussed in Chapter 6) they acquire, but, for example, "some experts note that judicial virtue has been tested more than usual of late by failure of salaries to keep pace with the earnings of private attorneys" (Lacayo, 1986:66). Furthermore, many public officials are severely constrained as to how and how much they can legally obtain beyond their public salaries. Thus, to the extent that public sector employment was chosen because it was an official's best alternative, a reasonably large expected payoff from corrupt activity will be tempting to at least some officials.

The magnitude of the potential payoff from corruption is determined by several factors. The expected value of the rights that the official is able to allocate is a prime determinant. If an official has allocative power over a number of different rights, the payoff could be large even though no single right has tremendous value. The Knapp Commission (1972:2–3) found, for instance, that "while individual payments to uniformed men were small, mostly under $20, they were often so numerous as to add substantially to a patrolman's income." Furthermore, for any particular right, *the greater the market distortion created by the laws being enforced*, the greater the potential payoff to officials doing the enforcing. When a market is entirely outlawed, as in the cases of drugs and prostitution, the potential payments to public officials for protecting a black market monopoly can be enormous. The Knapp Commission (1972:75) found evidence of payoffs to a plainclothes police officer from gambling interests in New York to range from $400 to $1,500 *per month.* But this is small time when compared to narcotics-related payoffs today, which can run into the hundreds of thousands of dollars, as noted below.[26]

When the discretionary power to allocate rights in a common pool is concentrated in the hands of a few officials, the corruption payoff to those individuals can be extremely large. Judges, for example, have near-monopoly control over the dispensation of cases that come before them. One of the judges found guilty as a consequence of "Operation Greylord" (a federal undercover operation to detect corruption in the Cook County, Illinois court system) was convicted of, among other things, accepting bribes totaling $400,000 in cash and eight automobiles. A New Jersey judge was convicted in 1982 of taking $22,000 to release one convict from prison and put another on probation (Gest, 1983:42). Investigating officers have similar monopoly powers. If an investigator puts together a case against a particular criminal (e.g., a drug dealer or user), then he or she is in position to extort money or accept a bribe from that offender. The Knapp Commission (1972:2) found that investigating detectives' "shake-downs of individual targets of opportunity" frequently "come to several thousand dollars."

If the power to influence a rights assignment is widely dispersed and difficult to coordinate, however, the payoff to any one official is likely to be relatively small. Organized crime may have to bribe several police officers, for instance, to assure the relatively unmolested operation of their underground markets in drugs and prostitution, but this means that the payoff to any one police officer will be relatively small and less acceptable.

Similarly, if a buyer of illegally allocated rights has several alternative sources (competitive corruption, if you will), then the return to any one corrupt seller is likely to be small. A pimp, for example, may be indifferent as to whether the prostitutes work in one or another of several geographically contiguous precincts or political jurisdictions.

An obvious determinant of the payoff to corruption is the private buyer's willingness to pay for an illegal governmental rights allocation. Naturally, buyers in the underground market for governmentally controlled property rights react to the same kind of incentives that participants in any illegal activity do. Is the potential return relatively large or small? Is the action likely to be detected? How severe might the punishment be if the activity is detected? Given the evidence of police and judicial corruption, a substantial number of private sector individuals find the potential returns from illegal dealings with officials to be high enough to be worth the risk (Sherman, 1974, 1978).

If there is a high probability that an illegal rights allocation will be detected and that a corrupt official will be identified and prosecuted, then officials are less likely to become corrupt. But, in general, very little effort has been made by voters or oversight sponsors to monitor law enforcement activities. When it comes to corruption, however, one might anticipate other sources of monitoring. For example, the news media are potential sources of monitoring. But there are reasons to expect that the news media will not present a major threat to most corrupt officials. Few members of the media devote much time to trying to detect corruption of criminal justice officials. Corruption exposed by others is certainly reported, but there are relatively few instances in which news personnel have actively sought out illegal activity. This is partly because newspapers and other media require daily output, and most reporters must concentrate on news that can be obtained easily and quickly. Detecting corrupt officials and proving their guilt are generally difficult and time-consuming tasks, and such efforts are likely to take place only when the potential payoff is substantial. A reporter might be willing to spend considerable time trying to demonstrate that an important public official is corrupt because the potential payoffs are large (e.g., front-page headlines, recognition by peers and citizens, and greater income opportunities), but he or she is unlikely to invest much time and effort detecting corruption by an ordinary police officer.

Peers can also be a source of monitoring for corruption. Most governmental institutions have established self-monitoring systems and have actually discouraged (and in some cases even prevented) monitoring from external sources. Police departments have their internal affairs divisions, for example, and court systems have judicial review boards. But such monitoring is not likely to be very effective. No matter what the goal of a governmental official might be, there are not strong incentives to expose corruption or inefficiencies within the governmental unit. Many police officials no doubt derive genuine satisfaction from working in law enforcement and are convinced, rightly so, that their agency's work is vital. But these officials may face a dilemma if, when they reveal corruption among their colleagues, the agency's effectiveness is jeopardized. Public-spirited individuals may try to suppress corruption internally, but they may be understandably reluctant to engage in all-out public campaigns to eliminate corruption from their agencies.

The Knapp Commission attributed to "intense group loyalty" police officers' extreme reluctance to bring evidence against fellow officers.[27] This in turn supposedly manifested itself in a "public-spirited" concern for the effectiveness and morale of the department which produced suspicion and hostility directed at any outside interference with the department: "This mixture of hostility and pride created the most serious roadblock to a rational attack on police corruption: a stubborn refusal at all levels of the department to acknowledge that a serious problem exists" (Knapp, 1972:6–7). Police are not the only bureaucrats with strong tendencies to protect their own. Most states have judicial review boards that involve judges in monitoring other judges, but "[s]ome critics complain . . . that judges cannot be counted upon to act against their own colleagues . . . the idea of firmly rooting out judicial corruption remains an especially sensitive one . . . [with] worries about the manifest danger of losing public respect" (Lacayo, 1986:66).

It must be emphasized that the kind of incentives and behavior discovered by the Knapp Commission (and many other investigative commissions) can easily be attributed to self-interested motives rather than public-spiritedness. For the public official for whom power and prestige are major sources of satisfaction, for example, revelations of corruption within his or her organization may lead to reductions in budget, discretionary power, and prestige. In fact, even basically honest "policemen work in such an incredible web of rules that all of them must sometimes violate some of the regulations and therefore are [potentially] subject to disciplinary action. To protect themselves against such a contingency, policemen engage in a gigantic conspiracy against the outside world and cover up for each other" (Jacob, 1974:10–11; and also see Westley, 1970, and Rubenstein, 1973). Finally, an official who may be corrupt or who wishes to keep the corruption option open obviously does not want to attract attention to the corruption potential of his or her position. This explanation is particularly compelling in the Knapp Commission (1972:61) case because "police corruption was found to be an extensive, department wide phenomenon, indulged to some degree by a sizable majority of those on the force."

It is not very surprising, therefore, to find that the few officials who reported corruption have often been ostracized by colleagues and superiors, denied promotions, and ultimately forced to resign. When honest officials face such potential costs, it becomes even clearer that corrupt officials probably have little to fear from their peers. Thus, "with extremely rare exceptions, even those who themselves engage in no corrupt activities are involved in corruption in the sense that they take no steps to prevent what they know or suspect to be going on about them" (Knapp, 1972:3).

Another source of potential detection comes from other governmental units. A legislature may choose to delegate the monitoring function to some other governmental unit. Results of the Federal Bureau of Investigation's corruption detection efforts, for example, have been quite visible. Similar efforts by state and local criminal justice agencies are also possible. Operation Greylord, for instance, produced initial expectations of indictments of thirty court officials, including ten circuit judges, on charges of fixing cases, bribery, extortion, mail fraud, and racketeering in the Cook County court system (Starr and Reese, 1983:21). But this was a unique case in that it was the culmination of an expensive three-and-a-half-year undercover investigation. Law enforcement officers are expected to enforce a wide range of laws with limited budgets, so resources devoted to corruption detection generally should not pose a great threat to the officials engaged in corruption. Expensive police efforts appear to involve a few possibly spectacular cases, such as Operation Greylord, perhaps in the hopes that the visibility of these actions will lead potentially corrupt officials to overestimate the risk of detection. A more compelling explanation for these efforts is that they reflect a temporary political commitment to investigate a highly politicized scandal. But there are problems with this "scandal reaction" approach to corruption control. Any "clean-up" that does not address the fundamental institutional issues—the information and incentives generating the corruption—is unlikely to be successful over the long run. Without changes in the fundamental institutions, the replacements for those who are convicted, forced to resign, or defeated in an election will face the same incentives to engage in corrupt activity (Smith, 1960:5–6). Thus, resources devoted to detect corruption should not generally pose a great threat to most officials engaged in corrupt behavior.

In many cases, the incentives for officials to monitor their counterparts in separate government bureaus are quite weak. Prosecutors' offices, for instance, might appear to be in a good position to investigate police corruption, but "in the case of the district attorneys, there is the additional problem that they work so closely with policemen that the public tends to look upon them—and indeed they seem to look upon themselves—as allies of the police" (Knapp, 1972:14). The Knapp Commission found citizens had a general mistrust of the district attorneys, primarily because of these close ties. One implication of this distrust, of course, is that many prosecutors were also involved in the corruption (Knapp, 1972:5). This leads to a related point. Government officials with the responsibility for preventing corruption by other officials have a potentially valuable right to sell: the right to be corrupt. They face the same kinds of incentives as officials who are supposed to prevent private sector illegal activities. Thus, it should not be surprising that public officials sometimes pay off police officers in order to practice corruption (Sherman, 1978:6).

Corrupt officials also may be relatively unconcerned with disclosure of their activities because investigations are costly. Most states, counties, and cities cannot commit significant resources to the monitoring of public officials. They rely on existing law enforcement agencies to monitor themselves and each other, at least until a major scandal erupts. But common pool problems provide those bureaucrats with a ready reason for not actively searching out corruption. In a situation where bureaucrats face excess demand and have substantial discretion to choose how to allocate their resources, they can easily ignore corruption, particularly if it is not brought to the public's attention. Whether the public is better served by use of those scarce resources in pursuit of corruption or in the provision of other services does not appear to be a question that is raised (Knapp, 1972:257).

An important potential source of disincentives for corruption is the severity of the punishment that arises when that corruption is detected. The impact of punishment is difficult to assess, however, since severity is a subjective concept. An official who obtains satisfaction from a prestigious position may view the embarrassment of public exposure for corruption, and the loss of a job, as severe punishment; another with attractive outside alternatives might view the exposure as an inconvenience. The same can be said of punishment as a deterrent to private sector illegal activity, so at least some inferences can be drawn from a comparison of the types of punishment that corrupt officials face relative to punishment given criminals in the private sector.

If it is correct that the incentives of officials who detect corruption in their own organizations are to suppress information and downplay its significance, then any internally generated punishment is likely to be relatively mild. Mild punishment should make the corruption appear to be relatively less significant to those outside the organization (e.g., legislators and private sector government-watch groups), thus minimizing the attention that exposure might attract. More severe punishment of a corrupt official might be expected when the conviction is a consequence of detection by another organization or a private government-watch group. One might even expect such punishment to be relatively severe if the strategy is to make examples of the officials who are caught, in order to deter other potential corruption. But this is not an appropriate deduction. Although there is little statistical evidence, public officials (particularly high-ranking officials) seem to receive relatively short prison terms and to be paroled relatively quickly.

> [The] Bronx County District Attorney testified before the Commission that light sentences were common in cases involving police officers. . . . It is clear that the risks of severe punishment for corrupt behavior are slight. A dishonest policeman knows that even if he is caught and convicted, he will probably receive a court reprimand or, at most, a fairly short jail sentence. Considering the vast sums to be made in some plainclothes squads or in narcotics enforcement the gains from corruption seem to far outweigh the risks. (Knapp, 1972:252–253)

Interestingly, from 1970 through 1973 in New York City there was also a 90 percent turnover in the rank of captain and above, apparently due to retirement in the face of misconduct charges; but almost every criminal charge was brought against those holding the rank of lieutenant or below. The obvious implication is that punishment for police corruption is likely to be relatively light and is likely to decline as the official's rank increases.

There seems to be little reason to doubt that corruption among police is quite widespread. Indeed it is, in all probability, true that "bribery and extortion rings exist in police departments all over the country" (Beigel and Beigel, 1977:xii). The same general conclusions hold for judges. Charles Ashman (1973:5) declared:

> We can no longer dismiss cases of corruption on the bench as isolated indiscretions. There are too many, too often. This book [*The Finest Judges Money Can Buy*] describes over seventy classic examples of judicial pollution. Unfortunately for each case discussed there is a handful we have not included, and for each handful not included there are scores yet undiscovered.

Many government officials would probably contend that the preceding arguments are incorrect. They would point out the stepped-up effort and success of law enforcement authorities, particularly at the federal level, in corruption detection in recent years. But the commitment of additional resources in the public sector does not guarantee that they will be used effectively; for all the reasons detailed above, existing public sector employees are reluctant to report corrupt acts by their fellow civil servants. Regardless of what officials claim, it appears clear that "Except in circumstances where the problem reaches outrageous proportions, nobody monitors the progress of criminal cases to detect abuses of prosecutional discretion; nobody raises money to support political campaigns of candidates who will eliminate police corruption; nobody watches the sentencing patterns of judges" (Neely, 1982:154).

Drug enforcement and corruption. The illicit drug market is probably the most lucrative source of police corruption that has ever existed in the United States, including the period of liquor prohibition (Ashley, 1972:136). "Significant levels of corruption" existed within the New York City Narcotics Division in the early 1970s, for instance (Moore, 1977:193–195). Similarly, Richard Kunnes (1972:43) reported, with regard to the heroin market:

> Profits are so great that corruption of law enforcement officials has become pandemic. In fact, the more officials hired for heroin suppression work, the more are bribed, or worse, become distributors themselves. Thirty federal agents within the last eighteen months alone have been indicted for being directly involved in the heroin (i.e., junk) trade.

Expansion of the cocaine market during the 1980s brought new allegations of widespread corruption. For reasons cited above, convictions for corruption may represent only the tip of illegal behavior by public officials. A fourfold increase in convictions of federal officials for corruption—from 115 in 1979 to 529 in 1988, most of which were connected with the drug trade—suggests that public officials have considerable opportunities to serve the illicit drug industry.[28]

Corruption is most likely to occur when the potential payoff is high relative to the risks of detection and opportunity for legal income. Exacerbating these risks is the undercover work that is typical of drug enforcement activities. Long-term association with criminal elements facilitates corruption, in part because of a gradual erosion of the officer's value system, increased sympathy for the criminal elements, and added exposure to opportunities for illegal behavior (Girodo, 1991). As Moore and Kleiman (1989:2) note, "the police executive knows from bitter experience that in committing his force to attack drug trafficking and drug use, he risks corruption and abuse of authority. Informants and undercover operations—so essential to effective drug enforcement—inevitably draw police officers into close, potentially corruption relationships with the offenders they are pledged to control." Risks of detection would appear to be modest since, as noted above, there are not strong institutional incentives to expose corruption. Similarly, opportunities for legal earnings by police are modest. The 1990 starting salary in the largest police departments for an entry-level police officer was about $26,000; for sergeants it was about $40,000, and for chiefs of police $85,000.[29] In smaller departments the entry-level salaries are only slightly lower than those in the largest departments, but more experienced officers are not rewarded as well. Police chiefs in departments serving cities with a population exceeding 1 million receive a salary that is 3.2 times that of the entry-level officer, while chiefs in cities with a population between 250,000 and 499,999 receive only 2.5 times the entry salary.

These salaries, like those of all public servants, are modest compared to the payments that can be offered by the illicit drug industry. In 1990, the markup on one kilogram of cocaine at the wholesale level in the highest cost markets was $135,000—enough to pay the annual salary of the chief of police, a sergeant, and offer $10,000 to a rookie officer.[30] Estimates of the markups in 1980 are considerably larger than the one offered here; but that is not surprising, since costs and prices will vary over time as the industry matures, creates new products, and responds to changing levels of enforcement.[31] Whatever the specific estimate, the potential payoffs are substantial relative to law enforcement salaries. Drug traffickers were reported to offer $100,000 to DEA officers "for openers," and one high U.S. Border Patrol official reported an offer of $5 million.[32] High returns can be achieved with little effort. In 1986 a federal prosecutor was charged with receiving payments of $210,000 and a boat in exchange for tipping off a drug smuggler to the evidence-gathering activities of U.S. Drug Enforcement Administration officers (Press and Starr, 1986:68). The illicit drug industry offers substantial incentives for corruption.

Accepting illegal payments does not require that police and other law enforcement officials reduce their drug enforcement efforts. Indeed, the market participants able to make substantial payments are the best established enterprises. Their interest is to have new entry discouraged by vigorous enforcement against emerging enterprises, thereby raising market prices while the established firms' costs do not rise except for the bribes paid to corrupt officials.[33] Since the less experienced drug dealers and nascent organizations are relatively easy to apprehend, it is possible for corrupt members of the law enforcement community to actively pursue drug offenders while providing valuable services to mature drug-trafficking organizations.

Law enforcement efforts against drug traffickers can even provide a way for a corrupt police official to enter the drug trade. Several examples of police officers seizing drugs and then selling them have been documented. For instance, the former sheriff of Nassau County, Florida, was convicted in July 1993 of distributing drugs from his department's property room.[34] He reportedly pretended to destroy marijuana and cocaine but sold it instead. In addition, he actually requested eighteen pounds of cocaine and 100 pounds of marijuana from other counties for use in "undercover" investigations by his partner in crime—one of his deputies—and then reported that the operations fell through and the drugs were destroyed, when in fact they were apparently sold. The sheriff supposedly earned between $175,000 and $225,000 from these drug sales.

As more police are assigned to the control of illicit drugs, more will be tempted by the huge payoffs available. Thus, another major unintended consequence of the war on drugs has to be the potential for an increased level of corruption and increasing costs of corruption control. When these costs are added to others already demonstrated, such as increased violence, higher rates of property crimes and other offenses, and overcrowding of the corrections system, one must begin to ask why the drug war is being waged. An answer to this question requires an understanding of the politics of drug crime and of police incentives relating to drug control—issues examined next.

Chapter 6

The Politics of the Drug War

A war on drugs was declared by President Reagan in October 1982 (Wisotsky, 1991). However, such an offensive has to be waged by state and local "troops." But the facts are that state and local law enforcement agencies generally did not increase their efforts against drugs dramatically until 1984, when a substantial reallocation of state and local criminal justice system resources toward drug enforcement began. In fact, while drug arrests relative to arrests for reported crimes against persons and property (Index I offenses) remained relatively constant at one to four from 1970 to 1984, the relative effort against drugs increased by roughly 45 percent over the next five years. By 1989, criminal justice resources were being allocated to make only about 2.2 Index I arrests for each drug arrest. Furthermore, state legislatures passed a large number of changes in their criminal codes, mandating more severe penalties for drug crimes during this period, and courts also responded with harsher sentences for drug convictions. Why did the state and local components of the criminal justice system respond to the federal call for a war on drugs after 1984?

Perhaps local elected officials, representing median voter preferences across the nation, simultaneously demanded that their police departments escalate the war on drugs. There are strong indications that this did not happen, however. For example, note that in 1985, the public opinion surveys discussed below suggested that drug use was not considered to be an especially significant problem. Section I of this chapter examines in more detail the role of public opinion with regard to legislative activity during the most recent drug war, in order to reject this explanation. Indeed, illicit-drug policy appears to be a case wherein policy changes have led public opinion, at least during the escalation of the drug war over the 1984–1989 period.

Another explanation for the trends in the allocation of local police resources over the 1984–1989 period is that powerful interest groups demanded the war. Indeed, it would be surprising if this were not the case, since as Chambliss and Seidman (1971:73) concluded, "every detailed study of the emergence of legal norms has consistently shown the immense importance of interest-group activity, not the public interest, as the critical variable." Similarly, Rhodes (1977:13) pointed out that "as far as crime policy and legislation are concerned, public opinion and attitudes are generally irrelevant. The same is not true, however, of specifically interested criminal justice publics." More recent research implies similar conclusions, but also makes it clear that one of the most important "specifically interested criminal justice publics" consists of law enforcement bureaucrats (e.g., Berk, Brackman, and Lesser, 1977; Benson, 1990:105–126).[1] In order to establish the argument that police bureaucracies have considerable power in the game of interest group politics, at least as it pertains to drug legislation, law enforcement influences on the historical emergence of illicit-drug legislation is briefly examined in Section II. The significant role that entrepreneurial bureaucrats have played in the development and evolution of this policy is emphasized as a prelude to Section III where federal legislation during the drug war period is examined from the same perspective.

Section III provides an explanation for state and local police involvement in the 1984–1989 drug war. Specifically, state and local policing officials faced what presumably was an exogenous change in bureaucratic incentives (although at least some of these police officials were important sources of the demand for the change), which induced an increase in drug enforcement efforts. In particular, one section of the Comprehensive Crime Act of 1984 established a system whereby any local police bureau which cooperated with federal drug enforcement authorities in a drug investigation would share in the money and/or property confiscated as part of that investigation. As a result, police in many states whose own laws or constitutions limited confiscation possibilities began to circumvent state laws by having federal authorities "adopt" their seizures.[2] Then, under the 1984 federal statute, a substantial percentage of these seized properties went back to the agency which made them, even if the state's laws mandated that confiscations go someplace other than to law enforcement. This legislation was demanded by federal, state, and local law enforcement bureaucrats, and largely reflects the bureaucratic competition and cooperation that Breton and Wintrobe (1982) describe.

Perhaps local police bureaucracies advocated such legislation and joined in the drug war because they perceived it to be in the "public interest." There is considerable evidence suggesting that the opportunity costs of resources allocated to the war on drugs have been very high,[3] however, and a good deal of evidence also indicates that many law enforcement bureaucracies created misinformation in order to exaggerate the potential benefits of a drug war (Michaels, 1987:311–324). This is relevant because if confiscations can be used at the discretion of local police bureaucrats to significantly enhance their own well-being, then this federal statute may explain a substantial portion of the changes in the allocation of local police resources after 1984. Local interbureau competition for resources may lead government decisionmakers (bureau sponsors) to treat confiscations as a substitute for ordinary appropriations. Therefore, an important component of Section III is the summary of a case study by Benson, Rasmussen, and Sollars (1992) of the budgetary impact of local police confiscations from the drug war. The findings are consistent with the hypothesis that confiscations legislation creates significant incentives to change the allocation of police resources.

As suggested in Chapter 1, there is significant variation in drug enforcement activity across states and cities, as well as through time. Therefore, if the "bureaucratic self-interest" story actually provides a strong explanation of drug enforcement policy, it should help explain cross-sectional variation in enforcement policy as well as time series variation. This question has been explored in a cross-sectional analysis of cities' drug enforcement policies (Rasmussen, Benson, and Mast, 1993). Since federally "adopted" seizures are only partially turned back to the local police (the federal authorities extract a 20 percent handling charge), police in states whose own laws allow them to retain seized assets are able to obtain even greater benefits from seizures than police who must involve federal authorities in the process. Thus, a self-interest view of police bureaucrats suggests that police in states whose laws allow the police to retain seizures will focus relatively greater efforts against drugs than police in states whose laws take such seizures away from the police. This expectation is supported by the empirical results in Rasmussen, Benson, and Mast (1993); and simultaneously, certain "public interest" explanations are rejected. These findings and their implications are explored in Section IV.

Law enforcement officials tell a very different story regarding the impetus for the 1980s drug war, focusing on their recognition of "public interest" reasons for the war even though the public might not have expressed such interest. Some of these public interest arguments are addressed in Section IV, but one frequently offered explanation of the increased focus on drug market activities is not: the so-called "crack crisis" or "crack epidemic," which allegedly has created a large-scale multi-dimensional crime and health problem and demanded an enhanced law enforcement effort. Section V examines this issue, concluding that like much of the crisis rhetoric that has accompanied political developments in the criminalization of drugs, many of the claims about crack were at least exaggerated if not intentionally false. Furthermore, the introduction of crack—first in New York, Miami, and Los Angeles—actually followed the advent of the drug war by well over a year, and much of the rest of the country did not see a developing crack market for some time after that. Thus, the argument that crack stimulated the war on drugs appears to be an ex-post effort at legitimization rather than a true ex-ante explanation for the drug war.

The escalation of the war on drugs ended in 1989. Indeed, since 1989, a substantial reduction in drug enforcement effort has occurred. The concluding section of this chapter offers several potential explanations of this downward cycle in drug policy, all of which are consistent with the bureaucratic self-interest arguments which explain the 1984–1989 escalation of drug enforcement.

I. Drug Legislation and "Public Opinion"

A system, defined to be a "combination of things or parts forming a complex or unitary whole," properly describes the institutions that maintain the law. The legislative branch presumably makes the rules, identifying the behaviors that are illegal and, under various determinant sentencing schemes, provides guidelines for punishment of offenders who are apprehended by the police and convicted by the courts. The component parts of this system—legislatures, police, prosecutors, and the judiciary—do not necessarily function as a coherent body determined to optimize some measure of public safety, however. Instead, the politicians, elected officials, and bureaucrats making the decisions for these component parts often have more self-serving interests in mind as they make policies that affect the administration of justice (Benson, 1990:87–175). The question addressed first is, what self-interest motives might explain the active participation of legislators to produce statutes intended to increase the severity of sentences for drug offenders, a change in policy which required that additional prison resources be allocated to the war on drugs?

Untangling the effects of public opinion about drug policy and the motivations of elected officials is useful in an effort to understand legislative behavior. Increasing minimum mandatory sentences for drug crimes, for example, might be hypothesized to be a reflection of the general electorate's preferences and therefore serve to enhance the politician's prospects for reelection. The coincidence of interest among the general public (voters/taxpayers) and their elected officials seem reasonable in a responsive political system. A substantial amount of research suggests that "public opinion" actually has very little to do with most legislation, however, including criminal legislation.[4] And, while the expectation that public opinion might be a significant constraint on the behavior of elected officials is superficially appealing, it turns out that public opinion polls actually provide little insight into the rationale for the statutory mandates for increasingly severe sentences for drug crimes that were passed during the 1980s. On the other hand, as suggested below, public opinion may come into play over the course of a policy cycle, as voters/taxpayers ultimately recognize that the alleged benefits of a policy are not materializing while the costs are higher than promised, and begin to demand accountability. Since it takes some time for people to recognize policy failures, public opinion often appears in the form of a delayed reaction or backlash.

Many citizens are clearly concerned with crime issues. Indeed, surveys of attitudes on crime during the 1980s confirm Zimring and Hawkins' (1991:203) observation that "the politics of law and order are a permanent feature of the administrative and legislative process at the state level." However, opinion polls actually provide some evidence that the drug war was escalated in spite of trends in public attitudes toward crime. Consider the case of Florida, a state whose legislature and law enforcement officials enthusiastically embraced the war on drugs. In public opinion polls from 1981 to 1991, the number of persons suggesting that combating crime was the top priority for increased funding peaked in 1982 at 28.5 percent of the respondents.[5] During the period of escalating drug enforcement, 1984 through 1989, the average percent of respondents who regarded combating crime as their top priority for increased spending was 19.4 percent. A similar pattern is revealed by national surveys of public opinion. In 1984–1987 about 66 percent of respondents believed more should be spent to combat crime—below the 69 percent sharing this opinion during 1981–1983.[6]

Nor was there a public outcry for a criminal justice system offensive against drugs specifically. The Gallup public opinion polls did not even ask whether drug abuse was "the most important problem" until 1985, and only 2 percent responded in the affirmative in January of that year. Figure 6.1 shows the drug problem did not merit great concern until 1988, after the drug war was well under way. In fact, the office of "drug czar" was created by the Anti-drug Abuse Act of 1988, prior to this apparent upswing in concern. After this bill was passed in November, the proportion of survey respondents proclaiming drugs the nation's number one problem rose rapidly, to 27 percent in May 1989 and 38 percent in November of that year. Thus, it might appear that legislative policy actually led public opinion, rather than the reverse. In fact, of course, policymakers do help form public opinion, as do powerful interest groups that have vested interests in particular legislative actions. In the area of drug policy, there are relatively few well organized interest groups with an alternative point of view to offset the views of the police (and prosecutors); and as suggested below, widely held beliefs (e.g., that drugs cause non-drug crime) have been promulgated by police interests.[7] Various elected officials clearly "jumped on the police bandwagon" in advocating legislation based on these beliefs, despite the lack of a high level of previously existing "public opinion" that would support such actions.

Perhaps such legislative action can be explained because the absolute level of public support for anti-crime and drug enforcement legislation is not as important as its relative level. An index of relative support may provide a better barometer of the opportunity costs that determine the importance of an issue for public policy initiatives. Assume that entrepreneurial legislators take the lead in proposing legislation and pursuing their agenda. Under such an assumption, drug policy was an unlikely candidate for major policy initiatives when the economy was mired in the 1981 recession, with inflation and unemployment rates exceeding 10 percent. An entrepreneurial politician, choosing at that time to focus on the ever present but relatively less important concern over crime, would be vulnerable because constituents would perceive it to be less pressing than "bread and butter" economic issues. As pressing concerns of the economy and foreign policy wane, issues such as crime and drugs will become more salient. Thus, legislative entrepreneurs might view the initiation of crime and drug legislation as a way of keeping themselves visible in the print and broadcast media and "doing something important," that is, satisfying constituent desires for a safer environment.

Anti-drug policy initiatives after 1984, which by a large margin constituted the greatest expansion of drug enforcement since the 1965–1970 effort, appear to fit this pattern. The political opportunity cost of a drug war was low during this period. Economic expansion was well under way and would become the longest period of sustained growth in the

Percent of Survey Respondents Saying Drug Abuse Is the Nation's Most Important Problem

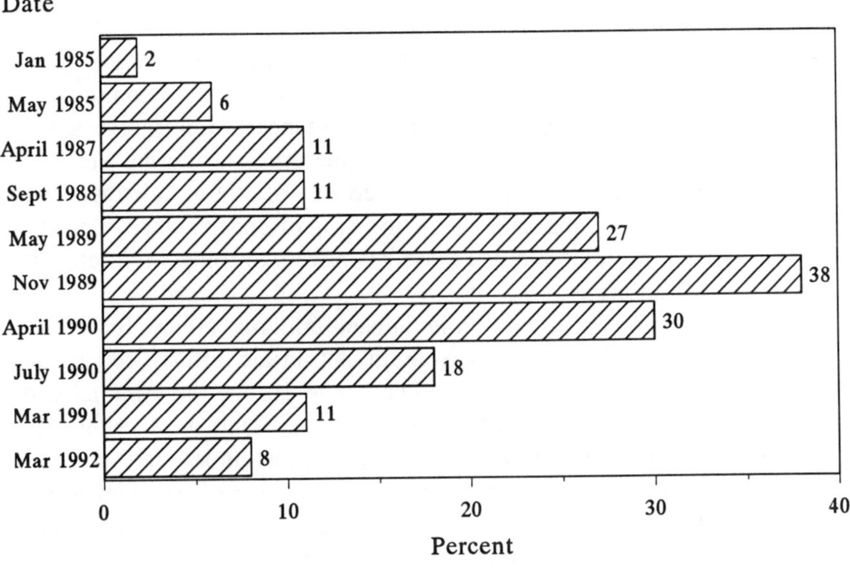

Figure 6.1

post–World War II era. No pressing foreign policy issues intruded. The drug war's escalation continued through 1989, with 1990 seeing a diminished emphasis on drug enforcement and the rise of competing issues in foreign and domestic policy.[8] Indeed, public concern over the drug abuse problem that rose so sharply in late 1988, as indicated by polls, quickly waned after April 1990 as economic issues moved back to the forefront (see Figure 6.1). Thus, escalation and subsequent deceleration of the drug war is consistent with this opportunity cost perspective. However, political entrepreneurs are undoubtedly motivated by many other factors. In particular, interest group demands must be recognized.

Despite the suggestion that legislative entrepreneurs might choose to take the lead and pursue a policy, the independent impact of legislators on drug enforcement policy is probably minimal. The fact is that few bills of any kind are actually initiated by or even written by legislators (Berk, Brackman, and Lesser, 1977).[9] Rather, legislators act as middlemen, sponsoring bills before the legislature that originate in the offices of interest groups; legislation is not customarily the creation of a lawmaker attempting to shape or respond to the "public" will. The well-organized interest groups prominently affecting the criminal justice system are those engaged in the law enforcement process—police chiefs and sheriffs, prosecutors, and judges (Berk, Brackman, and Lesser, 1977; Benson, 1990). These groups will have considerable impact on relevant legislation, offset only by the efforts of civil libertarian groups, defense attorneys, and, in the case of drugs, groups wanting to provide a treatment alternative or committed to the decriminalization of currently illegal substances. Legislative actions escalating the commitment of resources to the drug war during the 1980s were clearly consistent with the interests of those charged with apprehending, prosecuting, and convicting drug offenders, since opposition of these groups would naturally expose lawmakers to competition claiming they were soft on crime.

Legislators have relatively little impact on drug policy for another reason as well. Their primary role in anti-crime efforts—other than budgeting for prisons, courts, and police—is to change the criminal code. Code changes are a policy tool that is akin to pushing on a string, since application of the policy rests with the police, prosecutors, and judges. If minimum mandatory sentences or an increased range of penalties are not beyond the existing maximum penalty, for instance, the legislative initiative may have relatively little impact on the sentences actually meted out to drug offenders (Zimring and Hawkins, 1991:163). In fact, legislative attempts to reduce judicial discretion in hopes of providing relatively uniform sentences for similar offenders have, at most, met with only modest success.[10] These determinant sentencing schemes are frustrated by the police, prosecutors, and defense counsels bargaining over the charge in order to influence the sentence. Judges always retain some discretion under these initiatives, so their net effect does not necessarily reflect legislative intent (Tonry, 1988). The relative impotence of legislatures is reflected in the fact that states with similar criminal codes have very different rates of incarceration (Zimring and Hawkins, 1992:xii). Similarly, the power to set criminal justice budgets does not guarantee that criminal justice bureaucracies will allocate those budgets as the legislators expect (furthermore, it must be recognized that the level of the budgets are at least partially influenced by the demands of the bureaucrats). Police, prosecutors, and judges have so many mandated duties and so much discretion that legislators will be unable to control their activities through the budgeting process. Much more effective monitoring than that which actually exists would be required for substantive legislative control of these institutions (Stumpf, 1988; Williams, 1984). Legislators are perhaps best regarded as "second string" players on the criminal justice team, the first team being the professionals charged with the delivery of criminal justice services—police, prosecutors, defense counsels, and judges. These groups have a direct influence on legislation through their lobbying efforts and their "service" as sources of "information" due to their expertise.

II. Police Bureaucrats, Interest Group Politics, and Drug Legislation

There are many models of bureaucratic behavior based on self-interest assumptions. Tullock (1965) saw bureaucratic behavior driven by a desire for security. Chant and Acheson (1972) contended that bureaucratic behavior is driven by a desire for prestige. Niskanen (1968, 1971) assumed that a bureau manager could be characterized as a budget maximizer. Miqué and Belanger (1974) explained that budget maximization unduly limits the range of utility-maximizing efforts, however, and proposed that the bureaucrat seeks discretion, as reflected by a budget with excess revenues over actual costs (an argument Niskanen [1975] accepted).[11]

Public officials are presumably characterized by the same basic utility-maximizing behavior that motivates people operating in private markets. The institutional framework of public officials may differ from that of private sector employees, but their fundamental objectives do not. Employment security is a desirable job attribute in the private sector. The U.S. Department of Health, Education, and Welfare Task Force (1973) found that job security, along with interesting work and opportunity to develop special skills, were considered to be the most important features of job quality. Not surprisingly, civil service bureaucrats are also very concerned about job security (Johnson and Libecap, 1989). The same point can also be applied to elected officials, whose desire to be reelected is consistent with this broadly held desire for secure employment. Surveys of private sector employees identify other sources of worker satisfaction that may be equally applicable to elected officials: (1) good pay; (2) the discretionary authority, information, and opportunity to get the job done; and (3) seeing the results of one's work. Discretion to control the intensity and pace of work is another desirable job characteristic, and some research suggests that part of the wage premium paid to workers in very large manufacturing plants is explained by the absence of these job attributes (Stafford and Duncan, 1980). Thus, discretion itself may be a source of satisfaction for bureaucrats and public officials (Parker, 1992). Job characteristics that people value in a private setting are not likely to lose their allure just because someone is engaged in public sector employment. In this light, as Breton and Wintrobe (1982:27) noted, "In addition to size, budgets, discretion, prestige, and self-preservation, it has been suggested that security, the avoidance of risk or responsibility, secrecy, complexity, career promotion, leisure, internal patronage, and a bureaucrat's personal conception of the common . . . good are objectives of bureaucrats, either one at a time or in groups." They suggested that all of these factors may enter a bureaucrat's utility function and that no general theory of bureaucratic behavior can be built by specifying a particular objective. Thus, they assumed general utility maximization and focused on the institutional setting (e.g., the intensity of interbureaucratic competition for budget shares and intrabureaucratic competition for promotions and positions in networks; the existence of barriers to mobility; and the ability of superiors and sponsors to monitor performance) as the determinant of which particular objective will appear to dominate in a particular bureau. Breton and Wintrobe characterized the bureaucratic institutional process as one dominated by "entrepreneurial competition," wherein individual bureaucrats pursue their subjective goals by selectively seeking and implementing policy innovations.[12] This characterization fits the role played by law enforcement bureaucrats in the evolution of drug criminalization policy.

A number of self-interest political motivations for drug criminalization have been identified for both bureaucratic and non-bureaucratic interest groups. Some studies[13] have noted the incentives of professional organizations, such as the American Pharmaceutical Association, to create legal limits on the distribution of drugs (e.g., there was significant competition between pharmacists and physicians for the legal right to dispense drugs) while others have focused on the strong racial impacts of illicit drug laws and the desire by some groups to control racial minorities through the enforcement of such laws.[14] More importantly from the perspective stressed here, however, others have emphasized that the organized force of law enforcement bureaucrats was a major source of demand for the initial criminalization of illicit drugs.[15]

The analogies between Breton and Wintrobe's (1982:146–154) discussion of the development of wage and price controls and the criminalization of drugs is striking. For instance, one bureaucratic strategy to compete for resources is to "generate" demand for a bureau's own services through direct lobbying, policy manipulation, and the selective release of information to other interest groups and the media. This is done because bureaucrats must compete with other bureaucracies for the support and attention of sponsors (and individual bureaucrats must compete with other bureaucrats for benefits within a bureau), and because the control of resources is necessary before most of the subjective goals of bureaucrats can be achieved.[16] Indeed, Lindesmith (1965:3) contended that the nation's program for handling the "drug problem" was one "which, to all intents and purposes, was established by the decisions of administrative officials of the Treasury Department." For instance, for several years after its passage in 1914, the Harrison Act remained a rather unimportant source of taxes and regulatory measures (Reinarman, 1983:21), until criminalization of opiate users was instigated by the Federal Bureau of Narcotics raids on morphine treatment clinics in 1919.[17] King (1957:122) maintained that "the Narcotics Division launched a reign of terror. Doctors were bullied and threatened, and those who were adamant [about treating addicts] went to prison." Efforts by bureaucrats in the Narcotics Bureau led to a series of court decisions which reinterpreted the Harrison Act and became the pretext for criminalization of drug use (Reinarman, 1983:21). Furthermore, because of pressure from people in the same bureau, the Marijuana Tax Act was passed in 1937.[18] Some writers have stressed moral entrepreneurship by Narcotics Bureau officials (e.g., Becker, 1963), but others have focused on bureaucratic fiscal self-promotion (e.g., Dickson, 1968). Both views are consistent with the Breton–Wintrobe model, but the second appears to be particularly relevant since the bureau was in need of a new raison d'etre for continued funding in 1937; after all, it faced stiff competition from the FBI for the attention of the public and of Congress (King, 1978), so bureaucratic survival was certainly a probable motivation.

Breton and Wintrobe (1982:39) emphasized that bureaucratic release of both true and false information, or "selective distortion," can play significant roles in bureaucratic policy advocacy.[19] This has clearly been the case in the evolution of drug policy. For example, the bureaucratic campaigns leading to the 1937 marijuana legislation "included remarkable distortions of the evidence of harm caused by marijuana, ignoring the findings of empirical inquiries."[20] Marijuana was alleged to cause insanity, incite its users to rape, and to develop a delirious rage, making users irresponsible and prone to commit violent crimes. Furthermore, the bill was represented as one which was largely symbolic in that it would require no additional enforcement expenditures (Galliher and Walker, 1977).

The evolution of drug policy since initial criminalization has been, at least in part, shaped by competition between law enforcement and drug treatment bureaucrats over "ownership of the problem"—that is, over shares of federal, state, and local budgets (Gusfield, 1980; Morgan, 1983)—and between law enforcement bureaucracies themselves (e.g., between the DEA and the FBI [King, 1978] at the federal level, as well as between various local, state, and federal bureaucracies). This evolution also reflects another aspect of the bureaucratic process emphasized in Breton and Wintrobe (1982). As the perceived responsibility for some social ill (e.g., crime in this case, and inflation in Breton and Wintrobe) is shifted from outside forces to the government, and to the bureaucracy, bureaucrats seek to shift the blame elsewhere (Breton and Wintrobe, 1982:149). Blaming crime on people crazed by drugs provides an opportunity to shift blame. A good deal of false or misleading information emanating from police bureaucrats about the relationship between drugs and crime has clearly characterized the evolution of drug policy.[21] In fact, a primary source of the "information" (much of which was inaccurate and/or unsubstantiated [Michaels, 1987:311–324]) used to justify the 1984–1989 war on drugs was the police bureaucracy. It was largely as a result of information promulgated by police (Barnett, 1984:53) that it became widely believed that drug use is the root cause of much of what is wrong with society (e.g., see the Office of National Drug Control Strategy, 1989:2). In particular, drug use is claimed to be a leading cause of non-drug crime because, it is contended, property crime is a major source of income for drug users. This claim has been raised to justify political demands for the criminal justice system to do something about the drug/crime problem, demands which largely emanate from the police lobbies (e.g., see Berk, Brackman, and Lesser, 1977; Barnett, 1984); and in turn, it has led to an increasing emphasis on control of illicit drug traffic as a means of general crime prevention. State and federal legislators have been passing increasingly strict sentences for drug offenders, police have shifted resources to make more drug arrests, and judges have sentenced increasingly large numbers of drug offenders to prison. Such a reallocation of resources would appear to be justified if drugs truly are the root cause of most other crime; but as demonstrated in Chapter 5, these causal relationships do not actually hold. In particular, increased drug enforcement efforts tends to cause increases in crime as other crime types are less effectively deterred. Thus, the opportunity costs of the war on drugs appear to be quite high. This should not be surprising, given the history of failure of drug and alcohol prohibition policies (Thornton, 1991; Nadelmann, 1993). The question as to why this reallocation has occurred would appear to be even more pressing under the circumstances.

Breton and Wintrobe (1982:150–151) offer two reasons why bureaucrats advocate a policy of direct control of the source of blame, even though such policies have a history of failure. First, there is always opposition to such a policy; so when it fails, the opposition can be blamed for not allocating enough resources to combat the problem. And second, since the outcome of the policy depends jointly on the inputs of several different groups and bureaus, and since the set of possible control methods is very large, when the subset selected fails, the bureaucrats can make these arguments: (1) that while they favored a control policy they favored a different subset of control tools (e.g., more severe punishment of drug offenders; greater spending on interdiction efforts) so they are not responsible for the failure, and/or (2) that the other groups who had to contribute to make the effort successful (e.g., witnesses; judges; legislators who approve prison budgets; other law enforcement agencies) did not do their share. Indeed, a policy can fail completely while at the same time entrepreneurial bureaucrats expand their reputations and end up being substantially better off.[22]

Oerther (1991:20) suggested two other important factors, one of which harkens back to the discussion of corruption in Chapter 5. He contended that law enforcement bureaucrats are the interest group that benefits most from prohibitionary drug laws because prohibition policies put officials in a position to extract bribes from those who want to participate in drug markets, and because the officials gain the support of other prohibition advocates in their competition for budgets and discretion. The ongoing competition for a share of the total budget is always an important factor for a bureaucracy. After all, few of the subjective goals of bureaucrats can be achieved without a budget. Therefore, each bureau must demonstrate that it is doing a good job in serving its constituencies.

The function of police in the minds of most citizens is to "fight crime." But how can interest groups, voters, taxpayers, and/or elected representatives tell if police are doing a good job? The number of crimes prevented cannot be quantified. Therefore, police need statistical indicators of their "productivity" to use in their lobbying efforts for budgets (Sherman 1983:156). The number of arrests is a natural measure of "effectiveness," and this is a primary "statistic" that police focus on in the budget negotiation process. Others include response times following emergency calls, and, increasingly, seizures. Indeed, with drug prohibition, a source of arrests is created that does not require waiting for some victim to report a crime, and it provides a new statistical indicator of effectiveness: the value of drugs seized (and of non-drug property seizures, as discussed below).[23] Indeed, under prohibition, police incentives may be even more "perverted" than suggested so far: there are actually incentives to allocate resources in order to avoid deterring Index I crime. After all, while arrest statistics may be primary indicators of police performance used in the budget bargaining process, they are not the only important statistic used in such bargaining. As Milakovich and Weis (1975:10) note, police have a "vested interest" in keeping crime rates relatively high: if crime rates drop too much, then support for more police and larger budgets declines and "like all bureaucracies, criminal justice agencies can hardly be expected to implement policies that would diminish their importance." The economics-of-crime literature discussed in Chapter 3 indicates that higher Index I crime rates clearly are correlated with more police resources in "demand for policing" equations, supporting the assumption that political demands for police services rise if reported crime rates are high. But if police do respond to the incentives outlined here, additional funding need not lead to any decrease in reported crime rates. Police can focus resources on drug control, which can lead to both increased arrests and drug seizures as indicators of effectiveness, while simultaneously increasing Index I crime rates, as suggested in Chapter 5, thus implying a greater need for police services. These incentives have been in place since drugs were initially criminalized, however. Something else must have changed in 1984 to produce the significant reallocation of policing resources that are documented in Chapters 1, 2, and 5. Indeed, something else did change. A bureaucratically motivated policy innovation appears to have created explicit incentives for shifting resources toward drug enforcement. This innovation allowed police agencies to benefit through confiscations of money and property used in or purchased with profits from the drug trade.

III. Federal Confiscations Legislation and Police Interests

Government seizure of property used in criminal activity is actually a long-standing practice. It was one stimulus for the king's involvement in law enforcement as early as the ninth and tenth centuries (Benson, 1990), for instance, and was first used in the United States to combat smugglers who avoided import duties in the early nineteenth century. Now it is being used to combat the supply of illicit drugs. Federal officials confiscated over $100 million in 1983; and the Comprehensive Crime Act of 1984 broadened support for the practice, as the law required the Justice Department to share the proceeds with state and local agencies participating in the investigations. Perhaps as a result of the cooperation this produced, federal forfeitures were projected to be $700 million for 1991.[24]

The 1984 federal asset-forfeiture law was a bureaucratic innovation which allowed for an expanded interbureaucratic network of cooperation. As Breton and Wintrobe (1982:128) explained, cooperation through informal networks, both within and across bureaucracies, is an alternative to competition. A reduction in the intensity of competition allows bureaucrats greater discretion in the pursuit of their subjective goals.[25] On the surface at least, this innovation apparently allowed local law enforcement agencies to generate revenues that were not limited by the interbureaucratic competition for resources that arises in the local budgeting process, because the statute mandated that shared assets go directly to law enforcement agencies rather than into general funds, education funds, or other depositories that were mandated by many state forfeiture laws. An increase in the revenues from seizures creates the potential for bureaucratic managers to enhance their own well-being directly and indirectly by rewarding supporters in the managers' networks with various "perks" (Breton and Wintrobe, 1982:137). After all, in the context of a common-pool allocation process, police have considerable discretion in how they allocate the resources they control, and monitoring generally does not limit their discretion in any substantial way.[26] Therefore, inasmuch as this new source of revenue has increased the police's ability to control resources, it has probably increased their discretionary ability to generate perks.

Forfeiture has an obvious deterrent value in that it raises the costs associated with drug offenses. Forfeiture policies might also be justified in that they can be used to recoup public monies spent on law enforcement. This practical aspect was emphasized in a manual designed to help jurisdictions develop a forfeiture capability (National Criminal Justice Association, 1988:40). Pointing out that less tangible law-enforcement effects (such as deterrence) should be counted as benefits, the manual emphasized that the determining factor for pursuit of a forfeiture is "the *jurisdiction's* best interest" (emphasis added). This interest, of course, is viewed from the perspective of law enforcement agencies, a view that might put somewhat more weight on benefits for bureaucrats and somewhat lesser weight on the somewhat uncertain communitywide benefits of deterrence effects. After all, as Stumpf (1988:316; also see Blumberg, 1979; Benson, 1990) noted, we must "look past the external political and social determinants of criminal justice procedures and policies to understand the system in operation. The process is staffed by professionals and quasi-professionals who have their own agenda . . . [and] largely internal imperatives may be of even greater importance in explaining their outcomes." Indeed, if forfeitures are in the "public interest" because of their deterrent impacts, and if police are exclusively motivated to serve the public interest, then they should willingly cooperate in forfeiture efforts no matter what government agency's budget is enhanced by these seizures.

However, the 1984 federal confiscations legislation directed that all shared seizures go to law enforcement. This followed a period of active advocacy by federal, state, and local law enforcement officials who emphasized that it would foster cooperation between their agencies and increase the overall effort devoted to and the effectiveness of drug control; that is, law enforcement bureaus maintained that they needed to be paid to cooperate, whether the cooperation was in the public interest or not. For instance, in hearings on the Comprehensive Drug Penalty Act before the Subcommittee on Crime of the Committee on the Judiciary of the U.S. House of Representatives, held on June 23 and October 14, 1983, much of the testimony focused exclusively on the confiscations and forfeitures issue (U.S. Congress, 1985). Among the organizations and bureaucracies presenting testimony in support of the forfeitures-sharing arrangement were the U.S. Customs Service, various police departments and sheriffs, the U.S. Attorney's Office from the Southern District of Florida, and the U.S. Drug Enforcement Administration. There was no representation of local government oversight authorities (mayors, city councils, county commissions) either supporting or objecting to such legislation. Furthermore, when the innovation was first introduced, it appears that most non–law enforcement bureaucrats did not anticipate the bill's implications, probably due to the poor "quality" of information selectively released by law enforcement bureaucracies and their congressional supporters. The only group suggesting problems with the legislation was the Criminal Justice Section of the American Bar Association. Two groups involved in drug therapy (the Therapy Committees of America, and the Alcohol and Drug Problems Association) also supported forfeitures sharing, but proposed that a share also go to drug therapy programs. The law enforcement lobbies prevailed.

Following passage of the initial law, interbureaucratic competition for the rights to seized assets, as defined by federal statutes, intensified. It became clear to state and local bureaucrats, who compete with the law enforcement sector for the control of resources, that the federal legislation was being used to circumvent state laws and constitutions prohibiting certain forfeitures or limiting law enforcement use of seizures. For example, North Carolina law requires that all proceeds from confiscated assets go to the County School Fund. Law enforcement agencies in North Carolina, and in other states where state law limited their ability to benefit from confiscations, began using the 1984 federal legislation to circumvent their states' laws by routinely arranging for federal "adoption" of forfeitures so they could be passed back to the state and local law enforcement agencies. As education bureaucrats and others affected by this diversion of benefits recognized what was going on, they began to advocate a change in the federal law. They were successful: the Anti-drug Abuse Act of 1988, passed on November 18, 1988, changed the asset forfeitures provisions that had been established in 1984. Section 6077 of the 1988 act stated that the attorney general must assure that any forfeitures transferred to a state or local law enforcement agency "Is not so transferred to circumvent any requirement of State Law that prohibits forfeiture or limits use or disposition of property forfeited to state or local agencies." This provision was designated to go into effect on October 1, 1989, and the Department of Justice interpreted it to mandate an end to all adoptive forfeitures (U.S. Congress, 1990:166).

State and local law enforcement officials immediately began advocating the repeal of Section 6077. Thus, the U.S. House Subcommittee on Crime heard testimony on April 24, 1989, advocating repeal of Section 6077 from such groups as the International Association of Chiefs of Police, the Florida Department of Law Enforcement, the North Carolina Department of Crime Control and Public Safety, and the U.S. Attorney General's Office. Perhaps the most impassioned plea for repeal was made by Joseph W. Dean of the North Carolina Department of Crime Control and Public Safety (U.S. Congress, 1990:20–28),[27] who admitted both that law enforcement bureaucracies were using the federal law to circumvent the state's constitution and that without the benefits of confiscations going to those bureaus, substantially less effort would be made to control drugs.

> Currently the United States Attorney General, by policy, requires that all shared property be used by the transfer for law enforcement purposes. The conflict between state and federal law [given Section 6077 of the 1988 act] would prevent the federal government from adopting seizures by state and local agencies.
>
> . . . This provision would have a devastating impact on joint efforts by federal, state and local law enforcement agencies not only in North Carolina but also in other affected states. . . .
>
> Education is any state's biggest business. The education lobby is the most powerful in the state and has taken a position against law enforcement being able to share in seized assets. The irony is that if local and state law enforcement agencies cannot share, the assets will in all likelihood not be seized and forfeited. Thus no one wins but the drug trafficker. . . .
>
> . . . If this financial sharing stops, we will kill the goose that laid the golden egg.

This statement clearly suggests that law enforcement agencies focus resources on enforcement of drug laws because of the financial gains for the agencies arising from forfeitures. Perhaps it was not the fact that drugs are illegal, or that the president declared war on drugs, which induced the massive post-1984 police effort; a more likely stimulus was the 1984 legislation which mandated that forfeitures generate benefits for police.

The implication that law enforcement agencies benefit from the discretion arising through forfeitures was also corroborated by other testimony, including that of the Commissioner of the Florida Department of Law Enforcement (FDLE) (U.S. Congress, 1990:13–14). In fact, a statement by the U.S. Attorney for the Eastern District of North Carolina, in support of repealing Section 6077, actually implied that law enforcement agencies were focusing on confiscations as opposed to criminal convictions (U.S. Congress, 1990:26): "Drug agents would have much less incentive to follow through on the asset potentially held by drug traffickers, since there would be no reward for such efforts and would concentrate their time and resources on the criminal prosecution."

Indeed, forfeitures can be successful even if arrest and prosecution are not. Forfeiture laws are supposedly designed to protect lien holders and owners whose property is used without their knowledge or consent, but owners' rights are tenuous since most states prohibit suits claiming that the property was wrongfully taken. This prohibition, coupled with the fact that the procedure takes place in a civil forfeiture hearing, diminishes the capacity of property owners to defend themselves. Generally, owners whose property is alleged to have been used in a drug offense or purchased with the proceeds from drug trafficking have the burden of establishing that they merit relief from the forfeiture proceeding (National Criminal Justice Association, 1988:41). Not only must the owners prove that they are innocent of the alleged crime, but that they lacked both knowledge of and control over the property's unlawful use if someone else used it for criminal purposes. For example, if a drug seller places a drug order by phone from a friend's business, that property can be seized unless the owner proves both lack of knowledge and lack of control. Thus, forfeiture activity can be a lucrative source of revenue for a police agency, without regard to the actual criminality of the potential victim of such seizures. The power of confiscation is shown by a March 1991 drug raid in which federal agents confiscated three University of Virginia fraternity houses after they seized drugs valued at a few hundred dollars. The houses were valued at $1 million, and the rent from these buildings was subsequently paid to the U.S. Justice Department.[28]

Seizures can be particularly attractive for a local policing agency. For instance, the Volusia County, Florida, Sheriff's Department had a drug squad which seized over $8 million (an average of $5,000 per day) from motorists on Interstate 95 during a forty-one-month period between 1989 and 1992.[29] These seizures were "justified" as part of the war on drugs. Actually, however, most Volusia County seizures involved southbound rather than northbound travelers, suggesting that the drug squad was more interested in seizing money than in stopping the flow of drugs. In fact, no criminal charges were filed in over 75 percent of the county's seizure cases. More significantly, a substantial amount of money was apparently seized from innocent victims. And money is not returned even when the seizure is challenged, no proof of wrongdoing or criminal record can be found, and the victim presents proof that the money was legitimately earned. Three-fourths (199) of Volusia County's seizures did not include an arrest, and were contested. The sheriff employed a forfeiture attorney at $44,000 per year to handle settlement negotiations (he moved to private practice in mid-1990, after which he was paid $48,000 to continue working for the sheriff on seizure cases). Only four people ultimately got their money back, one went to trial but lost and has appealed, and the rest settled for 50–90 percent of their money after promising not to sue the sheriff's department.[30] How many were drug traffickers? No one knows, since no charges were filed and no trials occurred; but it is clear that several were innocent victims.

The Volusia County Sheriff's Department is not the only law enforcement agency that has benefited from asset seizure laws. Over 90 percent of the police departments with jurisdictions containing populations of 50,000 or more, and over 90 percent of the sheriffs' departments serving populations of 250,000 or more, received money or goods from a drug asset-forfeiture program in 1990, for instance (Reaves, 1992:1). Furthermore, the Drug Enforcement Administration seizes millions of dollars at ports, airports, and bus stations; Congress began investigating alleged abuses by the DEA in May 1992. Indeed, asset forfeiture by law enforcement agencies has become increasingly controversial throughout the nation. Highly publicized criticism in the print and electronic media has raised constitutional issues such as the erosion of Fourth Amendment rights, protection of innocent parties, and a lack of proportionality of punishment to the crime. Whether large portions of the seizures come from criminals or not cannot be determined since many do not involve arrests, and the costs associated with recovering wrongfully seized assets from the federal authorities can run into thousands of dollars. Despite the misuse of the forfeiture laws in Volusia County and all over the country,[31] however, the police lobbies won the battle over federal legislation. Section 6077 of the Anti-drug Abuse Act of 1988 never went into effect. Its repeal was hidden in the 1990 Defense Appropriations Bill, and the repeal was made retroactive to October 1, 1989. It appears that the police bureaucrats have won the competition over the property rights to forfeitures, at least as it has been waged at the federal level.

Competitors for budgets at the local level may recognize the significant discretionary gains that police enjoy as a consequence of asset seizures, however. If they do, then they might be able to convince local sponsors that police budgets should be reduced accordingly. That is, returns from asset forfeiture do not necessarily represent a net gain to local police agencies even when they are given to the agencies. Pressure from other local bureaucrats who are competitors for resources may lead administrators and politicians with whom bureaucrats bargain for agency budgets to view the flow of money from seizures as a substitute for regular budget increments. After all, one alleged purpose of asset forfeitures is to make drug enforcement efforts, to a degree, self-financing. If these gains are fungible in the budget bargaining and review process, and if local commissions, councils, and/or mayors face strong pressures to take full advantage of this possibility, they could refuse to approve police budgets that are not reduced to offset expected confiscations.

Asset seizures and police discretionary budgets. The extent to which police agencies can increase their budget via forfeiture activity is explored in Benson, Rasmussen, and Sollars (1992), using data from Florida policing jurisdictions. Confiscations were found to have a significant positive impact on police agencies' budgets after accounting for demand and local government budget constraints. As expected, the impact was larger in more populous jurisdictions. It appears that forfeitures offer police an attractive policy option: an activity that can be justified politically because of its potential strong deterrent effect and because it suggests that drug enforcement is, to a degree, self-financing, while it generates direct benefits to the police bureaucracy by increasing the bureau's discretionary budget. Relatively small amounts of money from seized assets can mean substantial increases in budget discretion. Florida data provide an indication of the importance of confiscations as a source of discretionary spending. Confiscations by law enforcement agencies in the state accounted for about 2.0 percent of the total 1989 law enforcement budget. However, relatively fixed obligations of personnel costs account for about 84 percent of all state and local police expenditures (Bureau of Justice Statistics, *Sourcebook, 1990*, Tables 1.4 and 1.13), and there are other unavoidable expenses; so administrators are likely to exercise discretion over less than 10 percent of the budget. For the average Florida jurisdiction in 1989, confiscations therefore account for at least 20 percent of its discretionary resources and perhaps as much as 30 percent for agencies with active forfeiture programs.

The estimated elasticity of non-capital expenditures with respect to confiscations is 0.04 for all jurisdictions in Benson, Rasmussen, and Sollars

(1992) and 0.07 for the larger ones; but this seemingly modest elasticity belies the potentially large impact of asset forfeiture on decisionmaking, since only a small fraction of non-capital expenditures are discretionary. The elasticity of discretionary spending with respect to confiscations can be approximated as the estimated elasticity divided by the proportion of all non-capital expenditures that are discretionary. Thus, if 10 percent of non-capital expenditures are discretionary, the relevant elasticity lies in the 0.4 to 0.7 range. Since the portion of budgets that is committed to specific uses is probably larger than assumed here, these figures probably represent a significant underestimate of the impact that confiscated assets can have on the discretionary budget.

These results, combined with the evidence of more intense drug enforcement after 1984, are consistent with the hypothesis that police have incentives to respond to the Comprehensive Crime Act of 1984 by focusing on drug enforcement. The asset forfeiture provisions of the federal statute created an exogenous change in state and local law enforcement agencies' bureaucratic incentives, inducing them to join in the federally declared war on drugs. Police agencies seeking to increase their budget discretion were tempted to use an increasing portion of their resources against drug offenders, and to devote fewer resources to other crimes. Thus, changes in police behavior since 1984 are consistent with the proposition that these agencies responded to the incentives created by this law. The relative allocation of state and local law enforcement resources has shifted dramatically toward drug enforcement, the major source of asset confiscations.

IV. Differences in Drug Enforcement across States and Cities

The federal confiscations statute appears to help explain the nationwide staging of a drug war, but it does not explain the large difference in drug enforcement activities across states and cities that is detailed in Chapter 1. However, under the federal adoption procedures, federal authorities keep 20 percent of the confiscated assets that they handle. Thus, there are incentives for police to avoid federal adoptions if their state laws allow them to keep seized assets, as a number of states do. In fact, the importance of the federal statute receded by 1990, as many state legislatures followed the federal government's lead and police bureaucrats' demands by incorporating the forfeiture process into their standard law enforcement procedures. Now, many more states have a forfeiture statute for controlled substances, and many police are no longer obliged to give

20 percent of their seizures to the federal authorities in exchange for adopting them. Items most often subject to seizure include material used in drug production, paraphernalia, containers, motor vehicles, and money, but most states also allow confiscation of real estate used in the "furtherance of illegal drug activity."[32] A growing number of states have more general forfeiture provisions, allowing seizure for "contraband" offenses and felonies. State racketeering laws that authorize the forfeiture of property obtained as a result of illegal activity are even more stringent. Nonetheless, state statutes are not all as accommodating to police as the federal statute, leaving the federal law as a useful vehicle by which some police bureaucracies can enhance their discretionary budget.

Given the variation in state laws regarding forfeitures, and given the costs associated with using the federal authorities, it might be that these factors help explain the cross-state variation in drug enforcement activities. Rasmussen, Benson, and Mast (1993) explored this issue in an econometric model using a unique data set that allowed for control of other potential explanations of this cross-sectional variation. The Drug Use Forecasting program has produced estimates of the level of drug use among criminal populations in twenty-four cities. By using these data, Rasmussen, Benson, and Mast were able to control for the level of drug use perceived by police, in order to see if variation in drug market activity explained the differences in drug arrests across these cities. Not surprisingly, the level of drug use is a determinant of drug arrests. This result is consistent with a "public interest" desire to control drug use or to control non-drug crime through a drug enforcement strategy. It is also consistent with a bureaucratic self-interest hypothesis, because a larger drug market implies that drug arrests are relatively easy to make. However, Rasmussen, Benson, and Mast also controlled for the level of property crime, in reflection of the public interest claims of police that drug enforcement is a general crime-control technique, and for various socio-economic factors.[33] The level of property crime was not significantly related to drug arrest activity, however, suggesting that the police do not actually act as if they believe the claim that making drug arrests will reduce property crime. In contrast, a state law that allows the police to keep any portion of seized assets was associated with significantly more emphasis on drug arrests. Indeed, the laws have a large and important impact on the allocation of police resources: the existence of a confiscation law that is favorable to the police raises the drug arrests/total arrests ratio between 35 percent and 50 percent, depending on the model specification. Allowing police to profit from the confiscation of assets from alleged drug offenders apparently provides a powerful incentive to law enforcement agencies—which, as expected, changes agency behavior.

Furthermore, it appears that the public interest explanation of drug arrest activity—that drug market control is intended to control the level of crime, which police claim is caused by drug use—does not explain the variation in policing behavior across jurisdictions. However, it may not be the level of crime related to general drug use, but rather the nature of the drug being used, that provides the public interest motivation for the latest war on drugs. In particular, the advent of crack cocaine is often cited as the reason for the sudden increase in drug enforcement during the most recent drug war.

V. The Crack Crisis: Is It an Explanation for or a Political Legitimization of the 1980s Drug War?

Crack cocaine was an innovation that clearly transformed drug markets during the 1980s. But was it an innovation that also stimulated the police to wage a drug war? The answer appears to be NO! The drug war was under way in 1984; but crack did not appear in any significant quantities in the United States until the latter half of 1985 or early 1986, and then only in a few urban areas. At the time of the publication of a book on *The Cocaine Crisis* in 1987, for instance, only three "principal trafficking areas" for crack had been identified: New York, Miami, and Los Angeles (Johnson, 1987:36). Indeed, the causal relationship between crack and the drug war is probably the reverse of that often alleged by policymakers and police: crack apparently was introduced into the United States in the 1985–1986 period because of the early drug war successes that law enforcement was having against marijuana (Thornton, 1991; Nadelmannn, 1993:45). Crack appeared in the Bahamas in 1983 (Allen, 1987:3), so the technology was available. Not surprisingly, this technology was transported into the United States sometime in 1985 as a substitute for marijuana.[34] After all, marijuana was the least expensive and probably the most widely used of the illicit drugs. Successful interdiction efforts during the early stages of the drug war made the marijuana trade riskier for sellers and raised its price to consumers, as noted in Chapter 4, inducing both consumers and producers to look for an alternative that could be transported with less risk and sold at a low price. Law enforcement officials often imply that crack use represents an increase in drug consumption. This may be true to a degree, because of its low price (it may have been a viable substitute for alcohol as well as illicit drugs, for instance); but in fact, a substantial portion of the increased use of crack appears to reflect a substitution of this drug for others which were more expensive and/or difficult to obtain. Thus, during the period when crack use was on the rise, marijuana and non-crack variations of cocaine were apparently declining in use (see Chapter 4).

Crack is allegedly a much more serious drug than either marijuana or other forms of cocaine, from both a health and a public safety perspective. But are these allegations accurate, or is this another example of the false or misleading "information" that has characterized bureaucratic advocacy of drug prohibition throughout the century? As usual, it is very difficult to sort out the truth from the half-truths; but let us begin considering the process by which this "crisis" has come to the public's attention.

Allen (1987:4) proclaimed that "the freebase or crack epidemic hit the Untied States [shortly after November 1985]. . . . Wreaking havoc first in New York City and California, the new form of the drug has spread to other parts of the United States, causing a public outcry and eliciting pledges from the White House to intensify the war on drugs." But there really was no "public outcry." Rather, was there some clever entrepreneurial maneuvering by law enforcement bureaucrats who recognized that this new, largely unknown variant of cocaine could provide them with the excuse to "intensify" the war on drugs which was already well under way?

One of the first bureaucratic entrepreneurs to focus on crack was Robert Stutmann, and he probably deserves much of the credit for creating the widespread impression that crack's unique characteristics were the source of large new social problems. Crack came to his attention on October 26, 1985, shortly after he became the head of the New York DEA office (Stutmann and Esposito, 1992:137). Stutmann was a man long accustomed to the processes of bureaucratic politics, who knew how to effectively manipulate the press in his efforts to gain support for greater budgets and power, and who enjoyed the media and political games.[35] Indeed, among the press who covered such activities, he was known as "video Bob" (Massing, 1992:44). The New York DEA office was focusing almost totally on heroin when Stutmann arrived, but he recognized a chance to make his mark by reorganizing and shifting the office's focus to crack. He immediately began such a reorganization, and started setting the stage for a "full-blown media campaign" (Stutmann and Esposito, 1992:148). He also visited prosecutors, local police, and judges, making deals and promises in order to gain their cooperation.[36]

The media campaign was in motion by late November when a *New York Times* (November 29, 1985) article first publicized crack's arrival in the city. Indeed, the media campaign was under way even before the reorganization was complete, but "Soon after crack began to dominate the news, the results of reshuffling our [DEA] case priorities began to filter in to an intelligence division now equipped to understand them" (Stutmann and Esposito, 1992:154).[37] Stutmann needed more than newspaper headlines, however; he needed the support of the DEA headquarters in Washington, which was reluctant to accept the claims that crack was of sufficient importance to warrant increased attention. Stutmann recognized that he "needed to make it [crack] a national issue and quickly," so he "began a lobbying effort and . . . used the media" (Stutmann and Esposito, 1992:217). But he also needed evidence that would be politically useful. Therefore, Stutmann and his assistant, "the DEA's leading cocaine conspiracy expert" who was transferred to New York in May 1986, designed a plan of action intended to simultaneously generate crack arrests and attract the attention of Washington (Stutmann and Esposito, 1992:211–226). They decided to target the Washington Heights area, in part because of its position at the end of the George Washington Bridge where it was easily accessible to suburban drug buyers from New Jersey and Westchester County. The first phase of their campaign was to seize crack buyers' cars in order to legitimize a claim that most crack consumers were politically important middle-class suburbanites and their children, rather than blacks and Hispanics from urban ghettos. Only after that would sellers be targeted, intentionally beginning with the street-level dealers in order to build up arrests *and* make deals for information about higher-ups. A bulletin for law enforcement officials was prepared and issued on May 26, 1986, explaining, among other things, that crack had a "very high addictive potential and that it causes medical and psychological problems." The report, which also implied that crack led to random acts of violence, was released to the press as well; so when the assault on Washington Heights began, the media were ready and willing to cover it.

The plan was explained to DEA administrator Jack Lawn in June 1986. Stutmann and Esposito (1992:219) noted that "the timing was perfect, although University of Maryland basketball star Len Bias might not have seen it that way. On June 19, the day Lawn arrived, we got the call that Bias had died. . . . The drug death of a young athlete, with all that signified to an America that worships sports heroes, had capped the groundwork that had been carefully laid through press accounts and [Stutmann's] public appearances. Crack was a national menace and 1986 was the year of Crack. From [Stutmann's] perspective, Len Bias had not died in vain." Lawn was given a full-blown presentation, focusing on two claims (1) that the over-whelming majority of crack users were middle-income working people and, perhaps more importantly, their high school and college-student children; and (2) that crack was a significant new cause of crime because the ghetto dwellers who used the drug had to steal, while the sellers protected their turf with violence. In other words, while crack threatened the politically important middle class, it was also responsible for rising property and violent crime. Lawn asked Stutmann to hold off on the car seizure program while he went back to Washington to begin lobbying for an expanded DEA budget to put twenty-four DEA crack task forces at the disposal of any region of the country that might need them. A request for a $10 million enhancement in the DEA budget for that purpose was presented, but it was turned down. Lawn then gave Stutmann permission to launch the seizure program in earnest with full DEA backing; and on August 4, 1986, the New York Police Department and the DEA jointly announced that the program had been implemented, with the seizure of forty-seven cars. The fruits of Stutmann's media campaign could also be seen in August: he had compiled a 199-page bound volume of articles from New York and New Jersey newspapers reporting a "surge of cocaine-related deaths," rising murder rates, crowded detox centers, and claims that all crimes except rape were up in New York and that crack was the cause. The national news media had also begun to pick up on the idea, with a *Newsweek* article appearing in June. Eventually, more than 1,000 cars were seized in the Washington Heights operation, and two crack rings were put out of business. Nonetheless, Stutmann and Esposito contend that Washington officials did not recognize crack as a problem warranting special attention until 1989 when newly appointed drug czar Bill Bennett decided to use DEA agents to police Washington itself. This does not mean that crack had no influence on criminal justice funding. The media campaign emanating from New York, and the arrival of crack in other parts of the country, provided state and local law enforcement officials with a new political tool in their budgetary battles. Thus, crack became the new drug scourge.

The crack scare is like many other drug scares that came before it. Indeed, innovations in drug markets often provide bureaucratic entrepreneurs with a new source of material to use in their competition for power and budgets, as suggested by the preceding account of Robert Stutmann's manipulation of crack. As Zimring and Hawkins (1992:50–51) explained, whenever a new drug variant such as crack has been introduced it has been presented as a new public policy problem because of the chemical, physiological, and psychological novelty of the new drug. This same argument has been applied to opium, heroin, marijuana, cocaine, and amphetamines. Each one has been declared to be "the greatest drug menace," and crack is simply the latest candidate. Zimring and Hawkins (1992:51) note that this occurs because "allegations of a drug's uniqueness can be used as a rhetorical device to shield proponents of a prohibitory policy from counter-arguments based on the history of earlier efforts at the state regulation of other substances or of the same substance in different forms or settings." Thus, a new variant of a drug provides the political entrepreneur with an opportunity for "selective distortion" à la Breton and Wintrobe (1982:39). Drugs do vary in their chemical properties, of course; but for the entrepreneurial criminal justice bureaucrat, uniqueness "represents the end point of analysis . . . [it] entails a corresponding distinctiveness in the social and law enforcement problems it generates, which make irrelevant any reference to past experience with any other drug" (Zimring and Hawkins, 1992:51). Crack, like all drugs, can have negative effects on users; but when such a drug is first introduced, it provides entrepreneurial bureaucrats with an opportunity to heighten political awareness of the "need" for a strong prohibitionary effort by exaggerating the negative effects of the drug before any evidence is available to counter those exaggerations, and even to make up some effects that are ultimately refuted by scientific evidence.

Not surprisingly, some of the early and often repeated claims about crack are now being revealed as false. While crack can be addictive, for instance, the Office of National Drug Policy now estimates that about one in ten who try it are likely to become addicted—the same percentage that is attributed to alcohol, and roughly half the addiction rate that was initially alleged to apply (Bennett and DiLorenzo, 1992:241).[38] Furthermore, the characteristics of crack addiction are different from the characteristics of heroin addiction; and on balance, crack is less addictive than heroin: withdrawal pain is less severe for cocaine than heroin, and the craving for cocaine comes from its euphoric effects rather than from avoidance of withdrawals (Gould, 1990:11). While crack is consumed by high school and college students, and by middle-income suburbanites, the claims that these groups constitute the overwhelming majority of crack users is "almost certainly untrue" (Massing, 1992:44). Crack is a very inexpensive drug and therefore a very attractive drug to poorer segments of the population. Furthermore, there is still no evidence to support the claims that crack causes crime—an issue addressed at length in earlier chapters of this book. Indeed, because crack is much cheaper than heroin or cocaine in non-crack forms, the "drugs cause property crime" argument is probably even weaker for it than for these other drugs. Violence associated with crack (e.g., turf wars) is more a function of its illegality than of its psychological effects.

Crack can kill its users. It boosts the heart rate and blood pressure, and therefore can lead to strokes, seizures, and heart attacks, as the Len Bias case demonstrates. However, its health effects are probably less significant than alcohol or tobacco and it certainly kills far fewer people than either of these legal drugs. Indeed, one of the most widespread alleged health effects—the "crack baby" phenomenon—has been revealed to be unsupported. Pregnant woman who use crack also usually drink alcohol, smoke heavily, neglect nutritional needs, live in poverty, and do not receive any prenatal care. Substantial evidence suggests that all of these factors affect the unborn child; and after accounting for them, medical researchers are now finding that the alleged effects of crack vanish (Bennett and DiLorenzo, 1992:243–245). No statistical relationship between crack consumption and such things as premature birth, low birth rate, or birth defects remains after these other factors are taken into account. This does not mean that crack consumption during pregnancy should be condoned, of course. But significantly, the crack baby scare may actually add to the problems of unhealthy newborns, rather than solving them. As Bennett and DiLorenzo (1992:244) noted, "The hysteria itself . . . may convince many mothers that their children are indeed hopeless. If [you find yourself to be pregnant, you consume crack regularly, and] you're told by authorities that you'll give birth to a zombie, why bother with prenatal care?"

Crack was not the impetus for the drug war. No doubt, crack use has grown dramatically since late 1985, in part as a response to the drug war's effects on substitute drugs such as marijuana. But how important crack really might have become is difficult to determine because of the success that bureaucratic entrepreneurs such as Robert Stutmann and Bill Bennett have had in pushing it into the political and media limelight. Politically, it has been important. Indeed, the advent of crack may well have allowed the latest drug-war policy cycle to last longer than it would have without the crack scare. Nonetheless, the expansion phase of the cycle has come to an end.

VI. Conclusions: The Drug War Winds Down

Escalation of the war on drugs, when measured by drug arrests relative to Index I arrests, apparently ended in 1989. In Florida the drug arrest/-Index I arrest ratio fell from .44 in 1989 to a 1990 figure of .37, a decline of 14 percent. For the entire United States this ratio fell 24 percent, from .46 to .36. This decline in drug enforcement is not inconsistent with bureaucratic incentives, however, including those created by asset forfeiture legislation. Police may be simply arresting "smarter," for example, concentrating on drug offenders with some potential yield via forfeiture. For instance, if police agencies are seeking seizure opportunities, they are likely to reduce juvenile arrests relative to adult arrests, as youthful offenders are less likely to own property that can be seized. This implication is particularly interesting because, from a theoretical perspective, increasing juvenile participation in the drug trade can be expected during the period of rising drug enforcement, as explained in Chapter 4. The war on drugs has included greater arrest rates for drug offenses, a greater probability of conviction given arrest, and longer sentences, but these increased costs have been primarily imposed on adults rather than juveniles, who generally receive relatively lenient sentences for an identical offense. Therefore, drug traffickers have had increasing incentives to reduce their risk by both lengthening the distribution chain and using more juveniles in the process. Yet, in Florida, juvenile arrests (under age eighteen) for drug offenses as a fraction of all drug arrests fell from 9.21 percent in 1984 to 7.34 percent in 1989—a 20 percent decline. Nationally, persons under the age of eighteen accounted for 11.95 percent of all drug arrests in 1984, but only 7.47 percent in 1990—a 37 percent decline. This reallocation of police effort against drugs is consistent with the hypothesis that police have been increasingly interested in the agency return from drug enforcement through the seizure of assets. As a high-ranking U.S. anti-drug official recently noted, "Increasingly, you're seeing supervisors of cases saying, 'Well, what can we seize?' when they're trying to decide what to investigate. They're paying more attention to the revenues they can get . . . and it's skewing the cases they get involved in."[39]

It is also possible that the opportunities for seizures are being reduced as drug market entrepreneurs adjust to the increasing focus on confiscations. For instance, marijuana growers are increasingly using national forests and other public lands rather than private land, because "this technique precludes the use by the government of the legal remedy of confiscation of the land on which the illegal activity is being perpetrated" (U.S. Department of Justice, Office of the Attorney General, 1989:12). Drug dealers can also rent or lease houses, apartments, cars, and other assets rather than purchasing them, and hide their own assets abroad. Indeed, increasingly sophisticated efforts to hide assets through money laundering and similar schemes make seizures more and more costly.

Another factor may be the growing recognition that the drug war has not lived up to its billing. Recall the discussion of the contrast between drug legislation and public opinion, and the fact that public opinion in support of the drug war seems to have decreased after 1989. Opinion polls report a consistent public preference for tougher treatment of criminals. But importantly, preferences regarding drug policy are becoming much more ambiguous and they do not necessarily support a law enforcement approach to the problem. Public opinion might be expected to support the continued "get tough" policies against drugs if the claims promulgated by law enforcement interests—that drugs are responsible for most crime—were widely believed. However, it is becoming increasingly clear that the war on drugs is not being won, and that the negative consequences of the war are substantial. Today, for example, many states are wrestling with the prison-crowding problem, which many citizens recognize is at least in part a consequence of the get-tough policies against drugs that occurred during the 1984–1989 period, including the large increases in arrests and convictions and the longer mandatory sentences. The Florida Legislature was forced to hold a special session in 1993, for example, in order to allocate more funds to prison construction and avoid the "gridlock" that was anticipated late in 1993 when no criminals eligible for early release would remain in the system (many prisoners cannot be released early under statutes regarding habitual offenders and various specific crimes, many of which are drug related). Given recognition that drug enforcement policy is a major determinant of recent trends in prison crowding, and that the drug war has not produced the benefits that its supporters claimed it would, public opinion may be turning against the drug war. It is clearly the case that the media have begun to focus on some negative consequences of the drug war, and the media's change in focus seems to be a reflection of changing public sentiments.[40]

When asked about the most effective way to deal with the drug problem, survey respondents generally favor treatment over incarceration. Fifty-seven percent of survey respondents in 1989 thought that building more federal prisons would not reduce illegal drug use, for example, while 80 percent thought that more money for drug treatment would be effective. Over 90 percent responded that more spending on drug education in schools would be effective in reducing drug use (U.S. Department of Justice, Bureau of Justice Statistics, *Sourcebook, 1990*, Table 2.95). A 1990 Gallup Poll revealed similar skepticism on the efficacy of arresting drug offenders. Only 4 percent believed the most money should be spent on arresting users and 19 percent thought arresting sellers was the most effective use of resources. In contrast, 40 percent thought early education was the best way to combat drug use while treatment to overcome addiction was preferred by only 5 percent of respondents in this poll (U.S., Bureau of Justice Statistics, *Sourcebook, 1990*, Table 2.96). In the face of apparent growing recognition by taxpayers that the war on drugs has not achieved its exaggerated purposes, police may be reducing their drug control efforts in order to control non-drug crimes. After all, as Breton and Wintrobe (1982:149) noted, as time passes, the perceived responsibility for the failure of a policy (e.g., crime control through the control of drug market activity) shifts from outside forces (e.g., the drug dealers, the recession, etc.) to the government; and within the government, it shifts to the bureaucracy, so pressure arises for bureaucrats to account for what is going on. Thus, policies tend to cycle. An uninformed public can be misled by bureaucrats and policymakers for a while, as the agencies push their own agenda; but if the policy does not work, it will ultimately have to be altered in recognition of its failure. This does not mean that a rollback to the pre-1984 level of drug enforcement is anticipated, but it does suggest that the increase in drug enforcement that characterized the 1984–1989 period could not be sustained forever.

Another important consideration for police in their increasing emphasis on non-drug crime after 1989 is that "a growing number of states, such as Texas, Florida, and New Jersey, apply their forfeiture laws to any criminal activity" (Reed, 1992:2). Police have learned from their drug forfeiture experience that seizures can be very lucrative. The 1984 federal statute pertained to drug crime alone; but with changes in state laws, forfeitures are increasingly targeted at property owners in general, not just criminally culpable property owners. A family home is fair game in some jurisdictions, for instance, if anyone (e.g., a son, relative, or friend of the owner or of the owner's family) uses the property unlawfully. But the spread of forfeiture activities to non-drug crime areas means "that property owners must police their property against all such activity, drug related or not" (Reed, 1992:2). In effect, property owners are being forced to act for the police in preventing all sorts of crimes on their property, and failure to do so can result in a very high fine: forfeiture of the person's property. With the ever broadening scope of forfeiture possibilities, drug activity is apparently becoming a less important target of police efforts, at the same time that it is probably becoming a more difficult target to attack, and a politically less viable policy to stress. Thus, a winding-down of the drug war appears to be the product of the same forces that led to its escalation: changing incentives that affect police bureaucrats.

Public opinion is easily swayed or dominated, at least in the short run; and alternatives to criminal treatment of the drug problem are also not likely to live up to the claims that their supporters (the treatment and education interests) propagate. Furthermore, crime is not going to go away, and the drug–crime connection is an easy one to argue, despite repeated falsification. It was used to justify initial criminalization of narcotics before 1920 and then of marijuana in the 1930s, and it was used to legitimize drug wars in the 1960s and 1980s. Citizens seem to have short memories. As treatment and education prove to be unsuccessful in solving the problems of drug use, and as police efforts to reduce crime in any dramatic way prove to be unsuccessful, another drug-war cycle is likely to occur. Uninformed public opinion will combine with bureaucratic interests sometime in the future to repeat what occurred between 1984 and 1989. Indeed, the opportunities for entrepreneurial bureaucrats to instigate a new drug war are probably an inevitable outcome of the drug market. As was suggested in Chapter 4, the incentives of drug market entrepreneurs to introduce new products and product variants are quite strong; and as these new varieties of drugs are introduced, prohibition advocates will be able to point to their uniqueness and claim that an increased effort is needed. The process is already under way: recriminalization of marijuana is being advocated in California, for example, as an advocate group has "sidestepped to its own satisfaction, the need to confront the long history of marijuana prohibition and its outcomes" by emphasizing that since the THC content of marijuana is much higher than it used to be, the drug is now "more dangerous" (Zimring and Hawkins, 1992:51).[41] As these kinds of opportunities arise, they are likely to be seized, because getting tough on drugs will again be safer politically, in part because officials will be susceptible to criticism for the inevitable failures of alternative policies, such as treatment and education programs.

Chapter 7

The Politics of Punishment

The escalation of drug enforcement by police during the 1984–1989 period was accompanied by higher incarceration rates and longer sentences for convicted drug offenders, reflecting the decisions of judges and prosecutors, and legislative mandates for harsher minimum sentences for drug offenses. Police involvement in the escalating drug war was, at least in part, a product of the changes in seizure laws, which to a large extent were a response to the demands of police themselves. But what explains the increased rates of drug convictions and longer sentences by the criminal courts? Part of the answer lies in the actions of the legislature in raising minimum sentences, but there is clearly more to it than that. After all, as suggested in Chapter 6, legislators merely play "second string" in the criminal justice system to the professionals charged with the delivery of criminal justice services: police, prosecutors, defense counsels, and judges. These groups can all have a direct influence on legislation through their lobbying efforts, but they also may have sufficient discretion to vary actual enforcement practices prior to legislative action, and to frustrate many effects of legislative initiatives that are counter to their interests. On the other hand, if the same interest groups influence both the legislature and the criminal courts, then legislated changes in the criminal code should move in the same direction as courtroom changes in conviction rates and sentencing. This appears to be the case with regard to the war on drugs.

I. Courthouse Bureaucracies and Interest Group Politics

Judicial independence—the insulation from political pressures—is commonly regarded as the distinguishing feature associated with this branch of government. The conventional "civics" interpretation of the courts ignores judges as people responding to incentives, and focuses on the judiciary as an institution, emphasizing that it is responsible for controlling constitutional excesses of the legislative and executive branches. However, judges actually reinforced the executive (police) and legislative "excesses" during the escalating war on drugs from 1984 through 1989 by crowding more and more drug offenders into the common-pool prison system. Sentencing patterns in U.S. district courts suggest that judges actively participated in the war on drugs, incarcerating more drug offenders and giving them longer terms. In 1985, 82.3 percent of traffickers convicted in these courts were sent to prison—a figure that rose to an estimated 91.5 percent in 1989. Sentence length for these offenders rose over 23 percent, from an average of 60.8 months to 76.1 months (U.S. Department of Justice, Bureau of Justice Statistics, *Sourcebook, 1990*, Tables 5.12 and 5.13). Indeed, getting tough on drugs was the norm for courts at every level of the criminal justice system from 1984 to 1989 (state court actions in this regard are discussed below). Question: why did the supposedly independent judiciary also participate in this reallocation of criminal justice resources?

Is the judiciary really independent? Incentives for federal judges to be attuned to interest group demands are often assumed to be minimal, effectively eliminated by lifetime appointment to the bench. While lifetime appointments were designed to insulate judges from short-term political pressures, a literature in political science has investigated courts as politically representative institutions (Pruet and Glick, 1986). Pressures for "representativeness" among the federal judiciary are suggested to be indirect, coming from changes in the policy environment. For example, draft evaders received more lenient treatment in federal district courts as organized opposition to the Vietnam War increased (Cook, 1979).[1] It is not surprising that federal judges' sentencing decisions will be influenced by their personal values and beliefs, and these beliefs certainly can change with prevailing political opinions which influence the policy environment. Judges' opinions might therefore be expected to bend somewhat in the direction of current policy demands, even without direct political pressure stemming from frequent reelection or reappointment.

Even more important factors may be at work. After all, not all judges have lifetime appointments, and even long-term judicial appointees must seek interest group support initially. Judicial appointments are some of the most prized positions in government because of their salary levels relative to workload, the nature of the work itself, the favorable conditions for tenure, and the prestige of the positions (Glick and Vines, 1973:37). Thus, appointments are pursued in a fashion similar to the campaign undertaken by a candidate for a high political office (Crow, 1963:275–289): interest groups such as labor unions, public utility firms, ethnic and minority groups, police, and lawyers are courted in an effort to mobilize the support that is vital for successful appointment. These groups will only support as potential judges those individuals whose beliefs are similar to theirs. There is no guarantee that the life-tenured judge will act as expected, *unless* the judge aspires to a higher judgeship or a political office which will require additional support in the future. But the incentives to keep such possibilities open will leave even appointed judges on any court below the highest to be somewhat attuned to the demands of powerful interest groups. And the fact that interest groups actively pursue their interests through the courts suggests that they expect to have an impact.[2] Thus, "the lower the level of the judge and the shorter his or her term of office, the more intense his or her political involvement tends to become" (Neely, 1982:27).

Unlike the federal judiciary, state and local judges who handle the vast majority of all criminal matters are explicitly tied to the political process because they are either elected or appointed for relatively short terms. These judges are selected in one of three ways: (1) by election (partisan or non-partisan); (2) by legislative or gubernatorial appointment; or (3) by a combination of the two, when, after a brief period of appointed office, the judge stands for election to determine retention.[3] Periodic review by the legislature, governor, or referendum means that political officials and organized interest groups can monitor a judge's behavior in virtually all states. While a few states have lifetime terms for judges, most judicial appointments are for terms from four to eleven years, with the modal term being six years (U.S., Bureau of Justice Statistics, *Sourcebook, 1990*). These methods of appointment and periodic review suggest that members of the state and local judiciary might pay relatively close attention to what they regard to be important underlying trends in political power. In addition, they may be also influenced indirectly by major changes in the political environment, just as these changes may affect the federal judiciary.

Since much of the work of state and local judges is invisible to the public at large, their incentives are to make decisions that are roughly consistent with the demands of informed and powerful interest groups.[4]

After all, there is also a practical antidote to this dose of political accountability. Generally, judges standing for retention do win the election, partly because they are often unopposed and voter interest in these elections is low (Dye, 1991). Nevertheless, when a judge has made decisions that attract the wrath of powerful political forces, elections can be highly competitive. Thus, regular retention decisions mean that state and local judges have an incentive to make rulings that are roughly consistent with the prevailing policy environment, although how important these direct political pressures are, relative to the more subtle forces discussed below, is uncertain.[5]

Judges, like most other public officials, have interests beyond retaining their position or moving up the political ladder. Discretion in sentencing, for example, may be an important source of job satisfaction. Discretion in sentencing is a practice challenged by the emergence of sentencing guidelines governing federal courts and some state courts, and judges resist these legislative schemes designed to reduce the range of judicial power.[6] More important in the context of the potential for interest group influences on the courts, judges also have an obvious interest in controlling their workload.[7] Writing a dissenting opinion is a voluntary increase in effort, for instance, and crowded dockets have been shown to reduce the number of dissenting opinions (Wold and Caldeira, 1980). Richard Neely (1982:44), a West Virginia Supreme Court justice, contended that "there are four personal advantages a . . . [judgeship] can offer: income (including all fringe benefits); power; prestige; and leisure. A fifth may be intrinsically interesting or worthwhile work, but I would subsume this under the category of power." This characterization sounds much like the bureaucratic model discussed in Chapter 6, with an emphasis on the importance of leisure in a judge's utility function. As Neely (1982:46) explained, a lawyer's reputation and income depend on winning cases, but a judge's salary is paid "regardless of whether he is good, mediocre, or abjectly incompetent." To be threatened with loss of job security, a judge must attract the attention of political activists; so what is important is that key political decisions be correctly made. The quality of other decisions is generally irrelevant, particularly if the judge continues to produce expected levels of observed output (i.e., case dispositions). Once again, public sector employees are not by nature bad people. But they are people, and most people respond to incentives. Judge Neely (1982:34) noted, "The point is not that human failings play a central part in the breakdown of the courts but rather that courts as an institution tend to breed many of the observed failings." Life tenure or long elected terms for judges, he observed, encourages "arrogance and indolence," while occupations such as working as a salesperson tend to mask these traits (Neely, 1982:35; also see Downie, 1971:186–189). Salespersons compete in markets for the expenditures of consumers, while judges supply a service within an institutionalized common-pool setting that requires potential consumers to compete for the judges' attention. Furthermore, like civil service bureaucrats, a judge's income is not based on the quality of his or her work; and so, incentives to efficiently provide quality justice are relatively weak. Thus, Downie (1971:160) maintained that "In the hands of legal bureaucrats of the trial courts, justice is subordinated to self-interest and bureaucratic ends, weakened by long delays and neglect."

Judges can determine their workload to a degree because they can often decide, for instance, which cases will be heard and which will be dismissed. Thus, they quickly indicate what type of cases will attract their attention, and those are the cases that lawyers pursue (Neely, 1982:25). The primary criterion for allowing a case to come to trial, according to one observer (Person, 1978:32), is that judges "ration justice by turning their backs to comparatively weaker claims and defenses that require additional judicial time to resolve fairly. By dismissing these 'weaker' claims and defenses, the overworked judge disposes of such time-consuming matters and gets on to the stronger (i.e., easier) cases, where the claims or defenses are more obvious and compelling." In this way, judges can consider more cases and have more free time.

It is obviously difficult to determine the degree to which judges respond to the incentives they face, since there are few comparable examples of judicial systems that provide different incentives. There is at least some evidence, however. According to Judge Neely (1982:198), when the fee system for county justices of the peace was eliminated in West Virginia and replaced by salaries, the number of hearings per day handled by each judge dropped dramatically, the quality of court paperwork deteriorated, and minor court dockets got crowded. When justices of the peace were paid by the case, they had incentives to dispose of cases quickly to make way for more cases. The justices of the peace also made fewer mistakes in the accompanying paperwork, presumably to avoid spending additional time on the same case later.

II. Bureaucratic Networks: The Courthouse Gang

The workload of judges is also significantly influenced by decisions made by the police, prosecutors, and defense counsels. Indeed, it is much more important that other bureaucrats within the judge's informal network are pleased with his or her output than that civil disputants, criminals, or crime victims are pleased. As with other bureaucratic organizations (Breton and Wintrobe, 1982:99), the informal bureaucratic network through which a judge cooperates in order to obtain various benefits, provides a primary force in determining judicial behavior. Thus, while judges have often been viewed as the key figure in trial courts, Pruet and Glick (1986) argue that the reality of criminal courts is shared power and group decisions negotiated among this network of players. This view is clearly consistent with the Breton–Wintrobe (1982) model discussed in Chapter 6 and with the evolving theory of judicial cooperation. The members of the "closed courthouse gang" (Downie, 1971:160–161; Jacob, 1974:12)—prosecutors, judges, defense lawyers, and their staffs, and perhaps police—operate in a "repeated game" environment. That is, they deal with one another over and over again. Under such circumstances, cooperation becomes the likely outcome, because over the long run the benefits of cooperation can outweigh any short-term benefits of not cooperating in one particular game (Axelrod, 1984; Luce and Raiffa, 1957). However, if the repeated game has a known finite time horizon, as it might, for instance, if a government prosecutor is known to aspire to a higher political office in the near future, or a public defender has designs on a position in a private law firm, non-cooperation could still prevail, but there is yet another force at work. The members of the courthouse gang (or informal network) must deal with each other day-in and day-out. A prosecutor (or defense attorney) has to deal with many different defense attorneys (or prosecutors and/or their assistants), and probably several judges. Similarly, a judge deals with large numbers of defense attorneys and several prosecutors or assistant prosecutors. Thus, reputation matters: failure of a judge to cooperate in a situation can result in an unwillingness of prosecutors or defense attorneys to cooperate with that judge in another situation where their cooperation benefits the judge. These reputation effects reinforce the repeated game incentives to cooperate (Tullock, 1985; Schmidtz, 1991). Thus, the criminal courthouse setting creates strong incentives to cooperate.

As shown in Chapter 2, criminal justice resources are allocated in a common pool environment. The consequence is chronic overcrowding and, for prosecutors, public defenders, and judges, pressure to increase output. But overcrowding of the system is likely to reduce job satisfaction among these elected and appointed officials, and the shortage of resources relative to the workload leads them to expedite cases through the system through cooperation in the form of plea or charge bargaining, rather than giving each case the attention it may, in their estimation, deserve. Cases can be rapidly processed through plea bargaining, but this process requires the agreement of the defendant, the defendant's counsel, the prosecuting attorney, and the judge. Judges clearly benefit as pressure on the court docket is relieved and cases are cleared; but given the wide range of views represented by these parties, it might be surprising to find them cooperating. In particular, it seems that defense attorneys and prosecutors should be at odds in this adversarial system. However, the key players have a shared interest in reducing their workload by lowering the number of trials, so they have incentives to convince the defendant to cooperate as well, as explained below.[8]

Most criminal cases—91 percent in state courts in 1990 (Dawson, 1992:6)—are plea bargained. Cooperation is crucial since plea bargaining is, among other things, a vehicle allowing public defenders, prosecutors, and judges to influence their workload. The importance of this cooperation is easily demonstrated. Suppose cooperation among these players erodes, and plea bargaining agreements can only be reached in 80 percent of the cases. If trials account for 10 percent of all cases initially, this reduced cooperation doubles the number of trials—from 10 percent to 20 percent of all cases. Thus, if prosecutors and/or public defenders were to refuse to plea bargain in good faith, a judge's workload would be increased substantially. It follows that since prosecutors and public defenders are chosen directly by the political process, and judges' control over their workload is dependent on the cooperation of these groups, the sentencing practices of judges might be closely tied to the political process even if the retention process itself is not a major influence.[9] Indeed, Downie (1971:161) argued that this group "works more toward preserving itself and its habitual ways than serving the needs of the public or the ends of justice. Each member is primarily concerned with protecting his job and the special privileges he has always enjoyed. . . . Each is careful not to spoil things for the other." Eisenstein and Jacob (1977:Ch.2); and Stumpf (1988:340–347) make similar arguments, suggesting that while external pressures may emphasize "doing justice" and disposing of cases, internal interests focus on "maintaining group cohesion" and reducing uncertainty. They further maintain that "although having a genuine need to appear to do justice, criminal courts are internally oriented to the efficient disposition of cases in a manner that produces few surprises and allow for a comfortable, predictable work environment" (Stumpf, 1988:341).

The incentives to cooperate come from more than simply the desire for congenial working environments: "group cohesion is pursued not for its own sake but to grease the internal workings of the system" (Stumpf, 1988:341). Each group in the closed courthouse bureaucracy has some power over the other to make their lives more difficult in the absence of such mutual support and cooperation. Downie (1971:161–162) discussed several examples of such power. For instance, when a few Washington, D.C., judges on the local trial court began to reprimand lawyers who failed to show up on time or who were obviously handling a client's case badly, the local bar announced it was going to investigate the conduct of the court's judges and possibly recommend removal. Similarly, a Detroit judge began scolding defense attorneys and prosecutors for plea bargaining cases where, in the judge's opinion, the defendant probably would have been acquitted in a trial; and the next day pressure was brought to bear on the presiding judge, who replaced the malcontent on the bench and made a show of quickly approving all plea bargains.

Reinforcing the incentives to cooperate: prosecutors. Prosecutorial incentives to plea bargain are very strong. For instance, government prosecutors' job security is influenced in a straightforward way: successfully prosecute a lot of criminals and do not botch any controversial cases. The "quality" of prosecutions in terms of their deterrent value or appropriateness as retribution from the victims' perspective, are not easily measured. Thus, as Schulhofer (1988:50) explained, "In choosing what charges to file, what cases to drop, what plea to offer, and which cases to steer toward trial, the prosecutor will be influenced by desires to enhance his office's batting average, to avoid the risk of an embarrassing trial loss, to gain credit for a dramatic trial victory, to cultivate good relationships with influential private attorneys, and any host of other factors" like cultivating good relations with police (Knapp, 1972:14). Similarly, David Jones (1979:201) found that prosecutors' incentives are tied to maximizing the number of *criminals convicted.* Such behavior is clearly predicted when prosecutors are considered in light of Wilson's (1980:374) characterization of "professionals" in the bureaucracy, given the inability to evaluate other aspects of the prosecutors' output. The dominant goal for such professionals is to demonstrate their legal talent in order to enhance their future market value. Therefore, they "prosecute vigorously" *but* selectively. According to Wilson, such professionals should favor trials for simple cases that can be investigated and prosecuted in a short time so that they can maximize the number of convictions they are responsible for.

Chambliss and Seidman (1960:84) found that criminal justice is a selective process in which the types of cases that most easily yield convictions for prosecutors are most likely to arise, as did Eisenstein (1973), Blumberg (1967), and Grosman (1969), among others. Furthermore, Eisenstein (1973:104–105) and Kaplan (1965:180) found that because the conviction rate is the main concern of most prosecutors, it becomes more important "not to lose than to win." As a result, plea bargaining is especially attractive to prosecutors because it produces convictions without the risk of acquittal associated with a trial; it also prevents even longer court delays that might make the prosecutor unpopular (Downie, 1971:185; Glick and Vines, 1973:73–74).

A prosecutor's self-interest motives behind plea bargaining appear be even more powerful in many places.

> [I]n all but the largest cities, the prosecutor's pay is so comparatively low for the legal profession that many prosecutors carry on at least part of their old private law practice on the side. The law usually allows this practice, which not only presents opportunities for possible conflicts of interest but also drains away that energy and dedication the prosecutor needs to bring to his performance if he is to do more than merely hammer out guilty pleas. (Downie, 1971:185)

In addition, as noted above, political support is vital for successful achievement of many of the long-term goals most prosecutors have (e.g., reelection and/or aspirations for higher office). This in turn implies that prosecutors are reluctant to take risks that might produce politically unpopular outcomes. One interest group that is a natural source of support for prosecutors is the police. Thus, it is important to maintain a high conviction rate in order to maintain their support.

Reinforcing the incentives to cooperate: defense attorneys. Public defenders have similar "bureaucratic" and/or reelection incentives to cooperate. Indeed, in almost a quarter of all counties, the public defender's office is an agency directly controlled by the judiciary (U.S. Department of Justice, 1984), so incentives to cooperate with judges are obvious. However, even when this is not the case, the public defender's office can be characterized as a bureaucratic agency, facing similar incentives to cooperate to control workload as those faced by judges and prosecutors. Many public defenders are, like prosecutors, elected and therefore subject to regular evaluation by interest groups. Their interests are similar to those of the legislature in that they want job security (reelection) and they share with bureaucrats an interest in bigger budgets and a high-quality work environment. Thus, a study of public defenders conducted by the Center for the Study of Law and Society at the University of California and discussed by Downie (1971:178–180) found that they

> came to think of themselves as part of the government team rather than as adversaries for client interests. They freely expressed their belief that most of their clients were guilty . . . they hated to impose on the prosecutor, judge, or themselves the inconvenience of trying cases of defendants who

> obviously appeared guilty. Defendants who insisted on trials in those circumstances were considered stubborn cases.

So, for instance, if a judge is under political pressure to process more cases faster, lawyers on both the prosecution and defense sides tend to cooperate by forgoing more trials through plea bargaining. Indeed, "In one courtroom, a plea may be promoted because the judge and prosecutor are in the midst of a jury trial on another case or because it is the end of the month and time to boost disposition statistics. In another courtroom or on another day, no one will press for a plea because there is time to hold a trial or because disposition statistics look all right for the moment" (Jacob, 1974:12). Similarly, if a prosecutor is under pressure to get tough on crime (or perhaps a specific kind of crime, like drugs), the judge tends to cooperate by handing down tougher sentences.

Non-publicly employed defense counsel can also benefit from cooperation. For instance, Stumpf (1988:344) pointed out that judges and prosecutors often delay a case while a defendant sits in jail until relatives agree to pay the defense attorney's fees (also see Blumberg, 1967). More significantly, as Schulhofer (1988:53) explained, the financial structure of the lawyer–client relationship generally reinforces the incentives to cooperate through plea bargaining. Most criminal attorneys work for a flat fee payable in advance. This occurs because attorneys generally cannot withdraw from a case once an appearance has been entered, and there clearly is no guarantee of payment, particularly if a client is found guilty. However, given this up-front payment, the attorney's incentives are to minimize the time and effort involved in the case: "the financial incentives to settle promptly are intense" (Schulhofer, 1988:54). Indeed, a high turnover rate is required in order to make a decent income from defending criminals who generally are not in a position to pay the large fees that could pay for a lengthy trial.

Even when an attorney is appointed by the court to represent a criminal defendant, the incentives to cooperate in plea bargaining are not likely to change. Indeed, in some jurisdictions, attorneys are required to serve "pro bono publico"; that is, they are expected to donate the time necessary to provide a defense, but they determine the actual amount of time. The incentives to cooperate by plea bargaining are even greater in this case. In other jurisdictions, attorneys actually volunteer for criminal appointments, of course, and their services are paid for by the state. However, flat fee cases are quite common, so the incentives to cooperate and settle quickly still exist. Even where hourly rates exist, nearly all states impose a maximum total payment, so the incentives are to simply work to the extent that payment can be justified. Thus, "[f]or the appointed attorney who chooses to go to trial, the financial compensation in many states is truly derisory" (Schulhofer, 1988:55). As a result, it is not surprising to find, as Blumberg (1970) did, that while defense attorneys supposedly work for the accused, they actually wind up representing the interests of the bureaucracy in selling a bargained plea to the defendant. As Stumpf (1988:345) explained, generally "the defense counsel gains most from going along with the system, working out deals with the prosecutor, and in general being a good team player."

Third-party effects: police, criminals,and victims. The courthouse gang deals with other parties as well. Police enter the picture because they are also in repeated games with prosecutors and judges. Thus, some police are likely to be part of the informal network radiating from the courthouse, and the cooperative environment includes consideration of those police interests.[10] In the case of drug market activity, for instance, police have demonstrated a long-standing interest in criminalization. Furthermore, since 1984 they have had an interest in legitimizing an increased emphasis on drug offenses. A prosecutorial/judicial crackdown on drugs clearly serves police interests by helping to legitimize their efforts. In addition, as explained below, many of the legislative-mandated sentences and the increasing ease of seizing assets have enhanced the ability of prosecutors to extract guilty pleas.

In contrast to their relationships with police, defense attorneys, and judges, however, prosecutors are in one-shot games with most crime victims. Thus, ceteris paribus, they are more concerned with the wishes of other members of the courthouse gang, including police, than with these one-shot contacts. As noted above, conviction statistics are of primary concern to prosecutors, so that the role the victims play in prosecution is generally conceived in terms of their function as witnesses (McDonald, 1977:302). It is not surprising that "The criminal justice system's interest in the victim is only as a means to an end not as an end in himself. The victim is a piece of evidence" (McDonald, 1977:299–300). Therefore, if the victim is likely to appear unconvincing or unsympathetic, if he (or she) has "done something stupid" and appears to deserve what he got, or if he has a criminal record, the prosecutor will dismiss the case or plea bargain in order to generate a conviction or avoid a loss. This reinforces the tendency for prosecutors to focus on those crimes that affect the well-to-do and politically influential members of a community. Lower income individuals are victims of a disproportionate number of crimes, but such victims are also more likely to have criminal records themselves and to make less articulate witnesses. "Thus, it is more likely that these cases are given away by prosecutors than those of higher income victims" (McDonald, 1977:300).

As a result of their incentives, many prosecutors dismiss cases and plea bargain, in order to obtain a large number of convictions at a low cost in terms of their own time and effort. Criminals are generally convicted on fewer or lesser counts and receive lighter punishment; but from the prosecutor's perspective, guaranteed conviction statistics more than make up for that. How much do prosecutors bargain away in their plea bargaining? It probably depends on the jurisdiction, but a New York study found that most people arrested as felons are not prosecuted and convicted as felons. The odds that a person arrested for a felony would be sentenced to prison was one in 108 (Neely, 1982:16). This rather startling figure represents more than just plea bargaining, however. Over 84 percent of New York felony arrests in 1979 (88,095 out of 104,413) were simply dismissed. Prosecutors pointed to a lack of staff and to police failure to secure items of evidence or lists of witnesses. And many cases are routinely dismissed because convictions are difficult to obtain. In 1979, of the more than 15 percent of the felony arrests (16,318) in New York that led to indictments, 56 percent resulted in guilty pleas to lesser felonies, 16 percent ended with misdemeanor guilty pleas, 12 percent were dismissed after indictment, 3 percent resulted in some "other" disposition, and 13 percent went to trial. Significantly, the largest number of sentences that did not involve a prison term arose due to prosecutors' willingness to permit felons to plead guilty to lesser charges. Indeed, defendants clearly recognize that if they "plead guilty and ease the job of prosecutor and judge [they] will be sentenced more leniently" (Glick and Vines, 1973:73).

The discussion of prosecutor incentives implies that criminals get off relatively lightly, because of cooperation within the courthouse gang. This certainly may be the case. After all, the defendant must also agree to the plea. The criminal who agrees to a plea bargain presumably gains in the sense that his or her punishment (or perhaps legal expenses) must be less than he or she expects it to be if the case goes to trial, although the entire courthouse gang has incentives to encourage and perhaps mislead the defendant to expect such gains (Stumpf, 1988:344–345; Schulhofer, 1988:56). Indeed, defense attorneys are in one-shot games with most of their clients, so their interests are more closely linked with the courthouse gang than to their clients. This, in combination with the financial incentives discussed above, suggests that defense counsel have strong incentives to "advise" their clients to plea, and as a result "settlements will occur in cases that a reasonably well-counseled defendant would prefer to see tried" Schulhofer, 1988:57). After all, as Schulhofer (1988:58) pointed out,

> Once the guilty plea route is chosen, the possibilities for cutting corners, for avoiding the effort that would be expected in a wholly dedicated, conflict-free plea negotiation defense, become almost unlimited. Legal defenses need not be researched or investigated, witnesses need not be located or interviewed, motions need not be filed. . . . The low visibility of the plea-negotiation process reinforces defense counsel's formal privilege to forgo investigation, and in practice outside parties can almost never review (or even perceive) the extent to which corners are cut.

Given that defendants are relatively unfamiliar with the internal workings of the criminal justice system, they are clearly among the outside parties that are unlikely to be able to fully perceive what motivates their attorneys' actions or advice. Furthermore, even if they can, the up-front payment and one-shot nature of their relationship with attorneys mean that they have little recourse other than changing attorneys, something that many criminals will be unable to do for financial reasons. The fact is that most criminal defendants lack both information and money (Schulhofer, 1988:59). Thus, while criminals may benefit from prosecutor incentives to plea, they can also be hurt by their own attorneys' incentives to plea, and the net effect is not obvious.

Plea bargaining and efficiency. Plea bargaining might be expected to improve the efficiency of the criminal justice system. Indeed, plea bargaining appears to relieve some of the pressure on the prosecutorial and judicial systems arising from non-price allocation of criminal justice resources and the resulting court-delay and waiting-time rationing process. This is, in fact, the typical justification for the widespread use of plea bargaining (e.g., see Easterbrook, 1983). But there is a significant difference between the goals of those participating in a market exchange and those participating in plea bargaining, as explained above (also see Benson, 1990; Schulhofer, 1988). Furthermore, the claim that efficiency gains occur should manifest itself in reduced caseloads and backlogs with plea bargaining. However, Jones (1979) found that guilty plea rates are not correlated with caseloads. In fact, he contended that prosecutors and judges have apparently established an "artificial quota" on the proportion of felony cases pending that can be taken to trial during any time period. The quota varies across jurisdictions, but is generally less than 10 percent. Furthermore, these quotas have remained at virtually constant percentages for perhaps as long as seventy years (Jones, 1979:81, 191, 193–197).

Plea bargaining is also rationalized on the grounds that rising crime rates necessitate the practice, but the historical data cast significant doubt on that argument. Even though crime rates increased steadily for the last thirty years of Jones' study, guilty plea rates remained almost constant for probably more than seventy years (Jones, 1979:81). Of course, prosecution and judicial bureaucrats have every incentive to claim that plea bargaining at its current (and historic) level is necessary because of the higher crime rates and caseloads that tax the bureaucracies' limited resources. In this way they can apply pressure for increased budgets and add leverage to their other demands.[11] As Cooper (1972:446) observed, plea bargaining is "less an independent ill than a symptom. More properly it is part of a collection of symptoms of a general sickness. It is but one manifestation, albeit a significant one, of a system which is not operating properly."[12]

III. Courts and the 1984–1989 Drug War

Because of the linkage of interests within the courthouse bureaucracies, Downie (1971:185) suggested that "in many ways, the prosecutor can be even more important in the criminal-court system than the judge," while Glick and Vines (1973:73) characterized the government prosecutor as a "de facto judge." The escalating drug war served the interests of prosecutors admirably. First, by focusing on drug crime, prosecutors could help police legitimize their focus on drug enforcement—a beneficial activity because of the important role police play in the prosecutors' informal network and because police can be an important source of political support for prosecutors. Second, and perhaps more importantly, the increased flow of drug arrests created the potential for raising one of the prosecutors' primary statistical measures of output: convictions. Raising the number of convictions increases the probability of retaining office and provides obvious evidence of a "need" for more resources. Third, legislation mandating longer sentences increased the bargaining power of prosecutors in the plea bargain process and, therefore, the probability of obtaining a guilty plea.[13] The higher minimum sentences passed by state legislatures and the Congress gave prosecutors a more significant threat that could be used to induce accused drug criminals to bargain, and plea convictions have "soared" as a result of these mandatory minimums (Cotts, 1992:39). Furthermore, the statutory changes that induced police to focus on confiscations also provided both a bargaining chip for prosecutors and a source of evidence.[14]

Asset seizures and the success of prosecution. Asset seizures provide police and prosecutors with two useful new avenues for generating convictions. First, when assets are seized, the police and prosecutors can use them as a bargaining chip: the defendant who cooperates might be able to keep his or her assets, but the dependant who does not will lose them

(Cotts, 1992:40). This has probably not been a particularly important bargaining tool in generating drug conviction pleas over the past few years, however, because a bigger threat has been the imposition of a mandatory minimum sentence if the offender does not plead to a lesser charge. However, it has been an important factor in obtaining another type of cooperation.

Recognize that the numbers of convictions are not the only important consideration for prosecutors. They are also likely to be interested in major, headline-grabbing prosecutions. While large numbers of arrests and convictions of drug buyers and street-level sellers can be made relatively easily, it is much more difficult to build a case against large-scale drug traffickers. In fact, in order to successfully prosecute anyone other than the minor players in the drug trade, the evidence of informants is almost always required. Thus, the police and prosecutors have incentives to induce cooperation from the small-time drug traffickers they arrest, in order to build cases against those who are higher up in the drug distribution network. The government can offer several different things in exchange for such cooperation: one is conviction on a lesser charge, another is the release of assets seized, and a third is a money payment. Thus, potential asset seizure can enter directly into this bargaining process; but significantly, it can enter indirectly as well. In the early 1980s, the DEA complained to Congress that it was short on PE/PI (Purchase Evidence and Pay for Information) money. These complaints had an impact. When Congress amended the asset forfeiture laws, as discussed in Chapter 6, they included a provision that allowed the DEA to use seized assets for PE/PI. As a result, the ability to pay informants increased dramatically. Federal law enforcement agencies paid $35 million to informants in 1987 and a record $63 million in 1989 (Cotts, 1992:38). Asset seizures accounted for more than a third of those expenditures. Furthermore, if an informer's information leads to asset seizures, the DEA can pay a commission of up to 25 percent of the seized assets, up to a maximum of $250,000. Some informants have become multi-millionaires by providing information on a number of different cases. The results are not surprising. First,

> The number of drug offenders who become informants has sky-rocketed in recent years. "I was in the U.S. Attorney's Office Annex in Miami today," says Ft. Lauderdale criminal defender Charles Wishna, "and the defendants were tripping all over each other. The assistants and the agents have to fight for the availability of rooms in which to debrief these guys." (Cotts, 1992:38)

And second, "all too often, informants simply can't be trusted. When prosecutors lay out the spectrum of rewards and punishments, the great temptation to lie is too great" (Cotts, 1992:40). A series of informant scams have come to light in recent years as it has been discovered that large numbers of convictions were based on falsified information. After one informant confessed to perjury in twelve separate cases in 1988, for example, the Los Angeles District Attorney's Office was forced to review more than ten years of convictions based on informants' information; and in 1989, the California Legislature passed a law requiring that juries be warned to view informants' evidence "with caution and close scrutiny" (Cotts, 1992:40). Nonetheless, information from informants has played an increasingly important role in generating arrests and convictions, and prosecutors continue to maintain that paid informants are vital if the drug trade is to be controlled. This may be true since voluntary drug transactions do not produce direct victims to file complaints, and since voluntary witnesses rarely come forward; but as Cotts (1992:41) concluded, the widespread abuses of the process suggest that the use of informants has been "over-zealous and unscrupulous."

Sentencing practices during the drug war. The most recent war on drugs, escalating from 1984 to 1989, provides a natural experiment in which criminal courts sentenced drug offenders in a changing political environment. This policy initiative provided judges with ample opportunity to reveal whether they are independent or whether their sentencing practices changed with the political environment. Kim, Benson, and Rasmussen (1992) used data from the State of Florida to explore two issues related to the role of sentencing in this war on drugs. First, they investigated whether drug offenders received more severe sentences during this period of escalating drug enforcement. Second, they explored the efficacy of drug-offense sentencing practices (i.e., to what extent did sentencing decisions serve the avowed goals of drug policy?). The findings are summarized here.

Data from Florida's Department of Corrections provide information on sentencing practices. Not all persons found guilty are included in these data, however. Offenders who are adjudicated guilty in state courts can receive a sentence that does not involve the Department of Corrections, an example being an offender who pleads guilty and is sentenced to time already served in a local jail. Others, coming under Department of Corrections control after being convicted, are sentenced to probation or incarcerated in the state prison system. These offenders were used in this study. One measure of the severity of punishment is the probability of being incarcerated rather than receiving a non-prison sentence upon convic-

Table 7.1: The Probability of Incarceration for Selected Offenses in Florida, 1984–1990

Fiscal Year	Unarmed Robbery	Burglary	Sale	Possession
1984–1985	.439	.321	.261	.073
1985–1986	.471	.339	.289	.093
1986–1987	.444	.326	.316	.132
1987–1988	.522	.360	.382	.176
1988–1989	.555	.394	.451	.194
1989–1990	.516	.374	.434	.225
Percent Change				
1984–1990	17.5	16.5	66.3	208.2
1986–1990	16.2	14.7	37.3	70.4
1987-1990	−1.2	3.9	13.6	27.8

Source: Florida Department of Corrections (various years).

tion. If sentencing decisions are dominated by prosecutors who have been influenced by the political environment of escalating drug enforcement between 1984 and 1989, we might expect the proportion of drug offenders sentenced to prison to rise relative to some other offenses.

Table 7.1 shows the proportion of convicted offenders who were incarcerated rather than put on probation among offenders whose primary offense was unarmed robbery, burglary, sale of narcotics, and possession of these substances. Punishment of offenders found guilty of unarmed robbery and burglary provide a control for any general trend toward getting tougher on crime.[15] The data clearly show that courts got tougher on drug offenders relative to property offenders over this period: the proportion of drug offenders charged with possession being incarcerated rose 208 percent and the percent of drug sale offenders incarcerated rose 66 percent, while comparable figures for unarmed robbery and burglary are 18 percent and 17 percent respectively.

An alternative explanation of the trends reported in Table 7.1 is that the composition of drug offenders changed over the period while the more homogeneous crimes of burglary and unarmed robbery did not. If during the 1984–1990 period drug offenders were being charged with increasingly serious drug offenses within the drug sale and possession categories, an increasing portion of those who pleaded or were adjudicated guilty could be expected to be incarcerated. Most drug offenses involve cocaine or marijuana, and cocaine offenses are more serious under Florida law than those involving marijuana.[16] Assuming that changes in the population of arrestees is reflected in the distribution of offenders charged, convicted, and coming under DOC control, the relative number of cocaine convictions—for both possession and sale—rose rapidly between 1984 and 1990. Cocaine offenses rose from 42 percent of drug sale convictions in 1984 to 78 percent in 1990. However, most of this increase occurred early in the period. By 1986, cocaine offenses accounted for 68 percent of the total; and by the following year, 76 percent. From 1986 to 1990, cocaine sale arrests rose 15 percent but the proportion of convicted offenders being sentenced to prison rose 37.3 percent. By 1987, cocaine arrests had neared their peak, increasing only 2.6 percent by 1990, while the percentage being incarcerated rose five times faster: 13.6 percent over the same period.

Similar patterns hold for possession offenses. Cocaine arrests rose relative to all possession arrests, rising from 24 percent of the total in 1984 to 55 percent in 1989. Between 1986 and 1989, cocaine possession arrests relative to total arrests rose 17 percent, but the percentage of all offenders convicted of possession going to prison rose over 70 percent. From 1987 to 1990 the proportion of offenders convicted of drug possession being sent to prison rose almost 28 percent, even though cocaine arrests as a proportion of all possession arrests grew only 5.8 percent during this period. Thus, a changing composition of drug offenses explains only a portion of the increasingly severe sentences meted out to drug offenders in Florida, particularly after 1986. Courts, on average, were getting tougher on drug offenders during the war on drugs. This change in criminal court behavior during the drug war is consistent with the hypothesis that they are responding, on the margin, to prosecutors' incentives as they are influenced by the policy environment.

Data on individual offenders in Florida provide another opportunity to investigate the probation/incarceration decision among a sample of convicted offenders who had been incarcerated for a drug offense in the past.[17] Allowing analysis of the probation decision affecting offenders returning to Department of Corrections control, these data can shed light on the probability of incarceration among drug offenders compared to offenders convicted of other crimes. The initial sample consists of 4,298 individuals incarcerated for a drug offense and released between March 1983 and March 1989. These data were updated to include subsequent returns to prison or probation prior to April 2, 1990. Since some individuals have been convicted more than once during the sample period, the number of releases from prison or probation (7,171) exceeds the number of persons in the sample. Of this total, 3,637 had been reconvicted and were subsequently sentenced; 559 or slightly over 15 percent of these were given probation upon conviction for a subsequent offense.[18] Since the initial sample included drug offenders who had been previously incarcerated, all individuals receiving a sentence have been convicted at least twice.

Table 7.2 summarizes some attributes of persons receiving probation as compared to those receiving a prison sentence. These data might appear curious since they uniformly suggest that the persons receiving probation appear to be higher risk offenders: (1) they had more prior felony convictions; (2) they had more prior prison sentences; (3) they had a relatively low opportunity cost of criminal activity since they were less likely to be employed at the time of arrest; and (4) they were more likely to have had a history of non-drug crime. Reflecting this apparent selection of relatively high risk offenders for the least severe punishment is the fact that the subsequent recidivism rate among probationers is 81 percent higher than that of offenders who were incarcerated—87 percent versus 48 percent.

Kim, Benson, and Rasmussen (1992) used a probit model to analyze the probation decision in greater detail, paying particular attention to the sentences received by drug offenders compared to persons convicted of other crimes. Probation is presumably a less severe sentence than incarceration. As such, a "public interest" theory of sentencing behavior, or a theory that assumes the goal of criminal courts to be the maximization of deterrent effects—as in Easterbrook (1983)—would suggest that probation is expected for persons convicted of less serious felonies, offenders with relatively modest criminal records, and those who are expected to be less likely to return to criminal activity. However, if sentencing decisions are responses to political demands for a war on drugs and to incentives judges have for cooperating with prosecutors waging such a war, then more severe penalties may be applied to those charged with drug offenders, regardless of these public-interest or efficient-deterrent considerations. The analysis also accounted for factors suggested by the economic theory of crime, such as the opportunity cost of crime.

Table 7.2: Attributes of Released Drug Offenders Returning to Florida Department of Corrections, by Type of Sentence

	Sentence	
Attribute	Prison	Probation
Percent employed at time of arrest	20.70	0.03
Average number of prior felony convictions	2.06	2.74
Average number of prior prison sentences	0.84	1.49
Percent having a history of non-drug crime	24.00	37.00
Recidivism rate	0.48	0.87
n	3078.00	559.00

Source: Florida Department of Corrections, (various years).

The hypothesized relationships based on the "public interest" or "deterrent maximization" propositions that probation would be awarded to persons with high opportunity costs and less extensive criminal records are generally rejected by Kim, Benson, and Rasmussen's empirical results. Persons employed at the time of arrest were more likely to be sent to prison, for example, as were older offenders and those who were married. Males and blacks were less likely to be sentenced to probation—a result consistent with studies that suggest males and blacks generally have a relatively high rate of recidivism.[19] Prior criminality as measured by the number of previous prison commitments and the length of the most recent sentence were associated with a greater probability of being sentenced to probation. In contrast, the hypothesis that the courthouse network cooperated in the drug war is generally supported: offenses of possessing illicit drugs and engaging in their sale—the categories which account for most drug offenses—are more likely to yield a prison sentence. Other drug offenders are more likely to be given probation, a predictable result since these offenses may be generally viewed as less serious than the possession and sale categories.[20]

These results reveal much about how courts treated drug offenses relative to non-drug offenses during the war on drugs, at least for this sample of convicted drug offenders. A drug offense was more likely to yield a prison sentence than other felony offenses, and committing a non-drug offense while under the influence of drugs significantly reduced the chances for probation. This fact, combined with the positive coefficients of the seriousness of a criminal's career as measured by prior sentences and their severity, suggests that the courts were particularly tough on drug offenders and relatively easy on offenders who were not demonstrably involved with drugs. The fact that the courts were especially severe on drug offenders also helps explain why opportunity cost, as measured by employment at time of arrest, is negatively correlated with the probability of being sentenced to probation. Gill and Michaels (1990) and Kaestner (1991) have investigated the impact of drug use on earnings and report a positive correlation between earnings and the use of illegal substances. Similarly, drug dealers in Washington, D.C., are reported to hold legitimate jobs for which they are generally paid considerably more than the minimum wage (Reuter, MacCoun, and Murphy, 1990). Thus, a higher frequency of employment among drug offenders may account for the result reported in Kim, Benson, and Rasmussen that persons with higher opportunity cost are the drug offenders whom judges seem most intent on incarcerating, rather than giving them probation.

Tougher sentences for drug offenders presumably served some judicial purpose: judges may have believed that they were combatting property crime by being tough on drug offenders; they could have been responding to the policy environment in order to enhance the probability of being reappointed; and/or their support of a "get tough on drugs" policy may have been the result of an implicit agreement between themselves and other officers of the court to handle the crushing workload generated by the rising number of drug arrests. In any event, the unintended consequences of their response to the drug war probably dwarf the intended effects. In Chapter 5, we argued that the war on drugs diverted police resources away from enforcement of property offenses, resulting in diminished deterrence and a correspondingly higher property crime rate. One motivation for the war on drugs allegedly was to combat property crime by eliminating the offenses supposedly caused by drug addicts driven to support their habit by burglary, larceny, and robbery. The opposite may have happened: reduced deterrence made property crime a more attractive source of income and the war on drugs may have actually increased the nation's property crime rate.

The courthouse gang's role in the drug war may have similarly contributed to a higher property crime rate. More severe sentences for drug offenders relative to others meant the judiciary was reinforcing the effects of changing priorities of the police—lowering the relative cost of property crime relative to other sources of income.

IV. Conclusions

Justification for the 1984–1989 war on drugs clearly cannot rest on the proposition that policymakers in the criminal justice system created policies that were effective in combatting drug use and other criminal activity.[21] Recall that this is a period when illicit drug use among high school seniors and persons in households already had been declining for half a decade. Furthermore, violent and property crime rates in 1985 were below their 1980 level, indicating that rising drug enforcement was not being driven by any hard evidence of increasing criminal activity. Nor did the drug war emerge as a result of strong public opinion: in fact, it is explained in Chapter 6 that drug enforcement escalated in a period of declining public support for crime control. Thus, drug enforcement started rising in a period of declining drug use, relatively low crime rates, and somewhat lower public support for increasing crime control. In addition, the war on drugs has been a textbook example of unintended consequences that result from a reallocation of criminal justice resources away from other law enforcement activities. In some states, increasing property crime has been the result of reduced deterrence due to a greater proportion of police and prison resources being devoted to combat drug offenses.[22] The ineffectiveness of drug policy is also suggested by declining cocaine prices, constant heroin prices, rising potency of marijuana, and rising use of heroin and cocaine over the 1983–1987 period (Moore, 1990). Cocaine prices were lower in 1990 than they were in 1985; the lower bound wholesale-price estimates fell by about two-thirds over this time period.[23] The war on drugs is a policy that has not had the intended effects on drug markets; it is not a highly successful policy created by enlightened public officials.

Developing a coherent drug policy is complicated by the fact that the criminal justice system is composed of individuals whose incentives to create such a policy are contorted by their place in the system. Treatment for drug abuse, for example, may not be a viable alternative to arresting and punishing drug offenders if police officials and prosecutors suspect their share of the public purse will shrink with such an effort. Criminal justice resources are allocated in a commons environment; each player in the system has some incentives to pursue short-term policies that are not particularly effective in fighting drug abuse and have unintended consequences that may in the long run reduce public safety. These factors, coupled with a careful assessment of the drug–crime link and other costs of drug abuse, must be considered when formulating a cost-effective drug enforcement policy. We now turn to this task.

Chapter 8

Drug Policy in the Criminal Justice Commons

Uncompromising and extreme rhetoric surrounds much of what passes for a debate on drug policy. Fear and moral outrage have been the cornerstones of America's policy of drug prohibition. Each new drug or drug variant is claimed to lead inevitably to a range of destructive consequences, including violence, property crime, the break-up of families, and many other social ills. So all drugs are ultimately seen as evil. The American people, who are inundated by such claims and rarely exposed to any serious counter-claims, naturally fear that their lives, their property, their children, and their society are threatened by the latest drug scourge. The 1984–1989 war on drugs is in this long-standing tradition, being based on the proposition that "clearly and emphatically . . . there is no such thing as innocent drug use."[1] The destructive consequences that drugs presumably have turned drug enforcement into a moral crusade actively supported by a wide range of people, including both public-spirited religious, academic, political, and bureaucratic activists and self-interested political and bureaucratic entrepreneurs. Even some of the nation's most preeminent scholars have joined in advocacy of this crusade. For instance, James Q. Wilson (1990a:523) offers a moral foundation for the prohibition of drugs, arguing that "The moral reason for attempting to discourage drug use is that the heavy consumption of certain drugs is destructive of the human character. These drugs—principally heroin, cocaine, and crack—

are, for many people, powerfully reinforcing. The pleasure or oblivion they produce leads many users to devote their lives to seeking pleasure or oblivion and do so almost regardless of the cost in ordinary human virtues, such as temperance, fidelity, duty, and sympathy."

The campaign for legalization is also seen as a moral crusade. Thomas Szasz (1984:271) believes, for example, "we have a right to eat, drink, or inject a substance—any substance—not because we are sick and want it to cure us, not because a government supported medical authority claims it will be good for us, but simply because the government—as our servant rather than our master—hasn't the right to meddle in our private dietary and drug affairs." Similarly, in *Towards a Moral Drug Policy* Richard Dennis (1990) writes that "Drug laws are a barbarous relic of an idea we rejected a long time ago—that people don't have an inherent right to do what they want with their lives as long as it doesn't directly harm another person."

Framing the drug policy debate in moral terms polarizes the debate into a discussion of fundamental beliefs which are, for most people, not subject to negotiation. Focusing the policy debate on legalization versus prohibition is probably counterproductive in the current political environment. It is partly irrelevant because opinion polls suggest considerable hostility to across-the-board legalization. Even for marijuana, the proportion of respondents agreeing with the idea of legalization has fallen from a peak of 30 percent in 1978 to a 1991 figure of 18 percent.[2] In fact, perhaps in recognition of political reality, some ardent advocates of legalization temper their position by recommending some restrictions on drug use—principally using excise taxes to discourage use, as well as regulatory restrictions on age of legal use, such as those applying to alcohol, and explicit limitations on time and place of sale for the purpose of controlling minors' access to these substances.[3] As a policy ideal, complete prohibition may be even more utopian than legalization. However much Americans profess interest in a "drug free" society (taking care to exclude alcohol, of course), it is obvious that the electorate prefers a limited war on drugs that does not require the massive infusion of funds which are required for a serious attempt to enforce prohibition.

Between the extremes of legalization and prohibition is a continuum of operational policy alternatives. America's desire to "solve" the "drug problem," reflected in the naming of a "drug czar" (as if the czars were noted for innovative policymaking), suggests a belief that appropriate policies can be adopted which will, if not solve the problem, at least limit its most serious consequences. An editorial in *Science* reflected this perspective as it considered the relative advantages of "war, program, and experiment" as a basis for drug policy.[4] Apparently in search of an economically and politically workable solution to the problem, the editors recommended a get-tough enforcement experiment which should be followed by legalization if the enforcement approach turned out to be ineffective.

The fact is that there is no magic policy bullet to kill the drug problem. Drug use has been a continuous feature of American life, and is best viewed as a chronic condition (Zimring and Hawkins, 1992:191). Furthermore, the drug problem inevitably changes over time, both in terms of the substances consumed and the social costs associated with their use. Today's solution may simply aggravate or even perpetuate tomorrow's problem. Predicting the unintended consequences of any particular policy alternative, including the extremes that dominate the debate, is difficult. Certainly, very few "drug warriors" would have predicted that reallocating criminal justice resources to control drugs would lead to an increase in non-drug crime; nor can any "legalizer" say with certainty what the consequences of legalization will be. Thus, a more pragmatic policy may be both economically and politically superior: a regime of local control and more or less "permanent experimentation," not seeking to solve the problem all at once with a federally mandated universal policy, but simply letting local officials make changes in policy that are politically feasible and likely to yield more benefits than costs.[5] The consequences of these changes can then be analyzed *and compared* so that decisionmakers in each jurisdiction can consider an array of new opportunities for policy innovation and imitation.

Even minimizing drug use—a diluted version of a drug-free society—is probably not an appropriate goal for federally driven public policy. Policy slogans such as "Just Say No" and "A Drug Free America" may be useful as exhortations to individuals not to abuse drugs, but they are counterproductive if they are used to justify a policy that focuses on drugs exclusively rather than drugs in the context of the entire criminal justice system. Such a policy is clearly misguided if the "just say no" campaign is based on either intentional or misinformed claims that exaggerate or falsify the adverse effects of drugs, claims that have typified the entire American experience with prohibition policy. The resulting short-term gains in reduced use can easily be offset by long-term losses. "Scare campaigns" directed at youth, which claim dire consequences from, say, marijuana use, are easily proven false by observing the behavior of the large number of those who use the drug. When anyone who decides to try the drug anyway finds out that these wild claims are significantly exaggerated, he or she may decide to experiment with heroin or some other riskier drug, believing that the claims about its consequences are also likely to be false. The idea that marijuana is a "gateway" drug, leading to the use of true narcotics, may become self-validating, not because of the drug itself but because experimentation with the drug proves that "reefer madness" scare tactics have little or no factual basis, causing users to discount claims made about narcotics as well.

There is an even more fundamental way in which a policy focusing exclusively on drugs is counterproductive, even if the policy could be truly factually based. As emphasized repeatedly throughout this book, any effective drug policy must recognize the fact that criminal justice resources are scarce. Allocating more resources to carry out a policy against drugs means that fewer resources are available for other purposes. Indeed, although it is not readily apparent in much public discussion, this proposition is widely accepted among policy analysts who have addressed the drug issue, except for the Office of National Drug Control Strategy (1989), which argued that no drug use is acceptable. James Q. Wilson, arguably the most thoughtful purveyor of arguments supporting a war on drugs, implicitly weighs the benefits of enforcement against the costs of drug use, for instance. He argues that the "moral and welfare costs of *heavy* [emphasis added] use are so large that society should bear the heavy burden of law enforcement, and its associated corruption and criminality, for the sake of keeping the number of people regularly using heroin and crack as small as possible" (Wilson, 1990a:527). In this and other passages he specifically mentions cocaine and heroin, generally ignoring marijuana,[6] and argues that the "question is this: how can we minimize the sum of law enforcement, moral, and welfare costs of drug use?" Rephrasing the question: do the moral and welfare benefits of reducing drug use outweigh the associated opportunity costs of forgone uses of law enforcement resources?

Although Wilson is often viewed as prohibitionist,[7] his description of the drug problem and emphasis on the drugs generally regarded as most dangerous, particularly heroin and cocaine, suggest that he in fact has in mind a prohibition policy for only specific drugs. Similarly, one of the doyens of legalization, Ethan Nadelmann (1989:945) argues that legalization is not an all-or-nothing proposition. Legalization of marijuana, he argues, could be tried without any dangerous experimentation such as reducing penalties for the harder drugs. Among the differences between "prohibitionist" Wilson and critics of the drug war, such as Wisotsky (1990), Szasz (1984), and Dennis (1990), are the different weights they place on the moral costs of drug dependency versus what might be called the moral costs of enforcement in terms of the erosion of Fourth

Amendment rights and human liberty. The crucial point is simple: most serious policy analysts actually agree on more than the mass media soundbites from the public debate on drug policy imply. In a localized experimentation approach to drug policy, particularly in the early years of such a regime, it appears that many prohibitionists and advocates of legalization would find considerable common ground.

Zimring and Hawkins (1992) are among the more pragmatic critics of contemporary drug policy, giving high praise for Kaplan's (1983) approach, which explicitly weighs the benefits and costs of criminalization or legalization on a drug-by-drug basis. Recognizing that there may be sharp differences in the evaluation of the specific economic and moral benefits and costs of particular drug policies, consideration of the explicit economic opportunity costs of drug enforcement policy—including the unintended consequences documented in this book—must be at least one cornerstone of a rational drug control effort that does not compromise the criminal justice system. Importantly, however, policies toward different drugs should not be formulated without explicitly recognizing the relationships between drug markets. As shown in Chapters 3 and 4, there is considerable evidence that alcohol is a substitute for marijuana among young drug users, and some evidence that crack cocaine was introduced because relatively successful interdiction efforts against marijuana led suppliers to look for a less bulky drug that could be smuggled more easily. Thus, the benefits and costs of a policy against one drug include that policy's consequences for other drug markets.

Strict prohibition is not likely to work if individuals want drugs: entrepreneurs seek out profit opportunities in both the legal and illegal sectors. The reality of effective black markets and the scarcity of resources for drug treatment, prevention, and enforcement indicates a need to use criminal justice resources efficiently, a goal that is undermined by the fact that many of these resources are allocated in a common pool environment. This chapter will suggest the first steps that need to be taken to allow local experimentation in drug policy, a strategy that might help overcome the tendency to use the criminal justice commons inefficiently. We do not pretend to know what the most efficient use of police resources to combat drugs might be, however. We are not experts in police tactics and, more important, there may be many potential areas of local policy innovation which we cannot anticipate, and many unintended consequences of various policy alternatives that will manifest themselves only after an experiment is under way. There actually are many localized experiments under way today, despite the efforts of federal policymakers to direct the nations' drug strategy. While these experiments do not yield definitive answers to the questions of optimal enforcement strategy, they are suggestive of potential avenues of experimentation. Our contribution in this regard is limited to the institutional setting in which these policies are implemented. The following section considers the federal government's role in drug policy, and the appropriate relationship among the various levels of government for the formulation of drug policy in a federalist environment. Section II deals with public policy toward drug markets, focusing on the opportunities for drug policy to control drug use by affecting various components of the full price of these substances. In Section III we explore ways to shape the incentives of policymakers in order to help reclaim the criminal justice commons, which has been degraded by an undisciplined war on drugs. Concluding comments are offered in Section IV.

I. Drug Policy in a Federalist System

Throughout this century the federal government has played an important role in formulating drug laws. The Harrison Act of 1914 was rooted in the belief that controlling the supply of drugs would reduce non-medical consumption of these drugs. U.S. commercial interests may have been paramount, however. China instituted a policy in 1906 to control opium consumption in order to facilitate its economic development, while at the same time it became embittered toward the treatment of its citizens in the United States. To mollify the Chinese so that our "aggressive commercial policy" in that country would not be compromised, the federal government entered into international negotiations which ultimately led to the passage of the Harrison Act in 1914 (Musto, 1991). Continuing federal leadership in drug policy is reflected in the asset seizure rules passed in 1984, as discussed in Chapter 6, and the Anti-drug Abuse Act of 1988, which created the "drug czar" to dramatize the national crusade against drug abuse.[8]

Actual substance use and potential related problems vary enormously among the states and policing jurisdictions of the nation, suggesting that there is no uniform "drug problem." The pattern of drug use among booked arrestees varies markedly among cities, for example. Cocaine was detected by urinalysis in 18 percent of males booked in Indianapolis during 1990, but in 65 percent of those in nearby Cleveland. On the other hand, only 3 percent of the males sampled in Cleveland tested positive for heroin, while 27 percent used this drug in Chicago. Only 2 percent of Denver's arrested males tested positive for heroin, while 24 percent tested positive for cocaine.[9] Local drug policy varies as well. Statewide drug arrest rates in 1989 ranged from eighty-eight per 100,000 population in West Virginia to 1,060 in California. Variation is even greater among cities. Consider differences in the drug arrest rate among cities with populations between 100,000 and 499,000. Madison, Wisconsin, had a low drug arrest rate of fifty-seven; Dayton, Ohio, had a rate (1,010) almost twice the U.S. average for 1989; while Oakland, California, made almost 3,500 drug arrests for every 100,000 residents.

Haaga and Reuter (1990) argue that a national policy is unlikely to offer the myriad of programs required to address the variety of drug abuse problems and their consequences that exist in local jurisdictions.

> Aside from marijuana, no drug other than cocaine has been the agent of a truly national epidemic. Even heroin has been confined primarily to a relatively small number of cities in the Northeast, northern Midwest, and West. The rest of the nation remained almost unaffected. Most other drugs, such as amphetamines and PCP, have been localized in a very small number of metropolitan areas. Sometimes they have occasioned short epidemics in other areas, but they have essentially disappeared after a few years.
>
> We offer no explanation for these varying patterns of use. What is important for all policymakers are the significant differences in drug consumption patterns across metropolitan areas . . . the trend toward centralization of drug policy making should be reversed. (Haaga and Reuter, 1990:8, 39)

Federal policy efforts are presumably most effective when the problem addressed is widely distributed among the states, a condition that obviously does not apply in the area of drug abuse. The costs of federal involvement in drug policy are substantial. To the extent that they "help" states with block grants of money, the political process is likely to disperse the resources more widely among jurisdictions than can be justified by the dimensions of the drug problem (Zimring and Hawkins, 1992:166). Indeed, even when matching funds are required, police and prosecutors in virtually all jurisdictions can conjure up a drug problem in the form of marijuana abuse. After all, marijuana arrests accounted for more than 50 percent of all drug arrests in twenty-four states in 1989. Any national effort to combat drugs will create incentives in states and communities to commit resources to this effort whether the local problem is severe or not. Mark Kleiman has suggested that the large number of marijuana cases prosecuted in the federal system could be the result of efforts of federal prosecutors in rural districts without other significant drug problems.[10] When a national agency emphasizes the importance of drug enforcement, its employees and employees of local agencies eligible for the agency's grant funds will find whatever drug abuse that can be found in their jurisdiction. Uniform national incentives to combat alleged drug abuse are not appropriate given the patchwork of varied substance use and potential related problems among U.S. communities.

Washington can also bully the states into policies that are not particularly appropriate for local conditions by requiring their adoption as a condition for receipt of other federal funds. The Office of National Drug Control Strategy (1989) proposed this mechanism to ensure state and local cooperation. In the environment prevailing during the 1984–1989 drug war, state and local politicians required little encouragement to reallocate resources to this enterprise, but the net effect of federal involvement probably increased non-federal spending on the drug war to levels higher than it otherwise would have been.

State policy has also been undermined by federal legislation. Federal asset forfeiture provisions adopted in 1984 are a primary offender in this regard. By requiring that local law enforcement agencies cooperating with federal agencies receive a share of seized assets resulting from these efforts, the Comprehensive Crime Control Act of 1984 actively encouraged these agencies to undermine many states' intended use of these monies. The subsequent practice of federal adoption of local seizures, whether cooperation was involved or not, made the incentives even stronger for police to circumvent state laws. Repeal of this provision in 1988 was short lived, as Congress in the 1990 defense appropriations bill retroactively reinstated the federal government's policy of superimposing its judgment over that of many state legislatures. This federal policy distorts the incentives for police to increase drug enforcement relative to other offenses, thereby contributing to many of the unintended consequences of the war on drugs. The 1988 repeal of this unwarranted federal intrusion into state drug policy was subsequently over-turned, but it should be reinstated.

First among federal reforms in drug policy should be a reduced role for or, perhaps better yet, elimination of the Office of the National Drug Control Strategy. Headed by the drug czar, this office has a strong symbolic aspect, providing a "bully pulpit" to cheer the country on in its fight against drugs. William Bennett, the first czar, was admirably suited to this role. The office was created during a climate of intense interest in the drug war, and its head was to whip up political support to solve the drug problem. As the drug war wanes, but the consequences of its trammelling of the criminal justice commons remain, it is time to reconsider the drug czar's role in federal drug policy. Even if we assume that the federal government has certain roles in which the states cannot take the effective lead, such as combatting the importation of drugs from abroad, limiting interstate commerce in illegal substances, and providing research and evaluation to guide policymakers in states and local jurisdictions, it does not follow that the drug czar has a unique role to play in these functions.[11] Interagency task forces can provide most of the coordinating activity required for interdiction of drugs from abroad and between states, and the Department of Justice has an active research and evaluation program that reports on the effectiveness of various policy innovations tried in states and cities.

A third federal reform appropriate in the drug policy experiment is both important and very modest: federal decriminalizing of marijuana possession.[12] It is important because it provides an environment for effective local experimentation with de-emphasis of marijuana enforcement. It is also a modest reform in many respects. Since marijuana possession is currently illegal in all states, there would be no fundamental change in the legal status of this offense. Federal practice would be altered little by this policy change: only 1.7 percent of federal prison admissions in 1988 were for marijuana possession. Finally, this reform is modest in that previous experiments with decriminalization at the state level do not indicate that there are major negative unintended consequences from this action even if states were to follow suit. There may even be substantial benefits, as noted below. Indeed, if state and local experiments with marijuana control lead in the direction and to the kinds of benefits anticipated below, then even further decriminalization at the federal level can be justified in order to facilitate localized experimentation with policies against other drugs.

There are many other changes at the federal level that would free state and local law enforcement officials from the constraints and incentives which tend to produce a relatively homogeneous national drug policy and discourage experimentation. Essentially, if the federal government were to adopt the role of facilitating each local jurisdiction's capacity to solve its most pressing problems, more creative solutions to specific local problems are likely to develop—solutions that are not likely to originate in Washington, if for no other reason than the difficulties associated with transplanting a successful program from one jurisdiction to another. Indeed, the federal government has, in recent years, tended to impose mandated expenditures on state and local jurisdictions, reducing their flexibility rather than enhancing it. Federal dollars to state and local communities could be best left untied, freeing up local resources to focus on programs that are most promising for the local community, perhaps but not necessarily including drug-related programs. In an environment less dominated by the need for

Congress and federal policing bureaucracies to appear tough on crime, some local communities might address drugs and their consequences in more creative ways that impose fewer costs on the criminal justice system.

No policy is a panacea, however, despite what some advocates at both extremes of the drug policy debate might allege. Even a localized drug policy can create problems. Indeed, decentralization of drug policy can be embraced with too much enthusiasm. Benjamin and Miller (1991) argue for a "Constitutional Alternative" to the existing drug policy in which local jurisdictions are charged with determining the sanctions for substance abuse. This local option approach is problematic because easily available drugs in one jurisdiction can spill over into adjacent jurisdictions desiring a relatively drug-free environment. Spillovers among jurisdictions as a result of differential drug enforcement are substantial.[13] Furthermore, if local jurisdictions are allowed to determine sanctions, they should also be required to bear the cost of imposing those sanctions. If a local jurisdiction decides to be "tough on drugs" by sending large numbers of drug offenders into a common pool state prison system, for instance, the costs on the rest of the state can be significant.

II. Drug Control as a Pricing Policy

Political reality suggests that politicians and bureaucrats at all levels of government will continue to want to influence drug policy. Many are likely to predict the worst conceivable outcomes of a decentralized experimental process. In order to counter such dire predictions, let us consider the potential margins along which experimentation is likely to occur. Most drug policy options that are likely to be tried can be viewed within an economic framework that emphasizes their effect on drug prices. That the quantity of a good demanded falls as its price rises is a basic tenet of economics. Most evidence suggests that even cocaine and heroin are probably "normal goods" in this respect, as shown in Chapter 3. Drug enforcement policies can attempt to raise price, which will reduce drug usage somewhat, and/or attempt to reduce the demand for these substances through treatment and education. Drug policy can affect the price of drugs in a myriad of ways because the "full price" of a drug is composed of several elements: money price; time costs associated with searching for drugs; risk factors such as the toxicity of adulterated products; chances of being harmed while engaged in black market activity; and the expected criminal penalties.

The current system emphasizes prohibition over alternative policies. Thus, for instance, the federal drug policy budget allocates at least $3 to criminal justice for every $1 allocated to treatment. Prohibition policies appeal to those who wish to limit drug use, because these policies are expected to raise every element of the drug's full price. Prohibition's effect on the supply of drugs has raised the money price of marijuana, cocaine, and heroin far above what it would be in an unregulated free market environment.[14] Search costs rise when these markets are disrupted by police sweeps and active street enforcement. Toxicity—including uncertain purity, which can lead to overdoses—and the risk of physical harm associated with dealing in black markets are products of prohibition. These risks are side effects of prohibition that are not generally an integral part of drug policy objectives.[15] Finally, risk of arrest and the penalties for drug users are obvious direct consequences of the predominant criminal justice tools of drug policy. Prohibition has other significant effects, however, many of which are documented in Chapters 2 through 5. For one thing, prohibition is differentially effective, so it alters the relative prices of drugs. In particular, because marijuana is bulky and more difficult to hide, law enforcement efforts tended to be much more successful against this drug than against cocaine during the 1980s, raising most components of the full price of marijuana. This success apparently has led drug suppliers to shift toward cocaine; and with the advent of crack, some drug users have also apparently substituted cocaine for marijuana. Furthermore, alcohol is apparently a substitute for illicit drugs like marijuana and cocaine, so the drug war has tended to increase alcohol use, alcohol-related health problems, drunk driving, and other related effects. In addition, drug enforcement requires the use of scarce police, prison, court, and prosecution resources that have alternative valuable uses. When local policymakers, uninfluenced by federal mandates, funds, and incentives, consider the costs and benefits of various drug policy alternatives, it may well be that they will move away from a prohibition strategy, at least on some dimensions. One option is legalization, and this is the option that prohibition advocates clearly fear the most.

The likelihood of legalization. Legalizing a drug has a dramatic impact on its full price. All elements of full price fall: the drug will be more accessible and freer of adulterants; participating in the drug market probably would be no more dangerous than in legal markets; and there will be no legal consequences of use or sale. When the sale of the drug is legal, the money price will also fall dramatically. Moore (1990:124) estimated that the money price of cocaine would fall to one-eighth its illegal price; marijuana would sell at one-fifteenth its controlled price; and heroin's price would shrink to less than 2 percent its illegal price. However, there are two reasons to expect that outright legalization of most illegal drugs will not occur under a regime of experimentation, at least at the outset. First, it is a drastic change in policy that is not likely to appeal to public officials concerned with job security. Second, and more important, the probable results, especially for cocaine and heroin, are likely to be perceived as undesirable by the majority of those who influence policy.

The premise that most people who do not currently use hard drugs will not use them when legalized is an article of faith among many advocates of legalization. It can be a glib argument: a speaker at a drug policy symposium asked the audience, composed mostly of middle-aged academics, if they would use cocaine if it was legalized. Since no one affirmed their interest in consuming the lower priced drug, the speaker claimed this supported the proposition that the quantity of cocaine consumed would not increase with a decline in price. In short, demand for cocaine is presumably price inelastic. This proposition is at the root of the "drugs cause crime" argument: drug-crazed individuals will do anything to support their habit. Virtually all research on the subject refutes this proposition, as shown in Chapter 4, at least over the range of prices that have been observed. And it may be wrong for drug legalization too (although price elasticity does tend to fall as price falls). Worse, the price elasticity might be highest among the group we are most keen on keeping drug-free: our young people who are at the ages where experimentation is expected. Youth might be more sensitive to price because they make less income, so the money price of drugs represents a much larger portion of their total income than it does for adults. Direct empirical evidence on this point is unavailable, but studies of drunk driving support the contention since they suggest that persons between eighteen and twenty-one are much more responsive than older drivers to price changes resulting from increased beer taxes.[16] However, it is only through experimentation that more accurate estimates of price responsiveness can be obtained. If significant increases in drug use occur, one alternative that is always available is reestablishment of stricter prohibition efforts.

Legalization does not necessarily imply the imposition of an unregulated market price. There could be elaborate controls on suppliers, for example, as there are in many states for alcohol, with an extreme case being one in which only physicians could supply some drugs. Less restrictive rules for sale, such as limited time of sale at specially licensed pharmacies, could be accompanied by a prohibition of advertising. Relatively high excise taxes are expected to offset the declining full price of heroin and cocaine under most proposals for legalization. In order to do so, however, these taxes would have to be draconian. If Moore's (1990) estimates are approximately right, the excise tax on cocaine would need to be about 1,200 percent just to prevent a decline in the money price. A higher excise tax would be required to offset the reductions in full price that result from reduced legal penalties and a safer market environment. Unfortunately, we have no reliable evidence on the relative elasticities of cocaine consumption with respect to the various components of full price. It is entirely possible that illegality and the threat of punishment have a much greater impact on the probability of consumption than any increase in money price. Further, the high excise taxes create an incentive for black markets to develop, as they have for tobacco products in states with high cigarette taxes; and the fact of legalization will make these markets less risky. Thus, it is not readily apparent that a system of taxation and restrictions on supply will control the use of the hardest drugs. Accordingly, such policies are likely to be considered only after many other policy experiments have failed an encompassing cost effectiveness test.

One of the more cogent arguments for the legalization of the hardest drugs is rooted in the libertarian position that freedom is the ultimate value and the state should not interfere with individual choices so long as they do not impose costs on others. Thus, the level of use is irrelevant from the libertarian perspective.[17] However, this libertarian argument is not likely to win the day, at least in most jurisdictions. Indeed, this argument actually has significant variations. Caveats usually are added to prevent children, variously defined, from having access to the drugs until they can make mature decisions. The nation's experience with alcohol makes it clear to most citizens that youth may not be reliably restrained from access to these drugs when they can be sold in legal markets, providing one reason to reject the individual freedom case for complete legalization. The libertarians' position regarding the value of freedom is not subject to debate; it is a belief that cannot be logically refuted.[18] However, pragmatic libertarians are likely to see that their view may be accommodated in the context of localized experimentation, since the libertarian policy perspective would suggest approval of the relaxation of any penalties, including those which are most likely to result from a policy regime that creates incentives for policymakers to accurately access benefits and costs of a policy. Movement in the direction of the legalizers' position are likely because, as explained in the preceding chapters, many of the alleged benefits of a drug war are either false or exaggerated, and many of the unintended consequences are undesirable. Thus, legalizers could support the start of an experimentation process that involves more modest changes in drug policy. After all, while the libertarian argument may have little chance in a national debate, it may have considerable impact in some jurisdictions, and if it is successful, it may spread through emulation. This expectation appears to be particularly likely for marijuana.

Weisheit (1992) suggests that the production and distribution of marijuana is much less violent than that of cocaine and heroin. Further, the social consequences of marijuana use may not be worse than those of legal drugs—tobacco and alcohol—thereby undermining one of the objective reasons for outlawing the substance. This argument must be viewed with caution since it says that illegal marijuana may yield fewer problems than legal beer: the real question is whether legal pot remains relatively benign. Existing evidence also suggests alcohol—particularly beer, which is the drink of choice among the young—is probably a substitute for marijuana.[19] This means that if the full price of marijuana falls, youths tend to substitute away from alcohol toward marijuana. Accordingly, a potentially potent policy to reduce marijuana consumption among this population is to reduce the full price of beer by lowering excise taxes levied on this drink of choice. Chaloupka and Laixuthai (1992) suggest that the net result of raising the price of beer relative to the full price of marijuana would be to reduce drunken driving and raise stoned driving. However, their empirical results suggest the net effect of relatively higher beer prices would be a reduction in the probabilities of non-fatal and fatal motor vehicle accidents involving youth.[20]

Some drug policy analysts have suggested a need for an integrated approach to substance abuse, considering tobacco and alcohol in the same context as the currently illegal drugs. Evidence presented here suggests this interdependence is particularly important for the discussion of public policy toward marijuana and beer, which are generally the substances of choice among the youthful population, making the immediate policy issue relatively simple: what should the price of beer be relative to the price of marijuana? Legalization of marijuana would change the current equation enormously: if Moore's (1990:124) estimates are accurate, the money price of marijuana would fall perhaps to one-fifteenth its illegal price. Falling search, toxicity, and safety costs, as well as elimination of legal penalties, would mean an enormous shift in incentives toward consumption of marijuana rather than beer. Indeed, public policy probably has implicitly encouraged beer consumption over marijuana over the past three decades. Besides the illegality of marijuana and rising penalties during the 1980s, the price of alcoholic beverages has been falling relative to the overall consumer price index, in part because federal excise tax on beer failed to keep up with inflation. Since the legal status of marijuana has an impact on the legal substitute, policy toward this drug should clearly be formed with recognition of its impact on beer consumption among youth. It would not be surprising to see some jurisdictions experiment with legalization of this drug. On the other hand, the first step in experimenting, even with marijuana, may be less dramatic, taking the form of decriminalization rather than legalization.

Decriminalization. Under an experimental regime of decriminalization, the penalty for possession of some drugs might be reduced to, say, a misdemeanor. As the penalties for supplying drugs remain intact, the money, search, toxicity, and victimization cost of drug use will not be seriously affected while the severity of expected punishment will decline sharply. In sharp contrast to legalization, it is possible that decriminalization represents a relatively small change in the full price of a drug. Reuter (1991) made an educated guess of the average risk of arrest for marijuana and cocaine users in 1988, concluding that marijuana users on average had about a 2 percent chance of being arrested during the year while cocaine users faced a 6 percent chance. Since the costs of supplying these drugs would not decline as a result of decriminalization and, in fact, may increase if some police and prison resources used to combat use are reallocated to combat the supply of drugs, the full cost of these drugs will only be affected to the extent that usage is sensitive to legal penalties.

It has been argued that decriminalization of marijuana would appear to be a relatively modest experiment. If legal penalties are a relatively small portion of the full price of marijuana, at least compared to cocaine and heroin, users would not be expected to increase their usage much unless the demand is highly elastic with respect to changes in the probability of arrest and the severity of punishment. Wisotsky (1990) has made this case, reporting that no significant numbers of new users or increases in frequency of use were found in evaluations of decriminalization in Oregon, California, and Maine. A more careful evaluation of the California study is less sanguine in this respect. Cuskey, Berger, and Richardson (1978) report that the prevalence rate rose only 6–7 percent for persons ages eighteen and over when marijuana was decriminalized. Among eighteen to twenty-nine year olds the prevalence rate rose 12–15 percent—not necessarily a trivial change, depending on the consequences of such increased use. Intensity of use rose somewhat, as did the duration of use. Shortcomings in the design of these state evaluations of decriminalization make it difficult to draw substantive conclusions about the effects of this change in policy, but the evidence is consistent with the proposition that lower prices raise the quantity consumed.

The limited decriminalization experiment in eleven states has revealed other important information to guide policy with regard to marijuana control. Decriminalization in these states allowed Chaloupka and Laixuthai

(1992) to analyze one important impact of such a change: did it make roads more or less safe? Their conclusion is that youths substituting marijuana for beer had, on net, a positive impact on safety. While their work is not the final word on the subject, it raises important questions about the wisdom of complete prohibition of marijuana. More importantly, the results of this study suggest that the change in the full price of marijuana resulting from decriminalization was large enough to solicit a significant substitution between beer and pot, further raising the credibility of the claim that usage rates will rise when user penalties are reduced.

Some states might choose to experiment with decriminalization of marijuana if this policy is adopted at the federal level, as suggested above. Operating as "laboratories of democracy," these states could introduce decriminalization legislation that sunsets after a period of time, say five years. The effects of this policy could be evaluated during this period, the results of which could determine if it should be continued. Among the issues to be addressed in such an evaluation should be the impact on youth substance abuse and the incidence of driving under the influence, taking care to consider that the costs of rising marijuana use may be partly offset by declining alcohol abuse. Impacts on the criminal justice system—including police enforcement, court crowding, and use of the prison commons—should also be considered. Finally, it might be possible to discern whether marijuana use is less likely to foster violent behavior than its alcohol substitutes. Such an evaluation, planned while the change in the law is being considered, is a good example of an experimental approach to changes in drug policy. States willing to serve as laboratories might even be deserving of federal support for the evaluations, since they eliminate the need for other states to undergo whatever uncertainty is associated with the experiment.

Stricter prohibition. The discussion up to this point suggests that experiments will probably be in the direction of less restrictive prohibition policies. This is not necessarily the case, however, without some significant changes in the way that criminal justice resources are allocated. For instance, if a local jurisdiction can "export" its drug problems by arresting and prosecuting large numbers of drug users so that they serve long sentences in a common pool state prison, then the incentives to experiment with innovative alternatives to prohibition are practically nonexistent. Those jurisdictions that experiment with less restrictive prohibition policies may have to bear the costs of whatever alternatives they adopt (e.g., treatment programs; treating possession as a misdemeanor subject to a local jail sentence or a community release program) while continuing to contribute taxes to pay for state prison systems that other jurisdictions crowd with drug offenders. Thus, local jurisdictions would be in a "prisoner's dilemma" situation because of the common pool problem of state prisons. In the face of such possibilities, all jurisdictions have relatively strong incentives to adopt a strong prohibitionist policy.[21] In order to create an environment that is conducive to experimentation, the incentives facing law enforcement officials must be recognized and taken into account.

III. Rationalizing Use of the Criminal Justice Commons

The criminal justice commons was abused during the 1984–1989 war on drugs. We have seen that every player affecting the criminal justice system—legislators, police, prosecutors, and judges—has incentives to use criminal justice resources to serve their self-interest. Putting the highest priority on the efficient use of criminal justice resources under these circumstances is unlikely. Viewing the criminal justice system as a commons, therefore, suggests that improving the allocation of these resources requires significant institutional change. These changes must attempt to harness the powerful incentives of agency self-interest and political survival so that they are more consistent with the rational use of criminal justice resources. Here we offer some examples of policy innovations that might contribute to this goal.

Police. Taxpayers' reluctance to fund law enforcement agencies at a level that allows them to pursue all types of crimes has turned police into entrepreneurial agencies. In this regard, the U.S. attorney general in 1992 argued that asset forfeiture is a valuable "double barreled weapon" against crime.[22] One weapon is the deterrence effect of taking away ill-gotten gains while the second is the "reinvestment" of the proceeds into the law enforcement effort. Our discussion of asset forfeiture in Chapter 6 suggests a very different interpretation, however. Police agencies have changed their priorities because of these incentives, resulting in increased drug enforcement with a possible decline in public safety. In light of this evidence, including asset forfeiture as a desirable strategy in a U.S. Department of Justice report titled *Combating Violent Crime* (U.S. Office of the Attorney General, 1992) seems strange. The incentives created by asset forfeitures do not encourage law enforcement to focus on violent crime per se, and potentially undermine efforts to fight crime against persons in two ways. First, police are likely to seek revenues via confiscations, leading to greater effort against drugs relative to other crimes. Second, since juveniles have few assets, this leads to a focus on adults in the drug market, producing adult drug arrests, which are relatively easily prosecuted, and contributing to the prison overcrowding which has resulted in the early release of some violent criminals.

Rather than being a double-barreled weapon against crime, asset forfeiture might at best be described as a single-barreled weapon with a very strong kick. Deterrence effects of forfeitures may be strong (although evidence of even this effect is not available), and thus a significant weapon against drug offenses if offenders believe that the probability of a seizure occurring is significant. Buyers of drugs can have their vehicles confiscated, for example, which they can buy back for a negotiated price. Tampa's program against buyers was believed to be effective when the media were used to get the message out that a "$20 rock may cost you a $20,000 car" (Kennedy, 1993:20). The kick from the asset forfeiture weapon, at least when police are allowed to keep the proceeds, is that enforcement efforts are distorted toward drug offenses, away from crimes in which some person is, at least potentially, explicitly victimized. One partial solution is straightforward, and already on the books in many states: police may use asset forfeiture to deter offenders, but the proceeds must go to general revenue rather than to the arresting agency.[23] This retains the deterrent weapon while eliminating the distorting effect of asset forfeiture on the allocation of police resources among crimes. A similar reform is needed for the federal enforcement agencies as well, and the federal adoption of state and local seizures should be stopped. Of course, local budget-setting authorities may want to reward police for their efforts to enhance general revenues through seizures. But at least police will have to compete for the revenue by convincing an oversight authority that their focus on seizures is an appropriate one; and if they cannot do so, they will clearly have incentives to redirect their efforts.

The point is that the nature of bargaining over police budgets in the public sector probably plays a role in the allocation of police resources. For police, an appeal of keeping the proceeds of seized assets is that discretionary budgets can be enhanced without having to justify their need in the face of competing demands from other community agencies. However, putting seizures into the general fund so that police must compete for them does not solve all of the problems of police resource allocation. Statistical studies of police budgets suggest that budgets rise with higher measures of productivity (as measured by outputs such as arrests) and rise with increased "need" (as measured by crime rates).[24] Budget bargaining over these measures of productivity and need has unfortunate consequences. For example, police agencies might be better off from a budget perspective if they arrest offenders after the crime is committed, rather than defending communities by preventing the crime from occurring in the first place (Sherman, 1983). Arrests for possession of small quantities of marijuana may be as effective in these negotiations as an arrest for a burglary, but searching for a burglar may be far more time consuming than finding drug offenders in open-air markets. The best police strategy to compete for public dollars might be to make as many arrests as possible and make sure that highly publicized crimes are solved. Indeed, by focusing on drug enforcement, both measures of output (e.g., arrests, drugs seized, assets seized) and measures of need (crime rates) can rise, as explained in Chapter 5, because with more police resources devoted to drug control, other crimes are less effectively deterred. Therefore, the budget-setting process itself also perverts police incentives.

Changing the budget negotiating process at the local level requires political action at the local level. Failures of past policies have led to increased pressure on police from individual victims and their families who demand justice and, increasingly, from communities that are victimized by the lawlessness which has plagued many neighborhoods. These community demands may provide significant changes in police behavior, given that their behavior is neither constrained nor dominated by incentives created by state or federal actions. The result could move criminal justice policy toward a greater emphasis on community safety, rather than generating statistical measures of output such as arrests. For instance, Tampa's drug problem had become so bad by the end of the 1980s—after several years of drug war—that community leaders began to put increasing pressure on the equally frustrated police. The result was an innovative program that was focused on community involvement for the purpose of making neighborhoods safer. Police officials knew that drug use might not be significantly changed by such a program. Indeed, they expected that "the best that might happen to the drug trade would be that it moved indoors. That seemed, nonetheless, a worthy goal" (Kennedy, 1993:18). Community policing and other such innovations in this direction require that, for budgetary purposes, the evaluation of police performance change to include more qualitative evidence and somewhat less reliance on quantitative measures. Political action by communities that demands safer streets will help encourage police to alter their strategies, concentrating their efforts to ensure public safety and putting a somewhat lower priority on fighting drugs per se.

Legislators. Legislatures at the federal and state levels often are enthusiastic supporters of legislation that symbolically gets tough on crime, while being understandably reluctant to finance more criminal justice resources through higher taxes. Their abuse of the commons comes in many forms. Legislators' aversion to having constituents pay for tougher en-forcement raises the appeal of the asset forfeiture legislation just discussed, for instance, because it appears to make incremental police activities "self-financing." The actual results are greater police efforts against drugs relative to other crimes, however, with the likely consequence of making the community less safe. Legislatures have further abused the criminal justice commons by passing minimum mandatory sentences for drug crimes, making it easy for prosecutors to get convictions for lesser crimes via plea or charge bargaining. The result is that more drug offenders are easily prosecuted, producing prison overcrowding and sometimes the early release of relatively dangerous offenders. Another result is the reelection of the get-tough legislators who are, in one sense, first in the line of players abusing the criminal justice commons.

The legislature actually has the power to codify, by statute, a mechanism that would move the allocation of scarce prison space toward its highest and best use. Sentencing guidelines are well suited to this task, in theory at least, although in fact they emerged in the United States after 1975 largely in an attempt to limit judicial discretion (which is characteristic of U.S. courts); and later alterations have reflected symbolic actions to demonstrate get-tough approaches to crime. If guidelines were to be used as a mechanism for allocating scarce prison space rather than for controlling judges and making symbolic get-tough gestures, guidelines would have been written in a way that determined the relative seriousness of crimes and criminal histories in light of prison capacity restrictions. Guidelines would be predicated on the assumption that offenders with similar criminal records should be given the same punishment when charged with identical offenses. Indeed, guidelines emerged because this elementary principle of justice was routinely abused in the courts. More significantly, however, while perhaps conceived to increase equity for treatment of each type of criminal, sentencing guidelines potentially could play an even more important role in enhancing the efficient use of prison space by explicitly considering the relative treatment of different types of criminals while simultaneously recognizing the limits on prison resources that exist.

Giving the judiciary a recommended sentence for burglary and robbery, for example, requires an explicit statement of the legislature's perception of the relative seriousness of these crimes. Sentencing guidelines, with or without allowance for judicial discretion, could provide a complete itemization of the legislature's perception of the relative seriousness of all crimes. This may in fact occur when guidelines are initially passed; but typically, once guidelines are passed, they are amended randomly one offense at a time, for politically motivated reasons that can actually add to prison overcrowding. But if guidelines are constructed simultaneously with consideration of the state's prison capacity and then only amended as an entire package, still recognizing prison capacity constraints, they can produce a coherent prison-rationing procedure. However daunting this task, it would be inherently valuable: without evaluating the relative seriousness of crimes while recognizing resource constraints that limit aggregate punishment capacity, it is impossible to know if the worst offenders are serving the most time. If prison space were in ample supply, a guidelines system could ignore efficiency and only address the equitable treatment of offenders. But this is unrealistic: taxpayers are generally not willing to pay for unlimited prison capacity. The norm will be a scarcity of prison beds. If guidelines are promulgated without reference to prison capacity, they become a symbolic wish list, unrelated to the reality of punishment. The result is prison crowding, so that desired sentences are subverted by early release and other methods of controlling the prison population. An integrated and disciplined criminal justice system is one that recognizes the scarcity of resources, thereby forcing decisionmakers to either proscribe punishment that can be delivered within the prison resources that taxpayers are willing to finance, or convince taxpayers that more resources are required.

No state has had the political will to provide such a system. Minnesota, a state with admirable intentions in this regard, set up its guidelines to allow for a constant prison population, although they could adjust over time with population growth. Tonry (1988) reports the matching of penalties with prison resources was intended to introduce the inevitable tradeoffs into incarceration policy, but the original intent was undermined by the desire of subsequent legislatures to increase penalties for drug and sex offenders without regard to prison capacity.[25] This is not surprising. Legislators benefit from the impasse in corrections by being able to promise constituents tougher penalties for some crimes without having to confront voters with the stark reality: either pay more taxes to build additional prisons, give up other public services, or abuse the prison commons—which could include the early release of some prisoners. The commons aspect of the prison system provides a convenient cover for prosecutors, judges, and legislators who can concoct politically popular policies that undermine the efficient use of prison resources. Sentencing guidelines, while providing a possible mechanism for the rational use of prison space, are undermined by the problem they could potentially correct: the tragedy of the commons.

The problem is political. So is the solution, to the extent that one exists. Perhaps one promising development is the rapidly evolving victims' rights movement, which may provide a countervailing influence to the traditional criminal justice lobbies—the law enforcement and civil liberties groups (Berk, Brackman, and Lesser, 1977; Benson 1990)—and may pressure legislatures to emphasize the punishment of offenders who have harmed individuals. A number of victim-oriented pressure groups have been formed, such as Parents of Murdered Children (POMC), Mothers Against Drunk Drivers (MADD), and Society's League Against Molestation (SLAM). These groups are now so numerous that they can support an organization in Washington that coordinates their lobbying efforts: The National Organization for Victim Assistance.[26] These organizations put pressure on legislatures to get tough on those offenders who have committed various violent acts. Other interest groups, such as police, have put pressure on legislatures to get tough on drugs. But such legislation has resulted in the early release of violent offenders; and the ensuing political pressure from victims groups apparently has begun to produce a strengthening of punishment for those offenses with victims, relative to those without victims (such as drug sales and possession). At least one study suggests these organizations might be quite effective. In an analysis of drunken driving in California counties, McCarthy and Ziliak (1990) show that an active MADD chapter has a deterrent effect on the incidence of alcohol-related accidents. While this does not directly measure the organization's effectiveness on the behavior of legislators, it suggests that these organizations might have a significant effect on public attitudes and policy, forcing legislators to recognize the consequences of their symbolic "get tough on drugs" legislation.

Successful political pressure, such as that provided by victims' rights groups, might move a state legislature in the direction of a rational sentencing guidelines program that reflects the relative seriousness of crimes and the limited capacity of prisons to punish. No such legislative action has survived, however, and it is doubtful that it will in the future. But there is an alternative solution: a solution that might be politically more viable and that is consistent with the recommendations for local experimentation made above. Rather than attempting to develop a state-wide mechanism for rationing the state's common pool prisons, the allocation of prison space might be localized by making prosecutors and/or judges responsible for rationing scarce prison resources.

Prosecutors and judges. The courts are particularly prone to abuse of the common pool of prison space. Prosecutors are elected officials sworn to punish those who break the law, and are likely to adopt what Zimring and Hawkins (1992) call a "legalist" approach which is consistent with a war on all drug use, finding serious fault in the behavior of both casual and addicted drug users. From a legalist perspective, casual drug users—those who are not addicted or otherwise criminally inclined—can be the worst role models because they "are most conspicuously thumbing their noses at the state authority" (Zimring and Hawkins, 1992:16). In this spirit the Office of National Drug Control Strategy (1989) could say there is no such thing as innocent drug use. By inclination, government prosecutors view themselves as administrators of punishment to those who break the law; since they are elected, they can best defend their record if they generate a high rate of convictions. Having the incentive and inclination to be tough on crime, prosecutors have played a major role in crowding the prison commons with drug offenders during the 1984–1989 period.[27]

Prosecutors and judges have what is perhaps the clearest incentive to abuse the criminal justice commons. Consider an example. A person is charged with writing a bad check. The prosecutor, seeing that the person has had a lengthy record of such offenses, decides to prosecute. The judge recognizes that this offense is not "very" serious, but is so frustrated with the continued unlawful behavior that the offender is sent to prison. Because the state prison system is under court order to limit its prison population, an early release mechanism releases an inmate in order to make room for the bad-check writer. A violent criminal who has served a substantial period of time is released, but to a county in another part of the state. Neither the prosecutor nor the judge has to consider the consequences of their decisions in this case, because another community is most likely to suffer the consequences. This example, unfortunately, closely approximates an actual series of events in Florida. Within several days of his release, the violent offender had killed two policemen.

The crucial question is this: would the prosecutor and judge have behaved differently if they knew the person to be released would be returned to their own community where the people who voted them into office would be directly affected? The answer would surely be yes. What prosecutor would like to seek reelection when the opponent could argue that the incumbent is willing to let out a murderer to punish a bad-check writer? Judges would likewise consider that bad press. Stopping the abuse of the prison commons requires that prosecutors and judges consider the consequences of their actions: what is the cost of incarceration and who might be let out early when a person is convicted to a prison term?

When considering this problem, it is important to recognize that not all courthouses crowd the prison commons. Southeast Florida has been a major area for drug trafficking, for instance; and yet, adjacent counties have very different policies in this regard. Broward County—notorious in Florida for its willingness to arrest and prosecute drug users—had 9.7 percent of the state's population but accounted for 12.1 percent of the prison inmates in 1991. Nearby Dade County had a higher crime rate and accounted for about 15 percent of the state population, but only 13.9 percent of the prison inmates had been committed from Dade. Put another way, if every county crowded the commons like Broward County, Florida's prison system would have to expand by about 24 percent. However, if every county used the alternative measures employed in Dade County, the prison system would have about 7 percent fewer inmates.[28] This difference is at least partially due to the creation of an innovative "drug court" which provides a diversion and treatment program for drug offenders charged with possession or purchasing drugs. Persons with a history of violent crime, with more than two previous non-drug felony convictions, and drug traffickers are not eligible. The program costs less than imprisoning these offenders, has a relatively low recidivism rate, and saves prison space for more dangerous offenders.[29]

In the absence of very specific sentencing guidelines that reflect real prison-resource constraints, some courthouse gangs are likely to continue crowding the common access prisons unless their incentives are changed. Indeed, an alternative to such guidelines is an institutional change that alters sentencing incentives for each court. This would have to involve major institutional reform, however, since incentives that encourage all prosecutors and judges to adopt innovative approaches toward non-violent criminals would need to be developed. The following discussion is intended to simply outline possible approaches without exploring all the details that would inevitably vary from state to state.

One approach is to have a "prison resource commission" assign each court a certain number of the state's prison beds. By "owning" a number of beds, the courts can incarcerate offenders without constraint until they are filled, after which they would have to release their own inmates who, presumably, would be released to the community.[30] If some local prosecutors and judges feel that the jurisdiction's allocation of prison space is inadequate to their needs, then they can attempt to convince local taxpayers to provide them with additional money for prison construction. Thus, if citizens of a local jurisdiction want a get-tough policy bad enough to pay for it, they can get one—but they will not be able to shift costs onto taxpayers from other jurisdictions who help fund a common-access prison system.

A more restrained variation of this approach is to limit to non-violent offenders the prosecutor's role in releasing prisoners, although we expect that most prosecutors would recognize the very strong incentives not to release violent felons early. The state could assume responsibility for housing all violent offenders, providing enough prison resources so these offenders would not be subject to early release. Courts (judges and/or prosecutors) would be given "title" to beds for non-violent offenders, requiring prosecutors to recommend a particular person for release when sentencing a new offender to a prison term when the court has no more beds in the prison.[31]

Even less encompassing institutional reform could move the criminal justice system toward a more efficient rationing of prisons by reining in the worst abusers on the prison commons. If a community's prosecutor and judge stray beyond some norm in terms of incarceration rates (e.g., their share of prison admissions exceeding their share of population, or perhaps of reported crimes, by 5 percent), the community could be required to pay for the extra burden imposed on the prison system. Assuming that the purpose is to deter prosecutors from seeking political benefit at the expense of the rest of the state, the payment could be in the form of a surcharge on state taxes if the local court's behavior does not conform to the standard within a specified time period which would allow the court to come back into compliance with the norm.[32] A simpler solution, but perhaps less obvious to voters, is a penalty system that would fine the local jurisdiction for each prisoner over the norm for every day it exceeds its allotted number of inmates.

Controlling the criminal justice commons is a political process in which prosecutors and, to a lesser extent, judges play an important role. While the suggestions provided here may not generate sufficient political support to implement them, they do represent the kind of institutional change that is required to bring a rational allocation to the criminal justice commons in the absence of a bold and innovative sentencing-guidelines program at the state level. Substantial change is required if prisons are to be used to protect citizens from the criminals who are most likely to harm them. Given the strong appeal of a "legalist" perspective that we should punish all those who undermine legal authorities, the political advantage that elected prosecutors gain by abusing the prison commons, and the appeal to legislators of passing symbolic anti-crime bills rather than packages of rational reform,[33] we cannot be sanguine about the prospects for the required institutional reform. The point is that criminal justice policy cycles, such as drug wars, will continue until reforms of the kind suggested here are tried.

IV. Conclusions

Why have we ended this book on drug policy with a discussion of institutional reforms for the criminal justice system as a whole? Because the problems associated with drug enforcement policy are, in large part, simply symptoms of a severely flawed criminal justice system. Indeed, the detailed examination of drug enforcement policy provided in this book has implications that go well beyond the drug issue. Although we have focused on drug policy, we have really been engaged in a case study which illustrates the kinds of problems that inevitably arise when criminal justice is provided as a commons. Prisons, courts, and police files would be crowded even if drugs were legal, forcing choices to be made with regard to the allocation of resources for which excess demand is the norm. As a result, criminal justice officials would still have considerable discretion in how to allocate scarce resources. A rational drug policy requires a rationalization of the criminal justice system. Those who have the discretion to determine how various criminal justice resources are to be allocated must have incentives to consider the real costs and benefits of their actions in order for those actions to produce an appropriate policy toward drugs and toward crimes against persons and property. A commons means that people are not liable for the costs of their actions, so they have at best only weak incentives to consider the consequences of those actions. If criminal justice decisionmakers could be held accountable for the negative consequences of their activities, they would have much stronger incentives to try to predict those consequences and take them into account.

The institutional changes we have discussed involve making at least some public sector decisionmakers more accountable. When rules, money, and incentives emanate from Washington, for instance, state and local officials can say "we are just doing what Congress mandates." Congress' mandates may be the policy desired by some communities, but only one congressperson can be held accountable by citizens of the other communities that prefer a different policy. The discussion in Chapter 6 of the federal seizure law passed in 1984 provides an excellent example of this problem. While many states have laws which reflect a preference that asset seizures not go directly back to law enforcement, the federal law overrode the states' laws by creating a way for law enforcement officials to circumvent any limitations on their access to seizures. Those states whose citizens prefer a different allocation of seized assets cannot hold Congress accountable for what they perceive to be a bad law.

Accountability is not the only reason for decentralizing the primary decisionmaking mechanisms for criminal justice, however. While criminal justice problems in general are ubiquitous, they vary considerably across the nation, and the impacts of many specific problems are, in fact, highly localized. Therefore, state-level decisions on criminal justice are likely to conform to the characteristics of a state's crime problems much more accurately than a congressional mandate is. A highly urbanized state like New York or New Jersey has a very different set of problems to deal with than a very rural state like North Dakota or Wyoming. Why should we expect that a homogeneous policy emanating from Washington would suit either of these kinds of states very well?

But state-level actions may be undesirable for the same reasons that federal actions are undesirable. Florida's experience with statewide sentencing guidelines and prison building provides a good example. A majority of the state's legislature, with its incentives to establish a symbolic get-tough policy, has created a commons problem of immense proportions. Prison crowding since 1987 has pushed more and more felons back out on the streets early. In an effort to prevent some kinds of felons from being eligible for early release, the legislature passed new statutes barring certain felons from early release and allowing prosecutors and judges to "habitualize" other felons with multiple convictions, thereby cutting them out of the early release program. But multiple drug felonies are just as easily habitualized as multiple violent felonies, so a court that wants to crowd the common-access state prisons with drug offenders still can. The result is near gridlock, as prisoners eligible for early release get out earlier and earlier until none remain, while the numbers of prisoners who cannot be released early grow. The threatened gridlock was alleviated at the last minute with a special legislative session in 1993 to allocate more money to prison construction rather than to attempt to rationalize the Sentencing Guidelines themselves. Such a rationalization of guidelines is unlikely, of course, because of the hard political decisions it would require. As with Congress, members of Florida legislative districts have little to gain from raising the tough issue that must be addressed in attempts to rationalize the criminal justice system. But the solution lies not in state policy per se: an alternative is increased reliance on local government. Dade County has demonstrated that it is willing to experiment with innovative programs that may reduce the need for prisons, for instance; but the state's undisciplined use of sentencing guidelines, and its siphoning off of tax revenues to build more common access prisons, constrain such experimentation. Why should it be constrained?

A policy of localized experimentation means that the officials who are elected locally are the ones who make the budgetary decisions that affect local citizens. Clearly, writing a letter to a county commissioner or a city council member is far more likely to stimulate a real response than writing to a state legislator or a member of Congress. The reason is that local officials can be held accountable for their actions, at least much more effectively than Congress or state legislators can. In this light, a policy that forces a local court to decide which of *its* prisoners to release when another prisoner is added to a crowded prison will induce the local courthouse gang members to recognize the consequences of their decision. They no longer have incentives to simply maximize the number of convicts that they can ship off to a common pool prison. Similarly, a police department that gets both its funding and its mandates regarding policing priorities exclusively through local channels is more likely to be responsive to the wishes of local citizens.

Will such localization really produce a rational drug policy as part of a rational criminal justice system? Perhaps, after all of the unconfirmed claims about the effects of drugs have been demonstrated to be either true or false. For one thing, through a process of localized experimentation, alternative policies are much more likely to be tried, so information about the consequences of various policy options is more likely to be available. If Dade County's experiments on alternatives to prison tend to reduce drug and crime problems more effectively than Broward County's "lock them up" approach, given that Broward County cannot export the costs of its approach, then Broward County citizens are much more likely to find out about it and demand a similar program. If Tampa's community-policing approach works better in producing a relatively safe environment than Fort Lauderdale's focus on drugs arrests and convictions, when Fort Lauderdale citizens bear the costs of its criminal justice approach they are relatively likely to demand community policing. The fact is that it is difficult to determine whether a policy is effective or not when the costs of some policies are localized while the costs of others are dispersed through the use of common access resources. Thus, experimentation is limited and there are fewer alternatives against which to compare any one policy.

Increasing the amount of information and the localization of costs and benefits would not just affect citizens' demand decisions, however. Although local bureaucrats have the incentives that are described in Chapter 6 to misinform when it is beneficial for them to do so, by making them at least relatively more liable for the undesirable consequences of misinformation, the chances of successfully rationalizing the criminal justice process would be relatively good. Police and prosecutors would have much weaker incentives to claim that drugs cause crime, simply to justify making seizures (particularly if they cannot retain them) or to build up their arrest and conviction statistics, for instance. After all, when they send a drug user off to prison, the result would be the release of another criminal back into the community. Thus, the tradeoff is localized and the question becomes: does the drug user pose a more severe threat to the community than the criminal who is released? Faced with this choice, police and prosecutors would have much stronger incentives to be concerned about the accuracy of their claims, both because information on alternatives is likely to be available and because the costs of their actions tend to be borne locally.

Consider an example. The uncompromising claim by so many criminal justice officials that drugs cause crime has prevented consideration of a policy experiment that might in fact reduce both crime and drug use. In today's criminal justice environment where courts, jails, and prisons are overflowing, a criminal generally has to commit and be arrested for a number of crimes before any real punishment is handed out. Anecdotes abound about juveniles committing and being arrested for dozens of car thefts before they are punished, for example. First-time offenders for most crimes are likely to get off with little or no punishment, particularly if they are juveniles. Convicted felons are about three times more likely to receive probation than they are to be incarcerated, and many probationers have multiple arrests and convictions. Prosecutors' say that their hands are tied by state statutes or by crowded prison facilities, or both, particularly for juvenile offenders. And they are, of course, at least to a degree. But prosecutors also exacerbate the problem when they apply policies that are based on a belief that drugs are the root cause of most of society's ills. If a juvenile crime cannot be shown to be "drug related," the crime can be brushed off as a teenage impulse that will be overcome with age. The result of such a belief, whether real or rhetorical, is that a drug offender is relatively likely to be given a prison term (or to be held in a juvenile facility), and that property or violent offenders are relatively likely to get probation or nothing at all. That this is the case is suggested by the fact that the portion of the prison population convicted for a drug offense grew dramatically throughout the drug war period. Beyond that, as suggested in Chapter 7, direct statistical analysis of the prison-versus-probation sentencing decision—using data from Florida—demonstrates that in Florida at least, drug crimes are more likely to produce a prison sentence than non-drug crimes.

Now step back from the belief that drugs are the primary cause of serious deviancy problems for a moment, and look at what might appear to be rather startling facts discussed in Chapter 3. Several studies of the temporal sequencing of drug use and non-drug crime among people who commit both types of offenses suggest that, for the majority, non-drug crime occurs *before* drug use starts. And this is not simply a matter of hours or days so that a person desiring drugs can accumulate money to make a buy. For example, a Bureau of Justice Statistics survey of prison inmates found that approximately half of the inmates who had ever used a major drug, and roughly three-fifths of those who used a major drug regularly, did not do so until *after their first arrest* for some non-drug crime, that is, "after their criminal career had begun" (Innes, 1988:1–2). Similarly, a survey of 395,554 jail inmates discussed in Chapter 3 found that more than half of local jail inmates who reported that they were regular drug users said that their first arrest for a crime occurred an average of *two years before their first use of drugs* (Harlow, 1991:7). Survey results may be questionable, of course, but these results are consistent with a number of other studies using other methods. The implication is that as individuals, and especially juveniles, get involved in the subculture of crime, they find that the criminal justice system actually does not appear to pose any real threat to them. Juveniles, in particular, are apparently very myopic. They consider only the immediate costs and benefits of their actions. When they learn that there are no real costs associated with committing crimes—even when they are arrested—because as first-time and even multiple-time offenders they get off with no real punishment, they tend to focus only on the personal benefits of the crime. Many of them apparently also begin to experiment with other illegal activities, including drugs.

A policy of punishing first-time criminals or even second-time criminals—so that they know that crimes are not costless—might not only divert such individuals from further crime, but it might move them out of the crime sub-culture where they eventually would find their way into drug use. However, for most criminals today, it is only after a large number of crimes and arrests that the rules are suddenly changed and a criminal finally gets some sort of punishment. By then the crime habit is firmly entrenched and, perhaps more significantly, the long record of criminal activity means that going straight may be impossible. Employers are not likely to consider someone with a record of large numbers of arrests, even if those arrests have not led to any punishment. By letting people commit a number of offenses before they are punished, a criminal cohort is created that has few options other than crime. A policy that tends to focus on drugs as the primary "evil" means that these kinds of individuals can move a long way down the path toward a "life of crime" before they are arrested for a drug crime (possession, sales, etc.) or a "drug-related crime" (i.e, a crime of violence associated with a drug deal, or a property crime with the proceeds used to purchase drugs) that warrants the attention of a "drug warrior" prosecutor.

Shifting criminal justice resources away from a focus on drugs toward a focus on non-drug crime, including early intervention and "treatment" of such crimes (perhaps traditional punishment; but perhaps alternatives such as a work program to earn money for mandated restitution to a victim, and efforts to enhance literacy), could actually prevent the development of both more significant criminal activities and of drug use among such criminals. This is important because there is substantial evidence that a very large portion of the crimes committed by drug users are committed by a very small portion of those users—the "career" criminal, so to speak. These are likely to be the kinds of individuals who commit large numbers of crimes before they are ever punished, perhaps despite a number of arrests. After all, most novice criminals are probably not very good at their crimes, so they are relatively likely to be arrested. When they discover that the costs of committing crimes are minimal, they can commit more, and they may learn how to commit them better. Thus, they reduce the probability of being arrested. Indeed, if they get good enough, they may be able to avoid arrest as they commit very large numbers of crimes before they get caught again, if they ever do. They are career criminals not because they are drug users, however, but because the criminal justice system has allocated its resources in such a fashion that they have been allowed to "go to school" and learn the criminal craft without paying any tuition.

Many people in the United States believe that criminals are not punished severely enough, while many other people, particularly in the academic community at least, believe that criminals are punished too harshly. But it may be that both of these views are correct for different subsets of criminals. In fact, as a direct consequence of getting tough on drugs, scarce criminal justice resources have been diverted away from the control of non-drug property and violent crimes. Empirical results discussed in Chapter 5 demonstrate that diverting police resources to make drug arrests can reduce the probability of arrest for other offenses, and therefore of punishment, and leads to more crime. Similarly, filling prisons with drug criminals forces the early release of other criminals. Getting tough on drugs has the inevitable consequence of getting soft on non-drug crimes. But because of the common pool nature of criminal justice resources, part of the costs of a jurisdiction's drug war are shifted onto citizens in other jurisdictions. Political action by citizens can ultimately slow the drug warriors' zeal, even without the reforms advocated here, because the costs do fall heavily on some people. Thus, victims groups, for instance, might put enough pressure on a state legislature or a local government to redirect the use of criminal justice resources toward the control of violent crime, at least for a period of time.

Nonetheless, we are left with a legacy from the drug war that continues to plague the criminal justice system, and with the potential for recurring policy cycles as new drugs are introduced and depicted as new sources of delinquency. Indeed, mandatory sentences for drug crimes, federal and state seizures laws, and other legislative actions produced in an effort to appear tough on drugs mean that drug control activity is not likely to return to its pre-1984 level, let alone to a level that might be an appropriate reflection of the true costs and benefits of drug enforcement. Significant changes in the institutionalized incentives facing criminal justice decisionmakers, from members of Congress down to patrol officers, are required to rationalize the system. Therefore, rather than fruitlessly advocate specific legislative actions regarding the criminalization or legalization of various drugs—which can subsequently be overturned by new legislative action—those who want a more effective use of criminal justice resources should be advocating greater decentralization of the criminal justice system. If drug warriors are correct in their claims that drugs cause many of society's problems, decentralized experimentation should provide evidence to that effect and the system will move toward stronger controls and more prisons. If legalizers are correct, the system will tend to evolve in the opposite direction. If neither side has all of their "facts" straight, something in between may be the outcome. As indicated throughout this book, the evidence as we see it suggests that the movement is likely to be away from a criminal justice focus on drugs toward a focus on community safety, and therefore on non-drug crime.[34] However, the evidence on the effects of drugs in a diversified society like ours is clearly limited by the relative homogeneity of criminal justice treatment of drugs across the United States. Perhaps localized experiments in criminal justice would prove us wrong. Whatever the outcome, however, it should involve a more efficient use of society's scarce criminal justice resources.

Notes

Chapter 1

1. The Gallup Poll, reprinted in the U.S. Department of Justice, Bureau of Justice Statistics (1991: Table 2.1).

2. Carmines and Stimson (1989: Ch. 1) contend that issue evolution is analogous to the natural selection process in biology. They argue that in both cases developmental paths are explicable after the fact, but are a priori unpredictable since they depend on context and chance. Carmines and Stimson believe that race is one of the rare instances of an issue with an enduring impact on U.S. politics.

3. Musto (1987:17 and 64).

4. The following quotations are drawn from Wisotsky (1991).

5. For an excellent discussion of America's historical experience with the prohibition of drugs and alcohol, see Zimring and Hawkins (1992:Ch. 3).

6. Schmoke (1989).

7. Wisotsky (1990), for example, identifies the launching of a drug war when President Reagan announced an increased commitment to tough drug enforcement in a radio speech on October 2, 1982.

8. We focus on state and local drug enforcement efforts, which account for the vast majority of the domestic effort against illicit drugs. Federal agencies take the lead in combating drugs when the source is in foreign countries and in efforts to curtail the importation of drugs. State and local agencies take the lead against the retail drug trade, while local, state, and federal authorities share responsibility for efforts directed against domestic production and wholesale distribution.

9. Recent books by Kleiman (1992) and Zimring and Hawkins (1992) are noteworthy exceptions to this tendency to polarize the debate on the proper role of law enforcement in drug policy.

Chapter 2

1. This does not necessarily mean that most property criminals are never caught, however. It actually means that many victims of property crime may have to wait a considerable period before the individuals who victimized them are apprehended, and that many may never actually recover their property or know that the individuals who stole from them have been arrested. For example, assume that half of all property crimes are reported (estimates on non-reporting from victimization surveys suggest that between 40 percent and 60 percent of various types of property crimes are not reported—see for example, Research and Forecasts, Inc. [1983:105]), so that the actual clearance rate is about 8 percent. The typical property criminal faces little risk of apprehension for a single offense; but

if he or she commits multiple offenses, the chances of being caught increase considerably. If the offenses are independent events, each with an 8 percent chance of apprehension, then the property criminal who commits five offenses faces a cumulative probability of arrest of .34. This cumulative probability rises to .56 to ten offenses, .81 at twenty crimes, and .92 at thirty. Of course, if property offenders also benefit from learning by doing, as it is suggested in Chapter 4 that drug suppliers do, then the crimes are not independent events and novices face a relatively high probability of capture (e.g., greater than .08 per offense) while experienced criminals face relatively low probabilities per offense. However, even for very experienced criminals the probability should not fall to zero, so eventually they should be apprehended. Imperfect policing does not necessarily mean that property criminals do not get caught; it means that they commit more crimes and create more victims before they are caught. And it means that while offenders probably are ultimately arrested, they generally are not punished for a large portion of the crimes they actually committed, so many victims never realize that the individual who victimized them has been arrested.

2. For general discussion of the commons problem see Hardin (1969), Gordon (1954), Johnson and Libecap (1989), and Hardin and Baden (1977). Applications of the commons analysis to the criminal justice system appears in Barnett (1986), Benson (1988, 1990, 1993), Benson and Wollan (1989), and Neely (1982, especially Ch. 6:164–186 on "Courts and the Tragedy of the Commons").

3. See Benson and Wollan (1989) for a brief discussion of such alternatives and additional references.

4. For example, a recent study stressed that "the war on drugs has led to an unprecedented growth in the nation's prison population, straining medical services in many institutions, which are being swamped by inmates. . . . In a study published last week in the *Annals of Internal Medicine*, three medical groups warn that massively overcrowded conditions in jails and prisons are creating a public health emergency" (Sandra G. Boodman, "Prison Medical Crisis: Overcrowding Created by the War on Drugs Poses a Public Health Threat," *Washington Post Health*, July 7, 1992:5). Overcrowding can result in multiple prisoners in single small cells, creating an environment that is much more conducive to the spread of diseases, while at the same time, medical staff and facilities are not being added at the same rate as prisoners are. For instance, in Illinois, where the prison population has grown rapidly in recent years, and money has been allocated to the construction of new prisons, there was no increase in the size of the Correction Department's medical staff. Medical expenditures per inmate have fallen dramatically. With approximately 10 million prisoners released each year, the increasing incidence of AIDS, hepatitis B, and especially tuberculosis in these crowded prisons also spills back out into the general population.

5. "More Judges Needed: While the Number of Drug Related Arrests and Cases Increase, a Serious Backlog Is Developing in the Courtroom," *Tallahassee Democrat*, May 28, 1991:3A.

6. Rationing by first-come-first-served adds to the commons problem because it means that resources do not necessarily go to their highest valued use. Consider an example. Many individuals and businesses have alarm systems with direct links to police stations. Studies of such systems have found a false alarm rate of over 95 percent (e.g., Kakalik and Wildhorn, 1971:29). The alarm industry itself has estimated a false alarm rate of between 95 and 96 percent. These false alarms have been attributed to a number of factors, including problems with equipment and subscriber error, with subscriber error accounting for 50–65 percent of the unwarranted calls. But a commons problem view suggests another consideration. Those using alarm services do not pay the cost of each policy response so they have no incentives to minimize those costs and, therefore, no incentive to minimize the number of false alarms. If users were liable for such costs, they would make far fewer "errors" and alarm companies would see that their equipment failed far less often. Recognize that the real cost of false alarms goes well beyond the outlay of police labor and equipment used to respond to these calls. The opportunity cost of those police resources must be seen as the alternative, considerably more valuable uses to which those resources could be put. Policy resources allocated to property crimes and police patrol resources respond, to a certain extent, on a first-call-first-served basis, so some real emergencies must wait to be served while police check false alarms. In many cases, delayed response can mean that a real crime will go unsolved. Furthermore, even if response to an actual crime is not delayed, police who are checking on a false alarm could be patrolling to deter crime (the use of police resources which may actually be the most cost effective way to address crime [Sherman, 1983]).

7. This section draws heavily from Benson and Rasmussen (1992).

8. These data on early release and prison construction are found in Illinois Department of Corrections (1989a:16–17).

9. Similar trends are indicated using "rating capacity" rather than design capacity. In 1984, for example, the Illinois prison population was roughly equal to rated capacity, but by 1988 the inmate population exceeded rated capacity by 1,384 inmates (Illinois Department of Corrections, 1989b:9).

10. See note 4.

11. About 11.6 percent of the crime victims in 1991 did not report the offense because they felt "police would not want to be bothered" or else were ineffective. Other reasons for not reporting crimes included "too inconvenient," "not important enough," and "other." Together these other reasons account for 17 percent of the 14.7 million crimes that were not reported, and also may be related to the quality of service. Assuming that having more criminal justice resources will result in better service and that victims would then perceive a decline in the implicit cost of reporting crimes together with enhanced benefits such as better prospects for prosecution, there could be a substantial increase in the caseload due to a higher percentage of victims reporting offenses (U.S. Department of Justice, Bureau of Justice Statistics, 1991, Table 112).

12. Discretion characterizes other bureaucrats in the criminal justice system as well. For instance, Phillips (1992) examined the consequences of the war on drugs for California prisons and parole agents. Between 1982 and 1988, drug admissions into the California prisons quadrupled from 8.5 percent to 35.4 percent of all prison admissions and increased the growth rate of new admissions by 25 percent. The increased flow of convicts into prison increased the outflow from prison to parole. Phillips (1992:98) found that as parole agent caseloads swelled, the agents were able to solve their crowding problem to a degree because the war on drugs had created a way for them to legitimately "exercise discretion." California parole agents have the ability to revoke parole if a parolee tests positive for drugs and they have the discretion to request such revocations. As their caseloads grew, their requests to revoke parole grew and, as a consequence, "the flow of parole violators returned to prison now exceeds the inflow of new admissions" (Phillips, 1992:99). Phillips' estimates suggest that this discretionary increase in parole revocations made the prison population approximately 25 percent larger than it would have been if parole agents had continued to supervise parolees in the same way that they had before 1982 when technical violations such as positive drug tests were much less likely to result in revocation.

13. These and following data come from Snell and Morton (1992).

14. These offenses include murder, manslaughter, sexual assault, robbery, aggravated assault, and burglary.

Chapter 3

1. Indeed, when addiction is defined as in Becker and Murphy (1988) to mean that consumption of a good in one period raises the desirability of consuming it in future periods, then the list of goods that are addictive goes far beyond those commonly identified drugs, including alcohol, nicotine, and caffeine. As Miron (1991:69–70) explains, if going to the opera for the first time teaches a person to appreciate opera, so that going to a second opera creates more enjoyment than going to the first, then opera is addictive. Similarly, if through repetition an individual gets better at something, like tennis, golf, or work, so that his or her enjoyment of the activity increases over time, then that activity is addictive. Thus the list of goods which economists traditionally study but which have addictive characteristics is probably huge.

2. Theft also fits this situation since it can be viewed as a production process with subsequent sale of the stolen property—for instance, see Vandaele's (1978) model of the market for stolen cars.

3. The preceding discussion focuses on the incentives to substitute in the face of a change in relative prices, but a price change has another effect as well: it changes the decisionmaker's overall purchasing power or "real income." Block and Heineke (1975) analyzed the criminal labor-supply decision in a way that is analogous to the usual work/leisure tradeoff in labor economics and showed that deterrence effects depend on whether leisure is a "normal" or "inferior" good (see

the next section for definitions of these concepts). This indeterminate effectiveness of enforcement holds when an explicit drug-supply decision is developed. See Rasmussen et al. (1990).

4. See Allison (1972); Fleisher (1966a, 1966b); Phillips, Votey, and Maxwell (1972); Leipziger (1975); Viscusi (1986); Myers (1983); Witte (1983); and Grogger (1991). In addition, almost all the literature cited on the deterrent effect of increasing the probability or severity of punishment also tests and supports the hypothesis that income and unemployment affect crime.

5. This appears to hold for drug dealers as well. Myers (1992) used a sample of California, Michigan, and Texas jail and prison inmates who were self-admitted drug dealers and found that the dominant factor contributing to entry into drug selling, particularly among black males, was unattractive market opportunities. Furthermore, racial differences in return to legitimate employment explained most of the gap between blacks' and whites' drug-dealing activities.

6. Much of this work has focused on recidivism. Recent examples include Kim et al. (1993); Myers (1980a, 1983); Hoffman and Beck (1984, 1985); Witte (1980, 1983); Trumbull (1989); Rhodes (1989); Schmidt and Witte (1988); and Barnett, Blumstein, and Farrington (1987, 1989).

7. The demand for insulin by diabetics is probably perfectly inelastic in relatively affluent societies.

8. There is a large literature outside of economics that addresses the issue of a drug–crime causal connection. See Wilson and Herrnstein (1985: Ch. 14) and Gottfredson and Hirschi (1990) for overviews on the literature. The "drugs cause crime" argument is based on the contention that drugs affect the mental and emotional state of users, making them aggressive or impulsive. The scholarly writing on drug policy generally recognizes the heterogeneity of drugs and drug user characteristics. However, this research does not suggest the simple connection between high rates of drug use and criminal activity that many policymakers perceive (Chaiken and Chaiken, 1990). Another view is that some of the same factors which influence the decision to commit crimes also influence the decision to consume illicit drugs; drug use and criminal activity are simply coincident symptoms of other problems including the lack of economic opportunity. Yet another characterization of the drug–crime relationship is that it is the illegality of drugs that produces the correlation between drug use and non-drug crime. Kaplan (1983) described four consequences of the fact that drugs are illegal: (1) the price of drugs is forced up, requiring users to acquire greater resources (this argument is discussed in more detail later in the chapter); (2) steady employment is difficult because of the time and effort required to find a safe source of supply; (3) holding any job becomes difficult because of arrests and general harassment by police; and, (4) drug users are forced into the criminal subculture by being forced to deal with criminals. These kinds of arguments all are predicated on the assumption that drug use and other crimes are highly correlated. Evidence discussed later in this chapter indicates that this may not be the case.

9. For a discussion of these issues see Rottenberg (1968), Erickson (1969), Koch and Grupp (1971), Holahan (1973), Eatherly (1974), White and Luksetich (1983), and Benson and Rasmussen (1991).

10. These points have been made by Gould et al. (1974); DuPont and Greene (1972); Levine, Stoloff, and Spruill (1976); Moore (1977); Silberman (1978); White and Luksetich (1983).

11. See Vaillant (1969), Silberman (1978), Baridon (1976), and Gould (1990:34).

12. It is a standard result of microeconomic theory that a monopolist will always maximize profit by setting price in the elastic portion of the market demand curve given no fear of entry and competition. Operation in the inelastic region of the demand curve in the short run might be explained as a promotional pricing scheme to stimulate long-term demand or as a deterrent to entry by competitive suppliers.

13. Estimates of the elasticity of drug demand are necessarily suspect. Even if accurate price data can be obtained by interviewing participants in the drug market, the quantity of purchases is extremely difficult to estimate. Quality of the product is also variable. In addition, as emphasized in Chapter 5, the ceteris paribus assumption might be violated if observed price changes reflect changes in enforcement effort, because a shift in enforcement effort may produce changes in income. If price increases due to enforcement activity are accompanied by increases in demand (not just movements along a stationary demand curve) because drugs are normal goods, then demand may actually be elastic.

14. It should be noted that heavy drug users (including addicts) can have several sources of income other than property crime, as explained in detail in Section IV. This is important because it illustrates how estimates of the level of property crime committed by drug users often are misleading. See Michaels (1987); Kaplan (1983). As Kaplan (1983) explained, these estimates often involve an assumption that all drugs are purchased with income obtained through property crime. Therefore the estimated amount of drugs consumed is multiplied by the estimated price of drugs to determine the predicted value of the property stolen to finance drug purchases. Through such a procedure, it was estimated that addicts supposedly stole ten times as much as was reported to police in all property thefts in New York City (Kaplan 1983:52). Underreporting of crimes by victims certainly cannot explain such a large discrepancy. Indeed, if the estimate of expenditures on drugs is anywhere close to being accurate, it would suggest that at most only about 20 percent of those expenditures could be generated through property crime. This acknowledges that victims apparently fail to report about half the property crimes they suffer (e.g., Research and Forecasts, Inc., 1983), and still assumes that all property crimes are committed by drug users. In other words, perhaps 80 percent or more of the drug using population are not involved in property crime. This is conjecture at this point, of course, but evidence presented later in this chapter suggests that this conjecture may not be too far off.

15. The possibility that rising drug prices do not lead to more property crime deserves more attention. After all, the downward-sloping portion of a backward bending labor supply curve is predicted on the notion that at some point a wage level is reached after which wage increases will induce the worker to choose more leisure and work less. In the case of rising drug prices and property crime, however, the illegal labor supply function is downward sloping at what presumably is a relatively low level of total income. This certainly suggests that drugs significantly distort the behavior of drug users in ways other than are often made explicit. The obvious question, however, is, why do these criminals not commit more crime when the real return to these offenses is higher? The traditional justification for the back-bending supply of labor is that as income becomes higher there is an incentive to reduce work effort in order to enjoy more leisure, but that does not appear to be a relevant option for low-income addicts. What then are addicts substituting for illegal work effort when the real return to such effort is relatively high?

16. Rasmussen et al. (1990) developed a criminal labor supply model that includes consideration of drug consumption and addiction as well as consideration of the impact of each on the decision to commit crimes. That model is summarized in this chapter without the technical (mathematical) analysis that is actually required to derive its conclusions.

17. Stigler and Becker (1977) and Becker and Murphy (1988) are the most prominent attempts by economists to model addictive behavior.

18. See Kozel (1985), National Institute on Drug Abuse (NIDA) (1988), and Kozel and Adams (1985) for discussions of fairly dramatic changes in drug use patterns.

19. The Becker and Murphy (1988) model of addiction is not directly adopted in the Rasmussen et al. (1990) model of criminal decisionmaking for a very simple reason. Becher and Murphy focus on the process of addiction, which requires a dynamic model. Rasmussen et al. (see note 16 above) were interested in generating comparative static predictions about the signs of various relationships in the context of the Block and Heineke (1975) criminal decisionmaking model. Therefore they accounted for many of the characteristics of addiction that Becker and Murphy did, but in the context of a static model. Varying levels of addiction can be accounted for in this case, but the dynamic reasons for these varying levels cannot be directly explained. They are discussed in Becker and Murphy.

20. Gill and Michaels (1990) and Kaestner (1991) use the National Longitudinal Survey (NLS) of the Work Experience of Youth in their analyses of the relationship between wages and drug consumption.

21. See Innes (1988). Among those inmates who had used drugs at all in the month prior to the offense, 35 percent had income from illegal sources, while 27.9 percent of those using drugs "regularly in the past" reported illegal income.

22. See Gandossy et al. (1980); Greenberg and Alder (1974); Innes (1988); and Harlow (1991).

23. See Anglin and Speckart (1988); Ball and Nurco (1983); Nurco et al. (1985); Nurco, Hanlon, and Kinlock (1991); and Johnson et al. (1985).

24. The figure (2.3 percent) approximates the proportion of a normal distribution that is more than two standard deviations above the mean number of felony arrests in the category. The source cited in Table 3.2 reports the mean and standard deviation for violent and non-violent felonies for each crime.

25. The 1987/88 *Annual Report* of the Florida Department of Corrections (various years) shows a marked difference between the average years of education claimed and the tested achievement level. For example, white male offenders admitted to state prison during FY 1987/1988 claimed 10.5 years of education, but tested at the 7.6 grade level. Black males claimed 10.5 years and tested at the 6.3 grade level.

Chapter 4

1. Moore is careful to point out the problems of estimating both the current price and the legal price. While too much should not be read into the precise estimates, there can be no doubt that the unregulated, untaxed cost of these commodities would be a fraction of their current street price.

2. Benjamin and Miller (1991) make this point that most drug users consume small quantities. They suggest that in the case of alcohol 10 percent of the drinkers account for 50 percent of total consumption. Tobacco, in contrast, has almost no casual users, with addicts accounting for almost 100 percent of the total consumption.

3. Estimates of the total consumption by frequent users are sensitive to assumptions regarding the number of users in any category. The 60 percent figure in the text assumes that users within the past year, month, and week each consume the drug twice during the relevant time period. NIDA's 1988 household survey yields a slightly higher estimate of the proportion of total consumption accounted for by frequent users (National Institute on Drug Abuse, 1988).

4. It should be noted that the number of frequent users rose to 862,000 in 1988 before falling to 662,000 in 1990.

5. As reported by NIDA in Drug Abuse Warning Network (DAWN) 1989.

6. Reuter, Crawford, and Cave (1988) and Cave and Reuter (1988) have argued this point, which is discussed in greater detail later in this chapter.

7. Buyers may be more valuable to sellers, since the seller must face added risk to replace a good customer. This suggests that there is an element of bilateral monopoly with uncertain price effects. However, to the extent that regular users are addicted to drug use, we would expect the seller to have an advantage in these negotiations.

8. Estimates of money prices are found in Moore (1990), and potency in Thornton (1991). As previously noted (see note 1), price data for illegal drugs are at best impressionistic and these conclusions must be viewed with caution.

9. *Narcotics Control Digest* (May 10, 1989); and Drug Enforcement Administration (various years), *Illegal Drug Price/Purity Report, United States 1987–1990*, March 1991.

10. See Moore (1990) and Thornton (1991).

11. Interdiction efforts are most effective against bulky shipments in non-commercial vessels, and the volume of marijuana necessary to make smuggling worthwhile means that much of it must be shipped in non-commercial vessels. Heroin and cocaine can be smuggled in economically profitable quantities that are much less bulky and, therefore, these drugs can be shipped in small private planes or in commercial vessels and planes. Note that increased interdiction efforts, which tend to affect marijuana more than other drugs, create incentives for smugglers to supply other drugs as well. See the discussion which follows in the text.

12. It was suggested above in the text that the price of marijuana adjusted for potency may have been fairly constant through the 1980s. The relative price of cocaine was falling over this period even when marijuana potency is taken into account, in part because law enforcement efforts against cocaine have been relatively unsuccessful.

13. Brecher (1972) and Siegel (1989) both suggested that marijuana and alcohol were substitutes because the first signs of large-scale marijuana markets appeared with the advent of alcohol prohibition. Similarly, following a highly publicized interdiction effort timed to coincide with the marijuana harvest in Mexico, a study of marijuana users was conducted to determine the impact of the resulting reduced availability. Over 50 percent of those surveyed reported an increase in alcohol consumption accompanying their decline in marijuana consumption (McGlothlin, Jamison, and Rosenblatt, 1970). A recent small-scale clinical study (Mendelson and Mello, 1985) further supports the expectation of substitutability as fourteen of the sixteen subjects studied consumed much less alcohol when both alcohol and marijuana were available. Thus, the results of the Model (1993), DiNardo and Lemieux (1992), and Chaloupka and Laixuthai (1992) statistical studies are not surprising. DiNardo and Lemieux (1992) found that a higher drinking age led to reduced alcohol consumption among high school seniors between 1980 and 1989, but it led to an almost one-for-one increase in marijuana consumption. Model examined the effect of marijuana decriminalization on hospital emergency room episodes (1993) and violent crime (1991), finding that decriminalization reduced episodes related to alcohol and other illicit drugs and reduced violent crime, and noting that a higher percentage of violent crime is alcohol related. Chaloupka and Laixuthai (1992) found that either lower money prices of marijuana or reduced legal sanctions against marijuana possession and use led to a substitution of marijuana for alcohol and to a significant reduction in non-fatal and fatal accidents from driving under the influence among youths. Similarly, higher prices of beer and increased drinking age led to more marijuana consumption and a reduction in traffic accidents associated with driving under the influence. Clearly, then, one unintended consequence of marijuana illegality is a greater level of alcohol consumption by youths, along with greater levels of traffic accidents and fatalities.

The implications of these studies will be discussed further in later chapters.

14. These effects are compounded because drug suppliers react to relative prices as explained further in the text.

15. Data on overcrowding come from U.S. Department of Justice, Bureau of Justice Statistics (various years, b), *Sourcebook, 1990*, Tables 6.51, 1.71; and U.S., Bureau of Justice Statistics (1992). See also Chapter 2.

16. See Chapter 2 and Benson and Rasmussen (1992).

17. A related effect may be at work. One factor that gives prosecutors bargaining power in a plea negotiation is that they can leave in jail an individual who cannot afford bail, waiting for a place on the crowded court docket. The longer the delay resulting from crowded courts, the stronger the prosecutor's bargaining position. In fact at some point this creates incentives for the criminal to plead guilty in exchange for a sentence of "time served." Thus, crowded criminal justice commons might increase the bargaining power of prosecutors. Of course, the prosecutor's bargaining strength may not actually increase at all if local jails become increasingly crowded and prosecutors face pressure to move cases along quickly to relieve this congestion.

18. See Chapple (1984) and Joe Davidson, "Marijuana Farming Buoys the Economy of Rural Kentucky," *Wall Street Journal*, December 24, 1992:1.

19. John-Thor Dahlburg, "Narcostan' Drug Land Rising from Soviet Union's Ashes," *Tallahassee Democrat*, June 7, 1993:4A.

20. These facts and figures were reported to one of the authors in a long meeting held on October 26, 1992, with Hernando De Soto, president of the Institute for Liberty and Democracy.

21. Kleiman (1992:299–300) points out there are strong incentives for sophisticated drug-dealing organizations to run a drug-free workplace because low-level dealers cannot support their habit on these illicit earnings.

22. Note that this discussion suggests that the individual's perception of the probability of arrest and of the severity of punishment depends on more than just observed data on arrests as a portion of total numbers of individuals involved in the activity. For individuals supplying their time to drug production and/or sales, perceived risks depend on characteristics of the individual as well as the law enforcement system. That is, individuals vary in their feelings about risk. For example, age may be a significant determinant of risk aversion. After all, punishment may be substantially less severe, in a relative sense, for a young person than it is for older members of society. In addition, an individual's opportunity costs (i.e., what the individual must give up when he or she is punished) influence his or her perception of the severity of punishment (Lott, 1990). Someone sentenced to a year in prison who could earn $100,000 during this same year will consider the sentence to be more severe than someone who can earn $10,000. Other individual characteristics can influence such perceptions (such as, someone who is married and has children may consider a jail term to be more undesirable than someone with no family).

23. *The Economist*, December 15, 1990:24.

24. Kleiman (1992:284) suggests that some marijuana growing shifted from Northern California to the mountains of Kentucky as a result of increasing enforcement. An unintended consequence of this change was to involve people whose cultural roots include moonshining and a history of violence, making the trade rougher than it had been before.

25. Reported by the Associated Press, "Billions Are Being Poured into a Losing Effort," *Tallahassee Democrat*, February 25, 1992:3A.

26. This subsection draws on Thornton (1991:Ch. 4).

27. This is supported by the fact that high school seniors report substantially increased availability of cocaine between 1985 and 1989.

28. Note that crack is not a "new" technology in the sense of being a new discovery. The knowledge necessary for producing crack has existed for some time. Indeed, virtually all of the technological changes that occur in the drug market involve the implementation of existing technology rather than new technology (Thornton, 1991). Below in the text, the reason for implementing previously known technologies in the drug market is explained further in the context of the discussion of increasing potency.

29. This subsection draws on Thornton (1991:Ch. 4).

30. It may be in the self-interest of law enforcement bureaucrats to make large seizures rather than small ones, so there may be a tendency to allocate relatively more resources to investigations that are likely to yield large seizures (see Chapter 6). Thus the probability of being detected with a large bundle of drugs is relatively high for yet another reason.

31. The limited number of observations meant that Thornton could not develop a more compelling test. Nevertheless, the results are consistent with prior theoretical predictions.

32. Zimring and Hawkins (1992:52) caution against using historical experience to evaluate current drug policies. The causal effects of prohibition will inevitably be affected by the very different social and political circumstances prevailing at that time. Nevertheless, it is useful to see if predictions based on economic theory are reflected in historical experience.

33. See Thornton (1991:100–105); Warburton (1932:148–166); and Fisher (1927b).

34. See Reuter, Crawford, and Cave (1988) and Cave and Reuter (1988). They emphasized drug smuggling, but the argument readily applies to all stages of drug production and distribution.

35. Note that a reputation for violence in the enforcement of contracts is valuable in a market where the legal apparatus of courts and police are not available for contract enforcement (Moore, 1990:139). Thus, as such a reputation develops over time, connections are less likely to break contracts and the need to use violence declines, both of which imply that transaction costs fall.

36. Furthermore, if the pool of experienced dealers becomes sufficiently stable, they may be able to form an effective cartel, thereby restricting the flow of drugs into the market and raising the price and their profits. In fact, Kleiman

(1985:Ch. 7) contended that since law enforcement efforts tend to eliminate the dealers who are least resistant to law enforcement efforts while leaving in place those who are most resistant, such efforts tend to exacerbate the organized-crime aspects of the drug problem. Of course the high profits earned by organized drug cartels make entry more attractive, so entry by novices would tend to limit the power of such a cartel.

37. See also Kleiman (1992,:Ch. 5).

Chapter 5

1. See Wisotsky (1992) for a summary of these issues.
2. See Furlong and Mehay (1981); Hakim, Speigel, and Weinblatt (1984); and Sollars, Benson, and Rasmussen (1992).
3. Benson and Rasmussen (1991); Benson et al. (1992); and Sollars, Benson, and Rasmussen (1992).
4. These calculations are drawn from Benson and Rasmussen (1991). The probability of arrest of .15 is the arrest/offense ratio for property crimes and is close to the U.S. average.
5. For the United States the drug arrest/Index I arrest ratio increased by 50 percent between 1984 and 1989. A 1 percent increase in drug arrests relative to Index I arrests led to a 0.199 percent decline in the probability of arrest for property crimes (Benson and Rasmussen, 1991:112).
6. Nationally, about one-third of all automotive fatalities are caused by drunk drivers (Kleiman, 1992:224).
7. Florida and Illinois may not be representative of all states in the nation, but they are typical of the large urban states which account for most of the anti-drug enforcement activity.
8. Kim, Benson, and Rasmussen (1992) reported that in Florida it appears that the courts followed the police lead in the war on drugs and metered out relatively tougher sentences to drug offenders than non-drug offenders during this same period. See also Chapter 7.
9. This discussion draws on Benson and Rasmussen (1991).
10. Illinois Department of Corrections, (1989a:21).
11. Of course some, like Florida, were under court mandate to restrict overcrowding.
12. Illinois Department of Corrections, (1989b:28).
13. See Kleiman (1992:62 and 140); Reuter (1991); and Miron (1992).
14. Reuter, MacCoun, and Murphy, (1990) indicated there was substantial risk of violence for drug dealers in Washington, D.C., during the mid-1980s. They estimated a regular drug dealer, defined as dealing more than one day per week, faced annual risks of 1.4 percent of being killed and 7 percent of being seriously injured. They argued that drug dealers in Washington, D.C., consider both the costs of violence and incarceration, suggesting that the high return to drug dealing was readily explained by the great risks of the enterprise.

15. For a more detailed analysis of spatial competition in drug markets, see Rasmussen, Benson, and Sollars (1992).

16. These and other unintended consequences of the Tampa Drug Task Force approach led to considerable dissatisfaction on the part of both citizens and police and ultimately to a new experimental program that changed the focus of policing in the city. This program is discussed in Chapter 8.

17. While this discussion focuses on adjacent jurisdictions, it readily applies to different precincts within a city.

18. This discussion is based on a large literature on the economics of location interdependence built on the work of Hotelling (1929).

19. There is virtually no evidence to support the frequently stated proposition that the demand for drugs is inelastic. Even heroin addicts change their use in response to price (Kaplan, 1983). For a summary of the evidence on this point, see Moore (1990), White and Luksetich (1983), Benson et al. (1992), and Chapter 3.

20. Goldstein (1989) discusses three sources of "systemic" violence in drug markets: (1) that resulting from competition among sellers; (2) that committed during robberies of drug market participants; and (3) violent acts between drug users, resulting from disputes over drugs. The latter is not likely to be affected by changes in the spatial distribution of drug markets so long as drug users do not change their place of residence as a result of changing drug prices. Goldstein is skeptical of the notion that much violence is spawned by the pharmacological effects of drugs. He also reports that there is little research evidence supporting the proposition that some drug users are compelled by economic necessity to engage in violence-prone property crime, (i.e., robbery).

21. See Sollars, Benson, and Rasmussen (1992); Mehay (1977); Kennett (1982); and McPheters and Stronge (1981).

22. The percentages of offenders under the influence of alcohol or drugs when committing property offenses were virtually identical, unlike the percentages for violent and public-disorder offenses. Of the property offenders, 48.9 percent were under the influence, with 18.2 percent using drugs, 17.9 percent using alcohol, and 12.8 percent using both (Harlow, 1991:10).

23. The director of the Federal Bureau of Prisons recognized in 1958 that "the drug user does not commit serious crimes of violence," and substantial amounts of evidence has come to light since then to support this conclusion (Miller, 1991:57–58).

24. This section draws on Benson (1981, 1988, 1990) and Benson and Baden (1985).

25. Most people want to think well of themselves, and many recoil at the idea that they or their colleagues could become corrupt simply because they have an opportunity for gain. However, almost everyone makes a distinction between "trivial breaches of policy" and corruption. Most people occasionally break speeding laws, for example—no doubt because of the small probability of being caught and the modest penalty. People are not bound to follow rules. Among persons in bureaucratic agencies, then, we expect a range of behavior—from a few

who slavishly follow procedure, those who have a flexible boundary that allows for variously defined trivial breaches of policy, and those whose scale of impropriety can only be labeled corrupt. To consider the possibility of corruption, therefore, should not be considered an insult to all public employees but instead is a simple recognition that no sector has a monopoly on virtue.

26. Testimony before the Mollen Commission, which was investigating widespread corruption among New York police officers in 1993, revealed that officers could make $8,000 per week protecting drug dealers (*New York Times*, September 28, 1993:A1).

27. This group loyalty among officers was also revealed in testimony before the Mollen Commission in 1993. One officer testified that instructors at the Police Academy instilled an "us against them" and "never rat against another cop" philosophy. The officer explained that "us were the cops and them were the public" (*New York Times*, September 28, 1993). Other testimony revealed that the Police Department systematically discouraged corruption inquiries (*New York Times*, September 29, 1993:A14).

28. *Tallahassee Democrat*, December 18, 1989:4B. Thornton (1991) notes that federal convictions of corrupt public officials increased from forty-four in 1970 to 1,067 in 1988.

29. Reaves (1992b).

30. These price data are for the fourth quarter 1990 from the Drug Enforcement Administration, *Illegal Drug Price/Purity Report*, United States 1981–1990, March 1991.

31. See Reuter and Kleiman (1986) for 1980 estimates of markups at different stages of production.

32. *Tallahassee Democrat*, December 18, 1989:4B. Compounding the financial incentives to cooperate with the drug industry is the implied threat if the offer is refused (Knapp, 1972:197).

33. See Cave and Reuter (1988) for a similar discussion of smuggling activities.

34. Ron Ward, "Ex-sheriff Convicted in Drug Case; Faces Sentence of Life in Prison," *Tallahassee Democrat*, July 16, 1993:2C.

Chapter 6

1. Bureaucrats often try to influence the demand side of the political process; see Berk, Brackman, and Lesser (1977); Congleton (1980); Breton and Wintrobe (1982); Benson (1983, 1990); Mbaku (1991). They have incentives to "educate" the sponsor regarding interest group demands which complement their own and to "propagate" their own agenda. Furthermore, they may have a relative advantage in the lobbying process because they have ready access to the sponsor, with whom they are often informally networked (Breton and Wintrobe, 1982:41–42), and they are naturally called upon due to their expertise. This is clearly the case with law enforcement bureaucracies (Glaser, 1978:22). Additional discussion of the role of bureaucrats as demanders of legislative action appears in Sections II and III of this

chapter.

2. Many states mandate that confiscated assets be turned over to a general government authority, while others require that some or all seized assets be used for specific purposes, such as drug treatment or education. Various states also limit the kind of assets that can be seized. For instance, in 1984, only seven states allowed seizure of real estate used for illegal drug activities. The federal statute had no such limitation.

3. See Reuter (1991); Benson and Rasmussen (1991, 1992); Benson, Kim, and Rasmussen (1994); Rasmussen, Benson, and Mast (1993); Benson et al. (1992); Sollars, Benson, and Rasmussen (1993); Rasmussen, Benson, and Sollars (1992); Zimring and Hawkins (1991); and see Chapter 5.

4. For example, see Stigler (1971); Chambliss and Seidman (1971); Peltzman (1976); Berk, Brackman, and Lesser (1977); Quinney (1970); McCormick and Tollison (1981); Neely (1982); and Benson (1983, 1990).

5. *Florida Annual Policy Survey*, Florida State University, Policy Sciences Center, 1991.

6. U.S. Department of Justice, Bureau of Justice Statistics (various years, b), *Sourcebook, 1990*:181. It is interesting that the percentage of respondents believing that more should be spent on crime rose noticeably in 1988 and 1989, the two years that also showed a marked increase in concern for drug addiction. These data suggest public opinion was following, not leading, public policy initiatives.

7. Fifty-eight percent of survey respondents in 1989 thought drugs were most responsible for crime in the United States. "Other" was the second most cited cause (19 percent), followed by unemployment (14 percent), and breakdown of family and society values (13 percent). U.S. Bureau of Justice Statistics, *Sourcebook, 1990*, Table 2.27.

8. This pattern fits what Downs (1972) called the "issue-attention" cycle, a tendency for initial enthusiasm for a policy initiative to wane as the cost and complexity of the issue becomes apparent. Breton and Wintrobe (1982:149) raise another possible explanation. In the face of the growing recognition by taxpayers that the war on drugs did not achieve its goals, perhaps police reduced their drug control efforts in order to control non-drug crimes. After all, as Breton and Wintrobe noted, over time, the perceived responsibility for the failure of a policy (e.g., crime control through the control of drug market activity) shifts from outside forces (e.g., the drug dealers, the recession, etc.) to the government; and within the government, it shifts to the bureaucracy, so pressure arises for bureaucrats to account for what is going on. The Breton–Wintrobe explanation is supported by the analysis and evidence which follows in the text.

9. In an as yet unpublished econometric study of congressional behavior in regard to drug legislation, Oerther (1992) found that some ideological factors relating to civil liberties and limited government did impact congressional voting on drug issues, but so did "drug prohibition pork-barrel spending." After controlling for these ideological and special interest factors, Oerther (1992:11) reported that the remaining determinant of legislators' support for prohibition is the

marginality with which they hold their office. The more a politician is in trouble with the voters and thus faces a significant challenge, the more is he or she likely to be a vocal promoter of prohibition and the traditional legal solution to drug problems. For the most part, this stems from the symbolic nature of drug prohibition as a patriotic but non-substantive issue, where the politician has little to lose and much to gain at election time by taking a get-tough-on-(drug)-crime and anti-civil liberties stance.

10. See Section 7(III) of the Anti-drug Abuse Act of 1988 for a detailed discussion of judicial discretion in this context.

11. A large literature has developed following in this Niskanen/Miquè–Belanger framework. See Toma and Toma (1980); Gonzalez and Mehay (1985); Benson and Greenhut (1986); Wyckoff (1988, 1989, 1990a, 1990b); Kress (1989); and Gonzalez, Folsom, and Mehay (1989).

12. This competition is multidimensional. It includes general competition for resources as well as competition for positions and promotions in the formal bureaucratic structure, along with membership in the informal networks that bureaucrats develop to facilitate non-market exchanges of benefits, information, and support between network members. Competitive strategies employed include the following: "(1) alterations in the flows of information or commands as these move through or across the hierarchical levels of the organization; (2) variations in the quality or quantity of information leaked to the media, to other bureaus in the organization, to special interest groups, and/or to opposition parties and rival suppliers; and (3) changes in the speed of implementation of policies as these are put into effect" (Breton and Wintrobe, 1982:37–38). These strategies and selective behavior in general are possible because of the way bureaucratic organizations and hierarchies work, including the fact that monitoring by sponsors is costly and the measurement of bureaucratic performance is generally difficult or impossible. Indeed, the use of such strategies can increase monitoring costs and make measurement of performance even more difficult.

13. See Musto (1987:13–14 and 21–22); Thornton (1991:56–60); Klein (1983:31–55).

14. Bonnie and Whitebread (1974); Helmer (1975); Musto (1987); and Nadelmann (1993).

15. See Himmelstein (1983); Becker (1963); Bonnie and Whitebread (1974); King (1957); Dickson (1968); Oteri and Silvergate (1967); Lindesmith (1965); Hill (1971); and Reinarman (1983). In fact, as Thornton (1991:62 and 66) and Morgan (1983:3) stressed, all of the various self-interests previously mentioned (bureaucrats; professionals from the American Medical Association and American Pharmaceutical Association; and groups attempting to suppress certain races or classes) interacted with still more groups (temperance groups, religious groups, etc.) to produce policies against drug use. Interest groups and bureaucratic entrepreneurs continue to dominate modern drug policy as well. These groups include "civil rights, welfare rights, bureaucratic and professional interests, health, law and order, etc." (Morgan, 1983:3). For instance, the pharmaceutical industry had a significant

impact on the Comprehensive Drug Abuse Prevention and Control Act of 1970 (Reinarman, 1983:19): "In this case as in most others, the state's policymakers were buffeted by law enforcement interests and professional interests."

16. See Stutmann and Esposito (1992) for a very revealing examination of the actual activities of a DEA agent and note the tremendous amount of time and effort that this agent spent in competing for resources. Note the significant role that politics played in determining the allocation of drug enforcement resources. The entire Stutmann–Esposito book could be easily set in the context of the Breton-Wintrobe model of bureaucratic entrepreneurship.

17. King (1957); Lindesmith (1965); and Klein (1983:32).

18. Becker (1963); Dickson (1968); Oteri and Silvergate (1968); Lindesmith (1965); Hill (1971); and Bonnie and Whitebread (1974).

19. This is suggested by the second strategy listed in note 12, and arises in part because of the high cost of monitoring bureaucrats.

20. Richards (1982:164). For details see Kaplan (1970:88–136) and Lindesmith (1965:25–34); Himmelstein (1983:60–62); Bennett and DiLorenzo (1992:237–239).

21. Lindesmith (1965); Kaplan (1970, 1983); Richards (1982); Michaels (1987); and Bennett and DiLorenzo (1992).

22. Note with Breton and Wintrobe (1982:152) that "one need not assume Machiavellian behavior, deceit, or dishonesty on the part of bureaucrats because in all likelihood the pursuit of their own interest will be as it is for everyone else veiled in a self-perception of dedication and altruism."

23. Once a prohibition policy is in place, police have incentives to make large drug seizures in order to demonstrate their effectiveness in controlling drug market activity, as noted in Chapter 4. In fact, as one of their "selective distortions," police have incentives to exaggerate the magnitude of the seizures they make. Thus drug seizures are always reported in terms of their "estimated street value" no matter what stage of the distribution and processing chain the seizure is made at. Claiming that pure cocaine has a value equal to its retail value after it has been processed and distributed as crack is like claiming that the two or three cents worth of wheat that goes into a loaf of bread is worth the dollar that consumers pay for that loaf of bread: it ignores the other inputs that must be added to turn the wheat into a marketable loaf of bread (i.e., transportation costs, processing costs, packaging, distribution costs, and advertising).

24. "Turning Drug Busts into a Profit Center," *Washington Post Weekly Edition*, April 8–19, 1991.

25. The role of informal networks within and across bureaucracies is very important in the Breton–Wintrobe model (1982:78–87, 99–106). These networks are the non-market institutions of exchange through which individual bureaucrats cooperate in order to obtain benefits. Thus, competition for positions in networks is also an important determinant of bureaucratic behavior (Breton and Wintrobe, 1982:99); and to the extent that this expanded network is able to generate more benefits for bureaucrats, competition to enter the network should intensify. However, competition for positions within a network actually tends to increase the

potential for discretionary or selective behavior in Breton and Wintrobe's (1982:103) model.

26. Stumpf (1988:327–332); Williams (1984:77-105); Benson (1990:132–146, 163–168).

27. Recall that North Carolina requires that all forfeited assets go to education.

28. "Turning Drug Busts into a Profit Center." *Washington Post Weekly Edition*, April 8–19, 1991.

29. This practice was revealed in a series of articles by Jeff Brazil and Steve Berry for the *Orlando Sentinel*, June 1992.

30. A twenty-one-year-old naval reservist had $3,989 seized in 1990, and even though he produced Navy pay stubs to show the source of the money, he ultimately settled for the return of $2,989, with 25 percent of that going to his lawyer. In similar cases the sheriff's department kept $4,750 out $19,000 (the lawyer got another $1,000), $3,750 out of $31,000 (the attorney got about 25 percent of the $27,250 returned), $4,000 of $19,000 ($1,000 to the attorney), $6,000 out of $36,990 (the attorney's fee was 25 percent of the rest), and $10,000 out of $38,923 (the attorney got one-third of the recovery).

31. Dennis Cauchon and Gary Fields, a series of articles on "Abusing Forfeiture Laws," *USA Today*, May 18, 1992.

32. As noted in note 2, only seven states allowed confiscation of real estate in 1984, but statutory changes increased this number to seventeen by 1988, and it reached forty-three in 1991.

33. A two-stage model was employed in recognition of the fact that the same things that influence the level of drug arrests in a state's major city might influence that state's asset seizure laws—a conclusion which was supported when the size of a state's police bureaucracy was included as an explanatory variable in the equation explaining the state's seizure law.

34. A National Institute of Drug Abuse (NIDA) field investigation in Florida and New York noted the existence of crack in the spring of 1985, but "the substance had limited recognition and availability" (Johnson 1987:36). The process through which crack came to the attention of policymakers and the public in late 1985 and 1986 is discussed below.

35. Stutmann and Esposito (1992:65–73) recount Stutmann's earliest entrepreneurial efforts as a DEA agent in Washington, D.C., whose initial work was directed against the heroin market. He then shifted his attention to marijuana on college campuses in 1966 after his arrest of an American University student for selling marijuana made the front page of the *Washington Post*. Indeed, Stutmann was ordered to drop heroin investigations and focus on marijuana because of the resulting publicity. When he arrested a congressman's daughter for possession of marijuana, the DEA's focus on marijuana in Washington increased even more, as "all of a sudden lawmakers were reading about their kids. Now they wanted marijuana stopped" (p. 66). Stutmann wrote that "in hindsight, I don't think any of these people should have ended up doing prison terms for using marijuana, but I don't have any regrets" (p. 67). Shortly after the arrest of the congressman's

daughter, Stutmann learned his "final lesson, one that would shape the remainder of [his] career": his supervisor ordered him to give a speech at a Lion's Club. Within a few months he was "speaking everywhere" and his "speech making began to get noticed in the higher reaches of government" (p. 72). He was on his way to becoming a very successful and competitive bureaucratic entrepreneur who could use the press and stir up interest group support through speech making and policy targeting. He learned that marijuana on campuses was a more politically viable target than heroin in the low-income ghettos; and this insight would serve him well twenty years later as he targeted his crack campaign, as discussed below in the text.

36. See Stutmann and Esposito (1992:150–153) for an interesting example of the networking process à la Breton and Wintrobe (1982), as Stutmann worked to establish relationships with various federal, state, and local police and with prosecutors and judges, and maneuvered around the demands and wishes of elected politicians (in this case, the mayor of New York).

37. Not surprisingly, with the de-emphasizing of heroin, the use of heroin began to expand in New York, particularly in the Chinese community (Stutmann and Esposito, 1992:154).

38. See the discussion of the implications of the NIDA surveys in Chapter 3 for similar conclusions about the addictive potential of cocaine.

39. "Turning Drug Busts into a Profit Center," *Washington Post Weekly Edition*, April 8-19, 1991:32.

40. For example, the *Tallahassee Democrat* has picked up a number of stories from other newspapers and news services with themes such as those in the following sampling: (1) from Knight-Rider's Washington Bureau: Aaron Epstein, "Tide of Opinion Turns Against Harsh Sentencing for Drug Offenders," May 7, 1993:4A; (2) from the Associated Press: Michael White, "Cases Indicate the War on Drugs May Be Overdoing It, " November 2, 1992:3A; (3) from the *Chicago Tribune*: Jon Margolis, "Punishment Should Fit Drug Crime," July 5, 1991:15A; and (4) from the *Miami Herald*: Ronnie Greene, "Skip Town, Judge Tells Drug Suspect," October 8, 1992:4C. Furthermore, significant negative coverage has been given to asset seizure policies; see the references to stories in *USA Today* (note 31) and the *Orlando Sentinel* (note 29), above. It is not obvious whether the media are leading or following public opinion in this regard.

41. But of course, the high THC content of marijuana being marketed today is a consequence of past and ongoing prohibitionary efforts, as explained in Chapter 4.

Chapter 7

1. Pruet and Glick (1986) argue that highly visible and controversial cases in which the "public interest" is obvious are not typical of the work of courts, and conclusions on the general representativeness of courts from such cases should be viewed with skepticism.

2. Peltason (1955:11) and Murphy and Pritchett (1961:274) both noted that

groups attempting to instigate wider roles for federal judges are typically those which consider their chances to be small when it comes to influencing selection of legislators and administrators who will represent their interests. Peltason listed several examples of this kind of interest group in the American experience, including Federalists, slave owners, industrialists, trade unions, racial minorities, and civil libertarians. Peltason's view of the court's role in the interest group form of government is consistent with the more recent position taken by Landes and Posner (1975), and supported empirically by Crain and Tollison (1979). These researchers argued that benefits gained through legislative actions are easily taken away if the beneficiary group is unable to maintain its position of strength. But it is more difficult for opposition groups to change rights assignments made by the courts, even if opposition groups become politically superior. As Peltason contended, groups that are not confident in their ability to obtain or maintain legislative support may attempt to gain their ends through the courts. Of course, one should not carry this argument too far. Court assignments of rights are not necessarily guaranteed. As Peltason (1955:55) noted, "No governmental agency necessarily has final word in any interest conflict. In the case of legislation or administrative agencies this is clearly recognized. . . . Yet a court decision is no more conclusive of interest conflict than a decision of other agencies. The constitution, or anything else, is what judges say it is only when the judges represent the dominant interest within the community." In the context of an interest group form of government, even the court's rulings are not permanent.

3. One of the most obvious channels of influence by interest groups is, therefore, in the recruitment of judges (and prosecutors). Eisenstein (1973:66–67) found that bureaucrats, lawyers, bar associations, and various other organized interest groups actively seek to influence judicial appointments at all levels of government. Several other studies have reached similar conclusions, including Schmidhauser and Berg (1972:81–99), Peltason (1955), and Blumberg (1970). There are good reasons for interest groups to try to influence judicial appointments. Some judges do not face reelection or reappointment, for instance; so, typical political tools of influence may be relatively ineffective (of course, if judges' interests in the criminal law arena are closely tied to prosecutors, as suggested below in the text, then the political pressures on prosecutors may feed through to judges). Thus, deciding who holds the office is a relatively more important avenue of political influence for judges than for legislators. Appointees may not wish to offend those who contributed to their past success. Indeed, judgeships are often "political rewards" for individuals who have demonstrated support for the desires of powerful interest groups. Those judges who do face reelection or reappointment or who aspire to higher appointment recognize that they will need the support of powerful groups, so they also tend to maintain the interests of their political sponsors. "In fact," Blumberg (1970:127) observed, "the *easy* decision is the one that is politically inspired."

4. Although elections are viewed as a real or imagined threat to the tenure of judges (Brace and Hall, 1990; and Drechsel, 1987), there seems to be a consensus

that judges' views on highly controversial issues are most likely to be influenced by the political demands. Kuklinski and Stanga (1979), for example, found California judges responded to the changing political environment regarding the possession of marijuana.

5. It should be noted that judicial behavior could be changed due to the direct incentive of a reduced chance of retention when judicial rulings represent unpopular views (e.g., relative leniency toward drug offenders) or by the fact that a judge's views are altered by the same forces affecting other members of society.

6. These determinant-sentencing plans attempt to reduce sentence disparities, so similarly situated offenders get similar sentences. In practice, judges retain considerable discretion under the guidelines, which usually allow substantial deviation when the judge provides justification. In Florida, for example, over 5,000 persons were sentenced to prison in 1990 even though the guidelines recommended a non-prison sanction (as reported at the Florida Joint Legislative Management Committee's Criminal Justice Estimating Conference in 1991). Similar discretion is allowed under federal guidelines (Katzenelson and McDanal, 1991). Legislatures may be more effective in limiting judicial discretion when they impose mandatory minimum sentences.

7. Anderson, Shughart, and Tollison (1989) suggest this possibility when they argue that chief justice salaries should be higher in states with a higher level of legislative activity since legislation raises the potential workload of the courts. Their empirical results are consistent with this hypothesis.

8. There is a natural divergence of interests between public defenders and prosecutors in this regard, for example. Public defenders will find their job easier when proposed settlements are readily acceptable to their client—an outcome that is most easily achieved when the penalty for the crime is relatively modest. Prosecutors can most easily get a conviction via an acceptable plea when the legislated penalty is severe, since the defendant will agree to a more stringent penalty as the potential penalty from a trial rises.

A recent effort to reform Florida's Sentencing Guidelines provides evidence in support of this concern for workload and divergent interests by observing how public defenders and prosecutors respond to proposed changes in sentencing. As part of this effort, in 1991 a division of the Joint Legislative Management Committee asked twenty public defenders and twenty prosecutors to evaluate a proposed ranking of offenses by degree of severity. Offenses were ranked from one to ten, with higher numbers reflecting greater severity. For each group a weighted average degree of severity was calculated for every offense. For example, if 90 percent of the prosecutors felt an offense should have a severity index of two while 10 percent believed it should be a level-three offense, the average weighted severity index would be 2.1 ([0.9 x 2] + [0.1 x 3]). This recommended severity index was compared to the severity level proposed in the report. Prosecutors and defenders were assumed to reject the proposed measure only when their recommended severity index differed from the proposed value by 0.5 or more.

The survey responses are consistent with the hypothesis that both prosecutors and public defenders advocate changes that make their jobs easier. The report ranked 167 offenses, and prosecutors had twenty-two instances when their weighted severity index differed from that of the report. Twenty of these discrepancies were in the direction of greater severity, while only two recommended a lesser penalty. Greater severity of punishment gives the prosecutors more leverage to secure a guilty plea bargain without going through a time-consuming trial. In sharp contrast, the survey responses of public defenders had a weighted severity index that differed from the report in thirty-five instances, thirty-four of which recommended a lesser sentence. By recommending a lower penalty applicable to an offense, public defenders can avoid trials by making it easier to secure a plea bargain acceptable to the defendant. When confronted with an opportunity to change the severity of criminal offenses, these public officials recommend changes that would tend to reduce their own workload. Despite this, however, the fact that the average level of plea bargaining has not changed markedly for decades and does not differ substantially across jurisdictions (Jones, 1979) suggests that these differing views do not stand in the way of cooperation.

9. One strand of the political science literature argues that judges, prosecutors, and public defenders create a courtroom elite and develop group norms regarding appropriate sentences (Pruet and Glick, 1986; Nardulli, 1978; Heumann, 1978). The argument presented here is not in fundamental conflict with this view, although here behavior is rooted in the personal interest of the players: concerns for retention may be limited to public defenders and prosecutors, while all are concerned with controlling the workload.

10. See Stutmann and Esposito (1992:150–153) for an example of the networking process involving the establishment of relationships and deals between the DEA and various federal, state and local police, prosecutors, and judges. For instance, when the New York DEA head was starting to redirect the focus of his office toward crack, as discussed in Chapter 6, he went to see his long-time friend, Special Narcotics Prosecutor Sterling Johnson, Jr., who "held the purse strings for state narcotics buy money" and who handled state court prosecutions in all five counties of the city. Stutmann told the prosecutor (p. 151): "You open your checkbook for my undercover. I'll bring my best cases to you when they don't have to go federal. I know you always want to prosecute hard." In Stutmann's mind he had "promised the prosecutor the one thing he wanted. Good cases"; and Sterling's chief assistant, Bob Silbering, responded, "Your guys stop acting like we're second-class citizens and Sterling will treat you right."

11. If judges have the same incentives as prosecutors and police, then the motivation for choosing the easy cases and avoiding the difficult, time-consuming ones might be to increase some statistical measure of performance. But it is not at all clear that this is the only, or even the primary, reason for such behavior. In this instance, the judicial bureaucracy may appear to differ from police and prosecutors. But remember that police rely on more than just arrest statistics to justify their budgets; high crime rates are also an indication of greater need for

police services. In the case of judges, the tremendous excess demand for their time arising in the common pool for court services may be a more powerful argument for an expanded budget than a statistical measure of output. Under these circumstances, indication of some "adequate" level of output given expectations based on historical performance may be desired, but production beyond that level could imply less need for additional resources. Therefore, "since judges can blame the court system's failure on others—on society's lack of consensus or society's parsimony in funding supporting services—there is no gnawing sense of shirked responsibility on the part of the judiciary. This is a convenient attitude; a gnawing sense of inadequacy would suggest a great deal of very hard work" (Neely, 1982:44).

12. The conclusions that Jones and other analysts reached may be too strong. Clearly, plea bargaining is a function of the court backlog, as judges and prosecutors claim—just not in the way that they claim it is. Because those who bring cases do not pay prices that cover the full marginal cost of trying those cases, the commons problem arises and court congestion results. Price is an allocating mechanism; and when price is not used, other discriminatory rationing mechanisms; take over. It is the congestion problem resulting from non-price rationing that gives prosecutors and judges the discretionary power to selectively ration trials and plea bargains. This does not deny the conclusions reached by Jones and others: it simply requires that they be reinterpreted. The evidence indicates that although plea bargaining occurs because of the case backlog, increasing resources allocated to prosecutors and the public courts to reduce the backlog are not likely to affect the portion of cases settled through plea bargaining. The congestion problem will not go away, at least not without a tremendous influx of resources, given the relatively low price of litigation (relative to costs). Besides, the bureaucratic incentives for expansion mean that the existence of delays and plea bargaining provide "justifications" for larger budgets and bureaus. Adding more personnel has never changed the ratio of plea bargaining cases to tried cases, as Jones demonstrated, and it is not likely to do so in the future.

There is little doubt that the level of plea bargaining is at least in part a function of the incentives arising in bureaucratic institutions of the criminal justice system. This rationing mechanism benefits bureaucrats by providing an argument for expanding bureaucratic budgets and resources and provides a means of generating conviction statistics without the danger of losses when cases go to trial. Criminal justice resources must be rationed, of course, because they are not allocated by a pricing mechanism and willingness to pay. Without such rationing mechanisms, congestion and delay would be even greater. Therefore, they often appear to be desirable. But other rationing techniques could be chosen (Benson, 1990; Schulhofer, 1988).

13. As an indicator of the increased bargaining strength of prosecutors, note that prosecutors have changed the rules of the game under which the plea bargain takes place. In 1974, 80 percent of the chief prosecutors in the state courts had explicit criteria and time limits on plea negotiations, but that percentage was down

to thirty-six in 1990 (Dawson, 1992:6). Prosecutors must feel that they are in a position to force pleas if they are willing to leave defendants in jail for uncertain periods. Of course, this change in the rules itself will create greater uncertainty for defendants and therefore create stronger incentives to plea.

14. Elected public defenders and private defense attorneys are in a more interesting situation since "success" means more accused offenders are declared innocent or get off with lesser sentences. However, the drug war unambiguously creates a greater workload for public defenders, and handling more cases strengthens their claim that more resources are required in order to facilitate the flow of offenders through the criminal justice system. Similarly, it created an opportunity for defense attorneys to increase their turnover. Given the evidence of long-standing plea bargaining arrangements, these parties should continue to cooperate with prosecutors and judges; but because they are bargaining from a weaker position due to legislated increases in potential sentences, the prediction made here is expected to hold.

15. Under Florida's Sentencing Guidelines repeat offenders are treated more severely than those appearing before the court for the first time. If more repeat offenders are convicted for one offense category, say burglary, we would expect a larger proportion of the population to be incarcerated. The increased rate of imprisonment reported here, then, provides an imperfect benchmark for comparison since the relative number of multiple offenders is not considered.

16. Cocaine possession is a second-degree felony, while possession of more than twenty grams of marijuana is a third-degree felony.

17. These data were provided by the Economic and Demographic Division of the Florida Legislature and updated by the Bureau of Planning, Research, and Statistics, Florida Department of Corrections. The data are discussed in some detail in Chapter 3.

18. This relatively large portion of repeat offenders receiving probation is an indication of the degree of discretion judges have under Florida's Sentencing Guidelines. Under these guidelines, virtually all persons previously sentenced to prison would be given additional points for each count of previous offenses, suggesting that a mechanical application of the guidelines would result in incarceration.

19. It is important to remember that the race variable can only be interpreted as a control variable, since many relevant human-capital and background variables that may be correlated with race are not included.

20. The coefficients for sale and possession are very similar, a surprising result if sale of drugs is viewed as a more severe offense than narcotics possession. In fact, the distinction between the two categories is muddied by the fact that sale includes "possession with intent to deliver." Charge bargaining also blurs the line between the two; so on average, defendants in the two categories may be quite similar for purposes of sentencing.

21. Indeed, many law enforcement officials will freely admit that their drug war efforts were in vain and probably never can be successful. For example, the former

New York DEA head noted (Stutmann and Esposito, 1992:225–6): "There is no way for law enforcement to keep up the kind of pressure that we applied to Washington Heights [as discussed in Chapter 6]. And that is what increasingly has troubled me about a law enforcement response to what is so clearly a social problem. . . . the effect [of breaking up two important crack rings] on crack dealing was, in the long run, minimal because [dealers]. . . are all easily replaceable if America continues to have an insatiable appetite for drugs. No cop with a gun will ever stop the craving, no occupying army can shut down the flow."

22. See Chapter 5.

23. Drug Enforcement Administration (various years). And see Chapter 4 for details.

Chapter 8

1. Office of National Drug Control Strategy (1989:17).

2. U.S. Department of Justice, Bureau of Justice Statistics (various years, b), *Sourcebook, 1991*, Table 2.83. Opinions regarding legalization are probably becoming somewhat more tolerant since the peak of the drug war in 1989. In that year 16.7 percent of college freshman thought marijuana should be legalized. By 1991 this percentage had increased to 20.9 percent. Surveys of high school seniors show a similar trend. See ibid., *Sourcebook, 1991*, Tables 2.68 and 2.70.

3. See Wisotsky (1990) and Nadelmann (1989). With respect to protecting children, Wisotsky writes that this priority "is self evident and needs no discussion . . . it is the only domain in which 'zero tolerance' makes any sense at all" (p. xxvii).

4. September 22, 1989.

5. Benjamin and Miller (1991) and Haaga and Reuter (1990) also advocate a decentralized approach to drug policy.

6. Wilson (1990a:23) explicitly recognizes that marijuana is substantively different from cocaine and heroin: "I do not here take up the question of marijuana. For a variety of reasons—its widespread use and its lesser tendency to addict—it presents a different problem from cocaine and heroin."

7. Zimring and Hawkins (1992:100) claim that "Wilson sees all illicit drugs as representing an equal threat to 'the moral climate' and as indistinguishable items in the total of 'tangible but real moral costs' of drug use." While the Office of National Drug Control Strategy (1989) can be tarred with this brush, it does not seem appropriate to use it on Wilson. In his discussion, Wilson uses the term "drugs" loosely, but he regularly emphasizes the egregious nature of heroin and cocaine, as noted in the passage cited in the text.

8. Alternative explanations for having a czar are the unlikely possibility that the name is associated with effective and efficient public policy or, more cynically to the point, a willingness to compromise fundamental constitutional rights to fight the war on drugs. For discussion of legal implications of rising drug enforcement see, for example, Wisotsky (1990).

9. These data are drawn from the National Institute of Justice (1991). Similar variation is exhibited in drug-related deaths; see Haaga and Reuter (1990).

10. A personal communication cited in Reuter (1991:10).

11. It is not even clear that these are appropriate roles for the federal government in all cases. For instance, if some state chooses to legalize the consumption of some drug, is it appropriate for the federal government to interfere with the importation of that drug? Furthermore, even if interdiction of imported drugs is an "appropriate" function of the federal government, there is substantial evidence that it is not likely to be very successful (see Chapter 4, and Cave and Reuter, 1988), and therefore, it is very possible that the costs will be greater than the benefits. Perhaps an interstate commerce function would remain if different states choose to treat certain drugs differently; but if some states wish to maintain relatively expensive prohibition policies, perhaps their citizens should also bear the costs of maintaining those policies, rather than shifting that cost into the common pool of federal revenues. Finally, inasmuch as the nature of the outcome of "research and evaluation" can be shaped by the political agenda of either the researcher or the persons controlling the source of the funds for the research, it may be that this could be an avenue through which federal influence can homogenize local policy. For instance, DiNardo (1992) reviews the studies which have attempted to quantify the costs of ADM (Alcohol Abuse, Drug Abuse, and Mental Illness) disorders and, by inference, the benefits of treating them. He finds that large numbers of studies focus on specific drugs and do not consider substitution effects. Thus, the costs associated with any particular drug's use tend to be exaggerated because efforts to limit that drug's availability produce substitution effects, and therefore raise the costs associated with other drugs. These substitution effects are important, as stressed in Chapters 3 and 4, helping explain the increased use of both cocaine and alcohol following law enforcement successes against marijuana. DiNardo (1992:20) concludes that he does not believe that the researchers who produce these studies "have an agenda or deliberately skew their arguments" but that these kinds of studies continue to proliferate "because there exists a demand for them" as "part of the claims making activities of government bureaucrats." The point is that both information and misinformation can be used to motivate a policy, as stressed in Chapter 6, so even the information-producing function of the federal government deserves close scrutiny.

12. Federal penalties for marijuana possession were made somewhat tougher in the Anti-drug Abuse Act of 1988 compared to the 1982 act. For multiple prior cases of possession, the penalty had been no more than a two-year prison term and no more that a $10,000 fine. The discretion left to judges to give lenient sentences was eliminated in 1988: the sentence length was between ninety days and three years and a minimum penalty of $5,000.

13. See Chapter 5. Also see Sollars, Benson, and Rasmussen (1994); and Rasmussen, Benson, and Sollars (forthcoming).

14. As noted in Chapter 4, Moore (1990:24) estimated that cocaine sold at about eight times its expected legal price, while marijuana and heroin sold at much

higher markups.

15. One could argue that spraying marijuana crops with paraquat, which increased toxicity, was an intended effect of the policy.

16. See Chaloupka, Saffer, and Grossman (1993), for example. Most econometric models of illegal drinking behavior generally ignore the effects of enforcement, and neglect the possibility that price can be capturing the effects of other attributes of states. In short, since these models may be misspecified, the conclusions of these studies should be viewed with caution.

17. Indeed Miron (1991) suggests that the increased consumption should be viewed as a benefit of legalization because when a fully informed individual chooses to consume something, including a potentially addictive drug, this choice is made because the individual expects the benefits of doing so to exceed the costs. If the externalities associated with drugs actually arise by and large as a consequence of prohibition, then they would tend to disappear with legalization, and all that remains is the personal net benefits of consumption. Thus, from this libertarian perspective, the fact that drug consumption might increase does not imply that legalization is undesirable. And even if there are still negative externalities associated with drug consumption under legalization, the relevant question becomes whether those externalities are greater than or less than the externalities that arise from the efforts to impose a prohibition policy (Miron, 1991:70–71).

18. There is an important caveat to this statement. A libertarian is willing to let individuals do anything they want as long as they are prepared to suffer the consequences. In modern societies, of course, drug users are often shielded from some of the consequences by the availability of welfare payments and subsidized medical care. With so many conditions of the libertarian's ideal world being violated, it does not necessarily follow that breaking one fewer condition is preferred. See Benson (forthcoming, b) in this regard.

19. DiNardo and Lemieux (1992), Chaloupka and Laixuthai (1992), and Kleiman (1992). Meier (1991) hypothesized that alcohol producers and tavern owners would lobby for tougher state laws against marijuana in order to stimulate demand for their products. The empirical results support this hypothesis for tavern owners but not for alcohol producers.

20. Cuskey, Berger, and Richardson (1978:520) argue that the "intoxicating effects [of marijuana] are usually non-aggressive in nature and may actually act as a deterrent to physically exertive criminal activities." Traffic safety may also increase if alcohol-impaired drivers are more aggressive than those under the influence of pot.

21. Indeed, as explained in Chapter 5, relatively aggressive drug enforcement policy tends to "export" problems related to illicit drug markets, even when not all drug offenders are successfully apprehended and sent to a state prison. As drug market participants move to less aggressive policing jurisdictions, they take with them the problems that arise with an active illegal market, such as violent confrontations over turf. Furthermore, less aggressively prohibitionist jurisdictions may attract more drug users who put a strain on the medical and welfare facilities

as well as increasing the level of violence and other crimes, to the extent that these crimes are associated with drug markets.

22. U.S. Department of Justice, Office of the Attorney General (July, 1992:22).

23. A similar issue arises in the anti-trust literature regarding potentially perverse incentives associated with treble damages. If the object of treble damages is to deter undesirable behavior, it is not apparent that the plaintiff should receive the trebled damages as compensation. Polinsky (1988) argues that the extra damages should be decoupled from the plaintiff's compensation.

24. See Benson et al. (1992); Benson, Rasmussen, and Sollars (1992); and Chapter 6.

25. Lawrence (1991) describes the breakdown of the Minnesota system. Florida, another innovator in using guidelines, created a system that ignored prison capacity. Over time, guidelines were eroded in a variety of ways, including the legislative approval of minimum mandatory sentences and habitual-offenders statutes. See Rasmussen, Benson, and Kim (1991) for an evaluation of the impact of these policy innovations on the allocation of prison space.

26. See Benson (1990:152–154) for a discussion of political actions by organized victims.

27. It is important to recall that prosecutors also play an important role in influencing crime policy by affecting legislation, as noted in Chapter 6.

28. This comparison is not strictly accurate in that the actual change would not be in the number of inmates, but rather in inmates serving a greater portion of their sentences. Nevertheless, these data give an accurate picture of how these counties vary in their use of the prison commons in Florida.

29. The Dade County prosecutor who cooperated in the creation of this program was Janet Reno, U.S. attorney general in the Clinton Administration. See Finn and Newlyn (1993) for a description of the court's development and activity.

30. A version of this approach is found in Benson and Wollan (1989). A common complaint to this proposal is that keeping track of these offenders would overly tax the prosecutor's office. In this era of inexpensive information management, this problem seems exaggerated. More to the point, since relatively few offenders are responsible for a large portion of crimes, one could argue that such a data base is required for the efficient operation of a prosecutor's office.

31. This policy obviously requires the same careful ranking of the seriousness of offenses that is needed for sentencing guidelines. The difference is that the ranking takes place at the local level in reflection of community concerns. As noted above in the text, this relative ranking of offenses is required for the efficient use of prison resources. With respect to drug offenses, we would expect that all persons whose record consists of possession offenses (perhaps including even those who have sold small amounts to support their drug use) would be in the pool of offenders to be sentenced to the courts' allotted prison space. Depending on the political preferences of the state and/or locality, however, persons whose drug use is combined with a record of violent crime might be considered for the state's pool of beds not eligible for early release. Drug use (including alcohol) could be

considered in sentencing and, in cases where the individual has a substantial record, could be an aggravating circumstance.

32. In states with a sales tax it might mean an increase in this rate imposed at the local level, while states with an income tax could simply add a fixed surcharge on returns filed from the offending jurisdiction.

33. An obvious problem in garnering substantive support for rational reform is the fact that it is much more difficult to explain to the public than a policy of "getting tough." Throwing criminals in prison is a policy that fits in a thirty-second soundbite more easily than an explanation of the tragedy of the commons. Perhaps one antidote to this problem would be rhetoric arguing that getting tough on minor drug criminals has the effect of being soft on violent crime.

34. It should be noted that our interpretation of much of this evidence is not unique. The "drugs-cause crime" hypothesis has been rejected by many others, for instance, as suggested in Chapters 3 through 5. Indeed the U.S. Justice Department's Bureau of Justice Statistics recently compiled a 208-page report on "Drugs, Crime and the Justice System" that concludes that the relationship between drug use and crime is far from certain. See a brief discussion of the report in Dan Baum's "Study Refutes Link Between Drug Use, Crime," *Chicago Tribune*, May 4, 1993, section 1, p. 2.

References

Allen, David F. "Introduction." In *The Cocaine Crisis*, edited by David F. Allen. New York: Plenum Press, 1987.

Allison, John. "Economic Factors and the Crime Rate." *Land Economics* 48 (May 1972):193–196.

Anderson, Annelise. *The Business of Organized Crime*. Stanford: Hoover Institute Press, 1979.

Anderson, Gary M., William F. Shughart II, and Robert D. Tollison. "On the Incentives of Judges to Enforce Legislative Wealth Transfers." *Journal of Law and Economics* 32 (April 1989):215–228.

Anglin, M. Douglas, and George Speckart. "Narcotic's Use and Crime: A Multisample, Multimethod Analysis," *Criminology* 26 (1988):197–233.

Ashley, Richard. "Heroin: The Myths and Facts." New York: St. Martin's Press, 1972.

Ashman, Charles R. *The Finest Judges Money Can Buy*. Los Angeles: Nash Publishing, 1973.

Axelrod, Robert. *The Evolution of Cooperation*. New York: Basic Books, 1984.

Ball, J. Shaffer, and David Nurco. "Day to Day Criminality of Heroin Addicts in Baltimore: A Study in the Continuity of Offense Rates." *Drug and Alcohol Dependence* 12 (1983):119–142.

Baridon, P.C. *Addiction, Crime, and Social Policy*. Lexington, Mass.: D.C. Heath, 1976.

Barnett, Arnold, Alfred Blumstein, and David Farrington. "Probabilistic Models of Youthful Criminal Careers." *Criminology* 25 (1987):83–107.

———. "A Prospective Test of a Criminal Career Model." *Criminology* 27, no. 2 (1989):373–388.

Barnett, Randy E. "Public Decisions and Private Rights." *Criminal Justice Ethics* (Summer/Fall 1984):50–62.

———. "Pursuing Justice in a Free Society, Part One: Power vs. Liberty." *Criminal Justice Ethics* 4 (Summer/Fall 1985):50–72.

———. "Pursuing Justice in a Free Society, Part Two: Crime Prevention and the Legal Order." *Criminal Justice Ethics* (Winter/Spring 1986):30-53.

Becker, Gary S., Michael Grossman, and Kevin Murphy. "Rational Addiction and the Effect of Price on Consumption." *American Economic Review* 81, no. 2 (May 1991):237–241.

Becker, Gary, and Kevin M. Murphy. "A Theory of Rational Addiction." *Journal of Political Economy* 96 (1988):675–700.

Becker, Howard. *Outsiders: Studies in Sociological Deviance*. New York: The Free Press, 1963.

Beigel, Herbert, and Allan Beigel. *Beneath the Badge: A Story of Police Corruption*. New York: Harper & Row, 1977.

Benjamin, Daniel K., and Roger L. Miller. *Undoing Drugs: Beyond Legalization.* New York: Basic Books, 1991.

Bennett, James T., and Thomas J. DiLorenzo. *Official Lies: How Washington Misleads Us*. Alexandria, Va.: Groom Books, 1992.

Benson, Bruce L. "Corruption of Public Officials: The Black Market for Property Rights." *Journal of Libertarian Studies* 5 (Summer 1981):305–311.

———. "The Economic Theory of Regulation as an Explanation of Policies Toward Bank Mergers and Holding Company Acquisitions." *Antitrust Bulletin* 28 (Winter 1983):839–862.

———. "An Institutional Explanation for Corruption of Criminal Justice Officials." *Cato Journal* 8 (Spring/Summer 1988a)139–163.

———. "Corruption in Law Enforcement: One Consequence of 'The Tragedy of the Commons' Arising with Public Allocation Processes." *International Review of Law and Economics* 8 (June 1988b):73–84.

———. *The Enterprise of Law: Justice Without the State*. San Francisco: Pacific Research Institute for Public Policy, 1990.

———. "Are Public Goods Really Common Pools: Considerations of the Evolution of Policing and Highways in England." *Economic Inquiry*, forthcoming, a.

———. "Third Thoughts on Contracting Out." *Journal of Libertarian Studies*, forthcoming, b.

Benson, Bruce L., and John Baden. "The Political Economy of Government Corruption: The Logic of Underground Government." *Journal of Legal Studies* 14 (June 1985):391–410.

Benson, Bruce L., and M. Greenhut. "Interest Groups, Bureaucrats and Antitrust: An Explanation of the Antitrust Paradox." In *Antitrust and Regulation*, edited by Ronald E. Grieson, 53–90. Lexington, Mass.: Lexington Books, 1986.

Benson, Bruce L., Iljoong Kim, and David W. Rasmussen. "The War on Drugs: Marginal Deterrence and Tradeoffs in the Allocation of Police Resources." (Working paper, Florida State University, Department of Economics, Tallahassee, 1992.)

———. "Estimating Deterrence Effects: A Public Choice Perspective on the Economics of Crime Literature," *Southern Economic Journal* (July 1994).

Benson, Bruce L., Iljoong Kim, David W. Rasmussen, and Thomas W. Zuehlke. "Is Property Crime Caused by Drug Use or Drug Enforcement Policy." *Applied Economics* 24 (July 1992):679–692.

Benson, Bruce L., and David W. Rasmussen. "The Relationship Between Illicit Drug Enforcement Policy and Property Crimes." *Contemporary Policy Issues* 9 (October 1991):106–115.

———. "Illinois' War on Drugs: Some Unintended Consequences." Chicago, Ill.: The Heartland Institute, April, 1992.

Benson, Bruce L., David W. Rasmussen, and David L. Sollars. "Police Bureaucracies, Their Incentives, and the War on Drugs." *Public Choice*, forthcoming.

(Working paper, Florida State University, Department of Economics, 1992.)

Benson, Bruce L., and Laurin A. Wollan, Jr. "Prison Overcrowding and Judicial Incentives." *Madison Paper Series* 3 (May 1989):1–21.

Berk, Richard, Harold Brackman, and Selma Lesser. *A Measure of Justice: An Empirical Study of Changes in the California Penal Code, 1955-1971.* New York: Academic Press, 1977.

Block, Michael K., and John M. Heineke. "A Labor Theoretic Analysis of the Criminal Choice." *American Economic Review* 65 (1975):314–325.

Blumberg, Abraham. "The Practice of Law as a Confidence Game: Organizational Co-option of a Profession." *Law and Society Review* 1 (June 1967):15–39.

———. *Criminal Justice.* Chicago: Quadrangle Books, 1970.

———. *Criminal Justice: Issues and Ironies.* 2d ed. New York: New Viewpoints, 1979.

Bonnie, Richard J., and Charles Whitebread II. *The Marijuana Conviction: A History of Marijuana Prohibition in the United States.* Charlottesville: University of Virginia Press, 1974.

Brace, Paul, and Melinda Gann Hall. "Neo-Institutionalism and Dissent in State Supreme Courts." *Journal of Politics* 52, no. 1 (February 1990):54–70.

Brecher, Edward M., and editors of *Consumer Reports. Licit and Illicit Drugs.* Boston: Little, Brown & Co., 1972.

Breton, Albert, and Ronald Wintrobe. "The Equilibrium Size of a Budget Maximizing Bureau." *Journal of Political Economy* 83 (February 1975):195–207.

———. *The Logic of Bureaucratic Control.* Cambridge: Cambridge University Press, 1982.

Brier, S., and S. E. Fienberg. "Recent Econometric Modelling of Crime and Punishment: Support for the Deterrence Hypothesis." *Evaluation Review* 4 (1980):147–191.

Brown, George F., and L. P. Silverman. "The Retail Price of Heroin: Estimation and Application." *Journal of the American Statistical Association* (1974):595–596.

Buchanan, David R. "A Social History of American Drug Use." *Journal of Drug Issues* 22, no. 1 (1992):31–52.

Byrne, James M. *Probation.* Washington, D.C.: National Institute of Justice, GPO, 1988.

Cameron, Samuel. "The Economics of Crime Deterrence: A Survey of Theory and Evidence." *Kyklos* 41 (1988):301–323.

Canadian Government's Commission of Inquiry. *Interim Report: The Non-Medical Use of Drugs.* New York: Penguin, 1973.

Carmines, Edward G., and James A. Stimson. *Issue Evolution: Race and the Transformation of American Politics.* Princeton: Princeton University Press, 1989.

Cave, Jonathan A. K., and Peter Reuter. "The Interdictor's Lot: A Dynamic Model of the Market for Drug Smuggling Services." *A Rand Note* (February 1988):1–36.

Chaiken, Jan M., and Marcia R. Chaiken. "Drugs and Predatory Crime." In *Drugs and Crime*, edited by Michael Tonry and James Q. Wilson. Chicago: University of Chicago Press, 1990.

Chaiken, Marcia R. "The Rise of Crack and Ice: Experiences in Three Locales." National Institute of Justice, *Research in Brief* (March 1993).

Chaloupka, Frank J., and Adit Laixuthai. "Do Youths Substitute Alcohol and Marijuana? Some Econometric Evidence." Mimeo, November 1992.

Chaloupka, Frank J., Henry Saffer, and Michael Grossman. "Alcohol-control Policies and Motor-vehicle Fatalities." *The Journal of Legal Studies* 22 (January 1993):161–186.

Chambliss, William, and Robert Seidman. *Crime and the Legal Process*. New York: McGraw-Hill, 1960.

———. *Law, Order, and Power*. Reading, Mass.: Addison-Wesley Publishing, 1971.

Chant, J.F., and K. Acheson. "The Choice of Monetary Instruments and the Theory of Bureaucracy." *Public Choice* 12 (Spring 1972):13–34.

Chapple, S. *Outlaws in Babylon: "Shocking True Adventures on America's Marijuana Frontier."* London, England: Angus and Robertson, 1984.

Chein, Isidor, Donald L. Gerard, Robert S. Lee, and Eva Rosenfeld. *The Road to H: Narcotics, Delinquency and Social Policy*. New York: Basic Books, 1965.

Church, Thomas, Jr., Kenneth W. Chantry, and Larry L. Sipes. *Justice Delayed: The Pace of Litigation in Urban Trial Courts*. Williamsburg, Va.: National Center for State Courts, 1978.

Congleton, Roger D. "Competitive Process, Competitive Waste and Institutions." In *Toward a Theory of the Rent-seeking Society*, edited by James M. Buchanan, Robert Tollison, and Gordon Tullock. College Station: Texas A&M University Press, 1980.

Cook, Beverly Blair. "Judicial Policy: Change over Time." *American Journal of Political Science* 23 (February 1979):208–214.

Cook, Philip J. "The Demand and Supply of Criminal Opportunities." In *Crime and Justice: An Annual Review of Research*, edited by Michael Tonry and Norval Morris, vol. 7. Chicago: University of Chicago Press, 1986.

Cooper, H. A. "Plea Bargaining: A Comparative Analysis." *International Law and Policy* 5 (1972).

Cotts, Cynthia. "The Year of the Rat: New Drug Laws Are Creating a Cadre of Unreliable and Unsavory Witnesses." *Reason* (May 1992):36–41.

Council of State Governments. *The Books of States*. Lexington, Ky.: Council of State Governments, various years.

Craig, Steven G. "The Deterrent Impact of Police: An Examination of a Locally Provided Public Service." *Journal of Urban Economics* 21 (1987):298–311.

Crain, Mark, and Robert Tollison. "Constitutional Change in an Interest Group Perspective." *Journal of Legal Studies* 8 (January 1979):165–175.

Criminal Justice Estimating Conference. Final Report of the Florida Consensus. The Florida Legislature, February, 1991.

Crow, John E. "Subterranean Politics: A Judge Is Chosen." *Journal of Public Law* 12 (1963):275–289.

Cuskey, W.R., L.H. Berger, and A.H. Richardson. "The Effects of Marijuana Decriminalization on Drug Use Patterns: A Literature Review and Critique." *Contemporary Drug Problems* (Winter 1978):491–532.

Dawson, John M. "Prosecutors in State Courts, 1990." *Bureau of Justice Statistics Bulletin* (March 1992).

Demsetz, Harold. "Toward a Theory of Property Rights." American Economic Review 57 (May 1967):347–359.

————. "Why Regulate Utilities?" *Journal of Law and Economics* 11 (April 1968):55–65.

Dennis, Richard. *Towards a Moral Drug Policy*. Washington, D.C.: The Cato Institute, 1990.

Dickson, Donald. "Bureaucracy and Morality: An Organizational Perspective on a Moral Crusade." *Social Problems* 16 (Fall 1968):142–156.

DiNardo, John. "A Critical Review of the Estimates of the 'Cost' of Alcohol and Drug Use." Irvine Economic Papers No. 90-92-18, March 1992.

DiNardo, John, and Thomas Lemieux. "Alcohol, Marijuana, and American Youth: The Unintended Consequences of Government Regulation." Irvine Economic Papers No. 90-92-17, March 1992.

Donegan, Nelson H., Judith Rodin, Charles P. O'Brian, and Richard Soloman. "A Learning-theory Approach to Commonalities." In *Commonalities in Substance Abuse and Habitual Behavior*, edited by Peter K. Levison, Dean R. Gerstein, and Deborah R. Maloff. Lexington, Mass.: D.C. Heath, 1983.

Downie, Leonard, Jr. *Justice Denied: The Case for Reform of the Courts*. New York: Praeger, 1971.

Downs, Anthony. *Inside Bureaucracy*. Boston: Little, Brown, 1967.

Downs, Anthony. "Up and Down with Ecology—The 'issue-attention cycle.' " *The Public Interest* 28 (1972):38–50.

Drechsel, Robert E. "Accountability, Representation, and the Communication Behavior of Trial Judges." *Western Political Quarterly* 40, no. 4 (December 1987):685–702.

Drug Enforcement Administration (DEA). Office of Intelligence, Strategic Intelligence Section, Domestic Unit. *Illegal Drug Price/Purity Report, United States*. Washington, D.C.: U.S. Department of Justice, Drug Enforcement Administration, various years.

DuPont, Robert, and Mark H. Greene. "The Dynamics of a Heroin Addiction Epidemic." *Science* 181 (August 24, 1972):716–722.

Dye, Thomas R. *Politics in States and Communities*. 7th ed. Englewood Cliffs, Prentice-Hall, 1991.

Easterbrook, Frank H. "Criminal Procedure and a Market System." *Journal of Legal Studies* 12 (June 1983):289–332.

Eatherly, Billy J. "Drug-Law Enforcement: Should We Arrest Pushers or Users?" *Journal of Political Economy* 82 (January/February 1974):210–214.

Ehrlich, Isaac, and Joel C. Gibbons. "On the Measurement of the Deterrent Effect of Capital Punishment and the Theory of Deterrence." *Journal of Legal Studies* 6 (January 1977):35–50.

Eisenstein, James. *Politics and the Legal Process*. New York: Harper & Row, 1973.

Eisenstein, James, and Herbert Jacob. *Felony Justice: An Organizational Analysis of Criminal Courts*. Boston: Little, Brown, 1977.

Elliot, Nicholas. "Economic Analysis of Crime and the Criminal Justice System." In *Public Law and Public Policy*, edited by John Gardiner, 68–89. New York: Praeger, 1977.

Erickson, Edward. "The Social Costs of the Discovery and Suppression of the Clandestine Distribution of Heroin." *Journal of Political Economy* 77 (July/-August 1969):484–486.

Fagan, Jeffrey. "Intoxication and Aggression." In *Drugs and Crime*, edited by Michael Tonry and J.Q. Wilson. Chicago: The University of Chicago Press, 1990.

Fernandez, Raul A. "The Clandestine Distribution of Heroin, Its Discovery and Suppression: A Comment." *Journal of Political Economy* 77 (July/August 1969):487–488.

Finn, Peter, and Andrea K. Newlyn. "Miami's 'Drug Court': A Different Approach." U.S. Department of Justice, National Institute of Justice, Program Focus, June 1993.

Fisher, Irving. "The Economics of Prohibition." *American Economic Review: Supplement* 17 (March 1927a):5–10.

———. *Prohibition at Its Worst*. rev. ed. New York: Houghton Mifflin Co., 1927b.

Fleisher, Belton. *The Economics of Delinquency*. Chicago: Quadrangle Books, 1966a.

———. "The Effects of Income on Delinquency." *American Economic Review* 56 (March 1966b):118–137.

Fleming, M. "The Laws' Delay: The Dragon Slain Friday Breathes Again Monday." *Public Interest* 32 (1973):13–33.

Florida Department of Corrections. *Annual Report*. Tallahassee, various years.

Furlong, W.J., and S.L. Mehay. "Urban Law Enforcement in Canada: An Empirical Analysis." *Canadian Journal of Economics* 14 (1981):44–57.

Galliher, J., and A. Walker. "The Puzzle of the Social Origins of the Marijuana Tax Act of 1937." *Social Problems* 24 (1977).

Gandossy, R.P., J.R. Williams, J. Cohen, and H.J. Harwood. *Drugs and Crime: A Survey and Analysis of the Literature*. Washington, D.C.: National Institute of Justice, GPO, 1980.

Gerstein, D.R., L.L. Judd, and S.A. Rovner. "Career Dynamics of Female Heroin Addicts." *American Journal of Drug and Alcohol Abuse* 6 (1979).

Gest, Ted. "Crackdown on Judges Who Go Astray." *U.S. News and World Report* (February 28, 1983):42.

Gill, Andrew M., and Robert J. Michaels. "Drug Use and Earnings: Accounting for the Self-Section of Drug Users." (Working Paper no. 11-90, Department of Economics, California State University, Fullerton, 1990.)

Girodo, Michel. "Drug Corruption of Undercover Agents: Measuring the Risk." *Behavioral Sciences and the Law* 9 (1991):361–370.

Glaser, Daniel. *Crime in Our Changing Society*. New York: Holt, Rinehart and Winston, 1978.

Glick, Henry R., and George W. Pruet, Jr. "Crime, Public Opinion and Trial Courts: An Analysis of Sentencing Policy." *Justice Quarterly* 2, no. 3 (September 1985):319–343.

Glick, Henry R., and Kenneth N. Vines. *State Court Systems*. Englewood Cliffs, N.J.: Prentice-Hall, 1973.

Goldstein, Paul J. "Drugs and Violent Crime." In *Pathways to Criminal Violence*, edited by Neil A. Weiner and Marvin E. Wolfgang. Newbury Park, Calif.: Sage Publications, 1989.

Gonzalez, Rodolfo A., R.N. Folsom, and Stephen L. Mehay. "Bureaucracy, Publicness and Local Government Expenditures Revisited: Comment." *Public Choice* 62 (July 1989):71–77.

Gonzalez, Rodolfo A., and Stephen L. Mehay. "Bureaucracy and the Divisibility of Local Public Goods." *Public Choice* 45 (1985):89–101.

———. "Economies of City Size in a Price Searcher Model of Local Government." *Public Finance* 42, no. 2 (1987): 236–249.

Gordon, H. Scott. "The Economic Theory of a Common Property Resource: The Fishery." *Journal of Political Economy* 62 (April 1954): 124–142.

Gottfredson, Michael R., and Travis Hirschi. *A General Theory of Crime*. Stanford: Stanford University Press, 1990.

Gould, Leroy C. "Criminal Episodes: An Interactionist Approach to Crime, Criminality and Criminal Behavior." Manuscript, Florida State University, Tallahassee, 1990.

Gould, Leroy C., Andrew L. Walker, Lansing E. Crane, and Charles W. Lidz. *Connections: Notes from the Heroin World*. New Haven: Yale University Press, 1974.

Greenberg, S. W., and F. Alder. "Crime and Addiction: An Empirical Analysis of the Literature, 1920–1973." *Contemporary Drug Problems* 3 (1974).

Greenhut, Melvin L., and Bruce L. Benson. *American Antitrust Law in Theory and Practice*. Aldershot, England: Avebury, 1989.

Grogger, J. "Certainty vs. Severity of Punishment." *Economic Inquiry* 29, no. 2 (April 1991):297–309.

Gropper, Bernard. *Probing the Links between Drugs and Crime*. Washington, D.C.: National Institute of Justice, 1985.

Grosman, Brian. *The Prosecutor: An Inquiry into the Exercise of Discretion*. Toronto: University of Toronto Press, 1969.

Gusfield, Joseph. *The Culture of Public Problems*. Chicago: University of Chicago Press, 1980.

Haaga, John G., and Peter Reuter. "The Limits of the Czar's Ukase: Drug Policy at the Local Level." *Yale Law and Policy Review* 8 (1990):36–74.

Hackett, Judith, Harry Hatry, Robert B. Levinson, Joan Allen, Keon Chi, and Edward D. Feigenbaum. *Issues in Contracting for the Private Operation of Prisons and Jails*. Washington, D.C.: National Institute of Justice, October 1987.

Hakim, Simon, Uriel Speigel, and J. Weinblatt. "Substitution, Size Effects, and the Composition of Property Crime." *Social Science Quarterly* 65 (September 1984):717–734.

Hardin, Garrett. "The Tragedy of the Commons." In *Population, Evolution, and Birth Control*, 2d ed., edited by G. Hardin. 367–381. San Francisco: W. H. Freeman & Co., 1969.

Hardin, Garrett, and John Baden, eds. *Managing the Commons*. San Francisco: W. H. Freeman & Co., 1977.

Harlow, Caroline Wolf. "Drugs and Jail Inmates, 1989." In *Bureau of Justice Statistics: Special Report*. Washington, D.C.: U.S. Department of Justice, Bureau of Justice Statistics, August 1991.

Hebert, Eugene E. "NIJ's Drug Market Analysis Program." *National Institute of Justice Journal*, no. 226 (April 1993):2–7.

Helmer, John. *Drugs and Minority Oppression*. New York: Seabury Press, 1975.

Heumann, Milton. *Plea Bargaining: The Experience of Prosecutors, Judges and Defense Attorneys*. Chicago: University of Chicago Press, 1978.

Hill, Stuart. *Crime, Power and Morality: The Criminal Law Process in the United States*. Scranton, Pa.: Chandler Publishing, 1971.

Himmelstein, Jerome L. *The Strange Career of Marijuana: Politics and Ideology of Drug Control in America*. Westport, Conn.: Greenwood Press, 1983.

Hoffman, Peter, and James Beck. "Burnout-Age at Release from Prison and Recidivism." *Journal of Criminal Justice* 12 (1984):617–623.

———. "Recidivism Among Released Federal Prisoners." *Criminal Justice and Behavior* 12, no. 4 (1985):501–507.

Holahan, John. "The Economics of Control of the Illegal Supply of Heroin." *Public Finance Quarterly* 1 (1973):467–477.

Hotelling, Harold. "Stability in Competition." *Economic Journal* 39 (March 1929):41–57.

Illinois Criminal Justice Information Authority. *Trends and Issues 89: Criminal and Juvenile Justice in Illinois* (March 1989).

Illinois Department of Corrections. *Adult Correctional Center Capacity Survey II*. Springfield: Illinois Department of Corrections, 1989a.

———. *Fiscal Year 1989 Annual Report*. Springfield: Illinois Department of Corrections, 1989b.

Innes, Christopher A. "Drug Use and Crime." *Bureau of Justice Statistics Special Bulletin*. Washington, D.C.: U.S. Department of Justice, 1988.

Jacob, Herbert, ed. *The Potential for Reform of Criminal Justice*. Sage Criminal Justice System Annuals, vol. 3. Beverly Hills: Sage Publishing, 1974.

Johnson, Bruce, Paul Goldstein, Edward Preble, James Schmeidler, Douglas S. Lipton, Barry Spunt, and Thomas Miller. *Taking Care of Business: The Economics of Crime by Heroin Abusers*. Lexington, Mass.: Lexington Books, 1985.

Johnson, Elaine M. "Cocaine: The American Experience." In *The Cocaine Crisis*, edited by David F. Allen. New York: Plenum Press, 1987.

Johnson, Ronald N., and Gary D. Libecap. "Agency Growth, Salaries and the Protected Bureaucrat." *Economic Inquiry* 27 (July 1989):431–451.

Jones, David. *Crime Without Punishment*. Lexington, Mass.: Lexington Books, 1979.

Justice Research Associates. "Quantitative Assessment of Factors Impacting Prison Populations." Report of the Office of Planning and Budgeting, Office of the Governor, Tallahassee, Fla., 1988.

Kaestner, Robert. "The Effects of Illicit Drug Use on the Wages of Young Adults." *Journal of Labor Economics* 9, no. 4 (1991):381–412.

Kakalik, James S., and Sorrel Wildhorn. *Private Police in the United States: Findings and Recommendations*. Santa Monica, Calif.: The Rand Corporation, 1971.

Kaplan, John. "The Prosecutorial Discretion: A Comment." *Northwestern Law Review* 6 (1965).

———. *Marijuana: The New Prohibition*. New York: World Publishing Co., 1970.

———. *The Hardest Drug: Heroin and Public Policy*. Chicago: University of Chicago Press, 1983.

Katzenelson, Susan, and Charles McDanal. *Sentencing Guidelines and Judicial Discretion in the Federal Court System*. Washington, D.C.: U.S. Sentencing Commission, GPO, 1991.

Kennedy, David M. "Closing the Market: Controlling the Drug Trade in Tampa, Florida." In *Program Focus*. Washington: National Institute of Justice, March 1993.

Kennett, David. "Standards and Procedures for the Distribution of a Public Service: Shoup Revisited." *Public Finance* 37, no. 1 (1982):80–97.

Kim, Iljoong, Bruce L. Benson, and David W. Rasmussen. "Courts Coddling Criminals: An Opportunity Cost of the War on Drugs." (Working paper, Florida State University, Department of Economics, Tallahassee, 1992.)

Kim, Iljoong, Bruce L. Benson, David W. Rasmussen, and Thomas W. Zuehlke. "An Economic Analysis of Recidivism among Drug Offenders." *Southern Economic Journal* 60 (July 1993):169–183.

King, R. "Narcotic Drug Laws and Enforcement Policies." *Law and Contemporary Problems* 22 (1957).

———. "Drug Abuse Problems and the Idioms of War." *Journal of Drug Issues* 8 (1978).

Kleiman, Mark A.R. *Marijuana: Costs of Abuse, Costs of Control*. New York: Greenwood Press, 1985.

———. *Against Excess: Drug Policy for Results*. Champaign, Ill.: Basic Books, 1992.

Klein, Dorie. "Ill and Against the Law: The Social and Medical Control of Heroin Users." *Journal of Drug Issues* 13 (Winter 1983):31–55.

Knapp, Whitman. *The Knapp Commission Report on Police Corruption*. New York: George Braziller, 1972.

Koch, James V., and Stanley E. Grupp. "The Economics of Drug Control." *The International Journal of the Addictions* (December 1971):571–584.

Kozel, Nicholas. *Epidemiology of Heroin: 1964–84*. Rockville, Md.: National Institute on Drug Abuse, 1985.

Kozel, Nicholas, and Edgar H. Adams, eds. *Cocaine Use in America: Epidemiologic and Clinical Perspectives*. Rockville, Md.: National Institute on Drug Abuse, 1985.

Kress, Shirley E. "Niskanen Effects in the California Community Colleges." *Public Choice* 61 (May 1989):127–140.

Kuklinski, J. H., and J. E. Stanga. "Political Participation and Governmental Responsiveness: The Behavior of California Superior Courts." *American Political Science Review* 73 (December 1979):1091–1099.

Kunnes, Richard. *The American Heroin Empire: Power, Profits, and Politics*. New York: Dodd, Mead, 1972.

Lacayo, Richard. "Passing Judgement on the Judges: A Spate of Legal Trouble for the Judiciary." *Time* (January 20,1986):66.

Landes, William M., and Richard A. Posner. "The Independent Judiciary in an Interest Group Perspective." *Journal of Law and Economics* 18 (1975):875–901.

Langan, Patrick A., and Mark Cunniff. "Recidivism of Felons on Probation, 1986–89." In *Bureau of Justice Statistics: Special Report*. Washington, D.C.: U.S. Department of Justice, Bureau of Justice Statistics, February 1992.

Lawrence, Richard. "The Impact of Sentencing Guidelines on Corrections." Paper presented at the annual meeting of the Academy of Criminal Justice Sciences, 1991.

Leipziger, Danny M. "The Economics of Burglary: A Note." In *Readings in Correctional Economics*, edited by Correctional Economic Center, 29–34. Washington, D.C.: Correctional Economics Center of the American Bar Association, 1975.

Levine, Daniel, Peter Stoloff, and Nancy Spruill. "Public Drug Treatment and Addict Crime." *Journal of Legal Studies* 5 (June 1976):435–462.

Lindesmith, Alfred. *The Addict and the Law*. New York: Vintage Press, 1965.

Lott, John R. "An Attempt at Measuring the Total Monetary Penalty from Drug Convictions." (Working paper, Anderson Graduate School, University of California, Los Angeles, July 1990.)

Luce, Duncan R., and Howard Raiffa. *Games and Decisions*. New York: Wiley Publishing Co., 1957.

Lukoff, Irving F. "Issues in the Evaluation of Heroin Treatment." In *Drug Use: Epidemiological and Sociological Approaches*, edited by E. Josephson and

E.E. Carroll. New York: John Wiley, 1974.

McCarthy, Patrick, and James Ziliak. "The Effect of MADD on Drunk-driving Activities: An Empirical Study." *Applied Economics* 22 (1990):1215–1227.

McCormick, Robert, and Robert Tollison. *Politicians, Legislation, and the Economy: An Inquiry into the Interest Group Theory of Government*. Boston: Martinus Nijhoff Publishing, 1981.

McDonald, Donald C. *The Cost of Corrections: In Search of the Bottom Line*. Washington, D.C.: National Institute of Corrections, 1989.

McDonald, William F. "The Role of the Victim in America." In *Assessing the Criminal: Restitution and the Legal Process*, edited by Randy. E. Barnett and John Hagel III. Cambridge, Mass.: Ballinger Press, 1977.

McGlothlin, W.H., D.M. Anglin, and B.D. Wilson. "Narcotic Addiction and Crime." *Criminology* 16 (1978).

McGlothlin, W., K. Jamison, and S. Rosenblatt. "Marijuana and the Use of Other Drugs." *Nature* 228 (1970):1227–1229.

McPheters, Lee R., and William Stronge. "Crime Spillover in the Boston Area." In *Crime Spillover*, edited by Simon Hakim and G. F. Rengert, 83–95. Beverly Hills: Sage Publications, 1981.

Massing, Michael. "What Ever Happened to the 'War on Drugs'?" *The New York Review* (June 11, 1992):42-46.

Mbaku, John M. "Military Expenditures and Bureaucratic Competition for Rents." *Public Choice* 71 (August 1991):19–31.

Mehay, Stephen L. "Interjurisdictional Spillovers of Urban Police Services." *Southern Economic Journal* 43 (1977):1352–1359.

———. "Burglary Spillover in Los Angeles." In *Crime Spillover*, edited by Simon Hakim and G. F. Rengert, 67–82. Beverly Hills: Sage Publications, 1981.

Meier, Kenneth J. "The Politics of Drug Abuse: Laws, Implementation, and Consequences." *The Western Political Quarterly* (1991):41–69.

Mendelson, Jack H., and Nancy K. Mello. *Alcohol: Use and Abuse in America*. Boston: Little, Brown, 1985.

Michaels, Robert J. "The Market for Heroin Before and After Legalization." In *Dealing with Drugs*, edited by Robert Hamowy. Lexington, Mass.: Lexington Books, 1987.

Milakovich, Michael, and Kurt Weis. "Politics and Measures of Success in the War on Crime." *Crime and Delinquency* 21 (January 1975):1–10.

Miller, Gary J. "Bureaucratic Compliance as a Game on the Unit Square." *Public Choice* 19 (Spring 1977):37–51.

Miller, Richard L. *The Case for Legalizing Drugs*. New York: Praeger, 1991.

Miqué, Jean–Luc, and Gerard Belanger. "Towards a General Theory of Managerial Discretion." *Public Choice* 17 (Spring 1974):27–43.

Miron, Jeffery A. "Drug Legalization and the Consumption of Drugs: An Economist's Perspective." In *Searching for Alternatives: Drug Control Policy in the United States*, edited by M.B. Krauss and E.P. Laze, 68–76. Palo Alto, Calif.: Hoover Institution Press, 1991.

———. "An Economic Analysis of Drug Prohibition." *Espana Economica* (April 1992):62–72.

Misket, T.C., and F. Vakil. "Some Estimates of Price and Expenditure Elasticities Among UCLA Students." *Review of Economics and Statistics* 54 (1972):474–475.

Model, Karyn E. "The Relationship Between Drug and Alcohol Use and Income: An Econometric Model." Mimeo, Harvard University, August 1991.

———. "The Effect of Marijuana Decriminalization on Hospital Emergency Drug Episodes: 1975–78." *Journal of the American Statistical Association* (1993):737-747.

Moore, Mark H. "Policies to Achieve Discrimination on the Effective Price of Heroin." *American Economic Review* 63 (May 1973):270–277.

———. *Buy and Bust: The Effective Regulation of an Illicit Market in Heroin.* Lexington Mass.: Lexington Books, 1977.

———. "Supply Reduction and Drug Law Enforcement." In *Drugs and Crime*, edited by Michael Tonry and James Q. Wilson. Chicago: University of Chicago Press, 1990.

Moore, Mark H., and Mark A. R. Kleiman. "The Police and Drugs," Perspectives on Policing No. 11. Washington, D.C.: National Institute of Justice, September 1989.

Morgan, Patricia A. "The Political Economy of Drugs and Alcohol." *Journal of Drug Issues* 13 (Winter 1983):1–7.

Murphy, Walter, and C. Herman Pritchett. *Courts, Judges, and Politics*. New York: Random House, 1961.

Musto, David F. *The American Disease: Origins of Narcotic Control*. New Haven, Conn.: Yale University Press, 1987.

———. "Opium, Cocaine and Marijuana in American History." *Scientific American* (July 1991):40–47.

Myers, Samuel L., Jr. "The Rehabilitation Effect of Punishment." *Economic Inquiry* 18 (1980a):353–366.

———. "Why Are Crimes Underreported? What Is the Crime? Does It Really Matter?" *Social Science Quarterly* 61, no. 1 (1980b):23–43.

———. "Crime in Urban Areas: New Evidence and Results." *Journal of Urban Economics* 11 (March 1982):148–158.

———. "Estimating the Economic Model of Crime: Employment Versus Punishment Effects." *Quarterly Journal of Economics* 98 (1983):157–166.

———. "Crime, Entrepreneurship and Labor Force Withdrawal." *Contemporary Policy Issues* 10 (April 1992):84–98.

Nadelmann, Ethan A. "Drug Prohibition in the United States: Costs, Consequences, and Alternatives." *Science* (September 1, 1989):939–947.

———. "Should We Legalize Drugs? History Answers Yes." *American Heritage* (February/March 1993):42-48.

Nardulli, P. *The Courtroom Elite: An Organization Perspective on Criminal Justice*. New York: Ballinger, 1978.

NASDAD (National Association of State Alcohol and Drug Abuse Directors). *Treatment Works*. Washington, D.C.: NASDAD, March 1990.

National Commission on Marijuana and Drug Abuse. *Drug Use in America: The Problem in Perspective, Second Report*. Washington, D.C.: GPO, 1973.

National Criminal Justice Association. *Asset Seizure and Forfeiture: Developing and Maintaining a State Capability*. Washington, D.C.: GPO, June 1988.

National Institute on Drug Abuse (NIDA). *National Household Survey of Drug Abuse*. Washington, D.C.: Department of Health and Human Services, GOP, 1985.

———. *National Household Survey of Drug Abuse*. Washington, D.C.: Department of Health and Human Services, GPO, 1988.

———. *National Household Survey on Drug Abuse: Main Findings, 1990*. Washington, D.C.: Department of Health and Human Services, GPO, 1991.

National Institute of Justice. *Drug Use Forecasting*. Washington, D.C.: U.S. Department of Justice, National Institute of Justice, 1990.

———. *Drug Using Forecasting: Drugs and Crime, 1990*. Washington, D.C.: U.S. Department of Justice, National Institute of Justice, August 1991.

Neely, Richard. *Why Courts Don't Work*. New York: McGraw-Hill, 1982.

New York State Narcotic Addiction Control Commission. *An Assessment of Drug Use in the General Population*. New York: New York State Narcotic Addiction Control Commission, 1971.

Nicholson, Walter. *Microeconomic Theory*, 3d ed. Chicago: Dryden Press, 1985.

Niskanen, William A. "The Peculiar Economics of Bureaucracy." *American Economic Review* 58 (May 1968):293–305.

———. *Bureaucracy and Representative Government*. Chicago: Aldine-Atherton, 1971.

———. "Bureaucrats and Politicians." *Journal of Law and Economics* 18 (December 1975):617-643.

Nurco, David N., John C. Ball, John W. Shaffer, and Thomas E. Hanlon. "The Criminality of Narcotic Addicts." *Journal of Nervous and Mental Disease* 173, no. 2 (1985):94–102.

Nurco, David N., Thomas E. Hanlon, and Timothy W. Kinlock, "Recent Research on the Relationship Between Illicit Drug Use and Crime." *Behavioral Sciences and the Law* (1991):221–249.

Nyswander, Marie. *The Drug Addict as Patient*. New York: Grune and Stratton, 1956.

Oerther, Frederick J. "An Economic Analysis of Victimless Crime Laws: Drug Law as a Negative Sum Game." Mimeo, Greensboro College, November 1991.

———. "Anti-Drug Pork Barrel, Ideology, and Marginal Politics: A Prohibition Index for the 102nd Congress." Mimeo, Greensboro College, August 1992.

Office of National Drug Control Strategy. *National Drug Control Strategy*. Washington, D.C.: GPO, 1989.

Oteri, Joseph, and Harvey Silvergate. "In the Marketplace of Free Ideas: A Look at the Passage of the Marihuana Tax Act." In *Marihuana: Myths and Realities*, edited by J. L. Simmons. North Hollywood: Branden House, 1968.

Parker, Glenn R. *Institutional Change, Discretion, and the Making of the Modern Congress*. Ann Arbor: University of Michigan Press, 1992.

Pate, Tony, Amy Ferrara, Robert A. Bowers, and Jon Lorence. *Police Response Time: Its Determinants and Effects*. Washington, D.C.: Police Foundation, 1976.

Peltason, Jack. *Federal Courts in the Political Process*. New York: Random House, 1955.

Peltzman, Sam. "Toward a More General Theory of Regulation." *Journal of Law and Economics* 19 (August 1976):211–240.

———. "Constituent Interest and Congressional Voting." *Journal of Law and Economics* 27 (April 1984):181-210.

Person, Carl. "Justice Inc." *Juris Doctor* 8 (March 1978).

Phillips, Llad. "The Political Economy of Drug Enforcement in California." *Contemporary Policy Issues* 10 (January 1992):91–100.

Phillips, Llad, Harold Votey, and Donald Maxwell. "Crime, Youth and the Labor Market." *Journal of Political Economy* 80 (June 1972):491–501.

Polinsky, A. Mitchell. "Detrebling versus Decoupling Antitrust Damages: Lessons from the Theory of Enforcement." In *Private Antitrust Litigation*, edited by L. J. White. Cambridge, Mass.: MIT Press, 1988.

Press, Aric, and Mark Starr. "The Friends of David T: A Prosecutor on Trial." *Newsweek* (February 10, 1986):68.

Pruet, George W., Jr., and Henry R. Glick. "Social Environment, Public Opinion, and Judicial Policymaking: A Search for Judicial Representation." *American Politics Quarterly* 14, no. 1–2 (January–April 1986):5–33.

Quinney, Richard. *The Social Reality of Crime*. Boston: Little, Brown, 1970.

Rasmussen, David W., Bruce L. Benson, and Iljoong Kim. "A Benefit–Cost Study of Alternative Sentencing Guidelines." Report prepared under contract with the Florida House Appropriations Committee, Tallahassee, July 1991.

Rasmussen, David W., Bruce L. Benson, Iljoong Kim, and Thomas W. Zuehlke. "An Economic Analysis of Drug Crime in Florida." Report prepared under contract with the Joint Legislative Management Committee of the Florida Legislature, Tallahassee, December 1990.

Rasmussen, David W., Bruce L. Benson, and Brent D. Mast. "Entrepreneurial Police and Drug Enforcement Policy." (Working paper, Florida State University, Department of Economics, Tallahassee, 1993.)

Rasmussen, David W., Bruce L. Benson, and David L. Sollars. "Spatial Competition in Illicit Drug Markets: The Consequences of Increased Drug Enforcement." *Review of Regional Studies*, forthcoming. (Working paper, Florida State University, Department of Economics, 1992.)

Reaves, Brian A. "Sheriffs' Department 1990." *Bureau of Justice Statistics Bulletin* (February 1992a):1–11.

———. "State and Local Police Departments, 1990." *Bureau of Justice Statistics Bulletin* (February 1992b):1–14.

———. "Drug Enforcement by Police and Sheriffs' Departments, 1990." In *Bureau of Justice Statistics: Special Report*. Washington D.C.: U.S. Department of Justice, Bureau of Justice Statistics, May 1992c.

Reed, Terrance G. "American Forfeiture Law: Property Owners Meet the Prosecutor." *Cato Institute: Policy Analysis* 17 (September 29, 1992).

Reinarman, Craig. "Constraint, Autonomy, and State Policy: Notes Toward a Theory of Controls on Consciousness Alteration." *Journal of Drug Issues* 13 (Winter 1983):9–30.

Research and Forecasts, Inc. *America Afraid: How Fear of Crime Changes the Way We Live*. New York: New America Library, 1983.

Reuter, Peter. "Eternal Hope: America's International Narcotics Efforts." *Public Interest* 79 (Spring 1985):13–94.

———. "On the Consequences of Toughness." In *Searching for Alternatives: Drug Control Policy in the United States*, edited by Edward Lazear and Melvyn Krauss. Pato Alto, Calif.: Hoover Press, 1991.

Reuter, Peter, Gordon Crawford, and Jonathan Cave. *Sealing the Borders: The Effect of Increased Military Participation in Drug Interdiction*. Santa Monica, Calif.: The Rand Corporation, National Defense Research Institute, 1988.

Reuter, Peter, and Mark A.R. Kleiman. "Risks and Prices." In *Crime and Justice: An Annual Review of Research*. vol. 7, edited by Michael Tonry and Norval Morris. Chicago: University of Chicago Press, 1986.

Reuter, Peter, R. MacCoun, and P. Murphy. *Money from Crime: A Study of the Economics of Drug Dealing in Washington, D.C.* Santa Monica, Calif.: The Rand Corporation, 1990.

Rhodes, Robert. *The Insoluble Problems of Crime*. New York: John Wiley and Sons, 1977.

———. "The Criminal Career: Estimates of the Duration and Frequency of Crime Commission." *Journal of Quantitative Criminology* 5, no. 1 (1989):3–32.

Richards, David A. J. *Sex, Drugs, Death, and the Law: An Essay on Human Rights and Overcriminalization.* Ottawa, N.J.: Rowman and Littlefield, 1982.

Rottenberg, Simon. "The Clandestine Distribution of Heroin: Its Discovery and Suppression." *Journal of Political Economy* 76 (January/February 1968):78–90.

Roumasset, J., and John Hadreas. "Addicts, Fences, and the Market for Stolen Goods." *Public Finance Quarterly* (April 1977):247–272.

Rubin, Paul. "The Economics of Crime." *Atlantic Economic Review* 43 (July/August, 1978).

———. "The Economic Theory of the Criminal Firm." In *The Economics of Crime and Punishment*, edited by S. Rottenberg. Washington, D.C.: American Enterprise Institute, 1979.

Rubenstein, J. *City Police*. New York: Farrar, Straus, Giroux, 1973.

Russell, Bertrand. *Power.* New York: Norton, 1938.

Saltzburg, Stephen A. "Another Victim of Illegal Narcotics: The Fourth Amendment." *University of Pittsburgh Law Review* 48 (1986):1–26.

Schelling, Thomas. "What Is the Business of Organized Crime?" *American Scholar* 40 (Autumn 1971):643–652.

Schmidhauser, John, and Larry Berg. *The Supreme Court and Congress*. New York: Free Press, 1972.

Schmidt, Paul, and Ann Witte. *An Economic Analysis of Crime and Justice: Theory, Methods, Applications*. Orlando: Academic Press, 1988.

Schmidtz, David. *The Limits of Government: An Essay on the Public Goods Argument*. Boulder, Colo.: Westview Press, 1991.

Schmoke, Kurt L. "Another Option: A Public Health Strategy." In *Understanding the Enemy: An Informational Overview of Substance Abuse in Ohio*. Columbus: State of Ohio Governor's Office of Criminal Justice Services, November 1989.

Schulhofer, Stephen J. "Criminal Justice Discretion as a Regulatory System." *Journal of Legal Studies* 17 (January 1988):43–82.

Sherman, Lawrence W., ed. *Police Corruption: A Sociological Perspective*. Garden City, N.Y.: Anchor Books, 1974.

———. *Controlling Police Corruption*. Washington, D.C.: National Institute of Law Enforcement and Criminal Justice, Law Enforcement Assistance Administration, 1978.

———. "Patrol Strategies for Police." In *Crime and Public Policy*, edited by James Q. Wilson. San Francisco: Institute for Contemporary Studies Press, 1983.

Siegel, Ronald K. *Intoxication: Life in Pursuit of Artificial Paradise*. New York: Dutton, 1989.

Silberman, C. E. *Criminal Violence, Criminal Justice*. New York: Random House, 1978.

Silver, S. *Punishment, Deterrence, and Police Effectiveness: A Survey and Critical Interpretation of Recent Econometric Literature*. New York: Crime Deterrence and Offender Career Project, 1974.

Silverman, Lester, and Nancy L. Spruill. "Urban Crime and The Price of Heroin." *Journal of Urban Economics* (January 1977):80–103.

Smith, Bruce, ed. *Police in the United States*. 2d rev. New York: Harper & Row, 1960.

Snell, Tracy L., and Danielle C. Morton. "Prisoners in 1991." *Bureau of Justice Statistics Bulletin* (1992).

Sollars, David L., Bruce L. Benson, and David W. Rasmussen. "Drug Enforcement and Deterrence of Property Crime Among Local Jurisdictions." *Public Finance Quarterly* 22 (1994):22–45.

Stafford, Frank P., and Greg J. Duncan. "Do Union Members Receive Compensating Wage Differentials?" *American Economic Review* 70 (June 1980):355–371.

Starr, Mark, and Michael Reese. "Stinging the Chicago Courts." *Newsweek* (August 22, 1983):21.

Stigler, George J. "The Theory of Economic Regulation." *Bell Journal of Economics and Management Science* 2 (Spring 1971):3–21.

Stigler, George J., and Gary S. Becker. "De Gustibus Non Est Disputandum." *American Economic Review* 67 (March 1977):76–90.

Stroup, Carl. "Standards for Distributing a Free Government Service: Crime Prevention." *Public Finance* 19 (1964):383–392.

Stumpf, Harry P. *American Judicial Politics.* San Diego: Harcourt Brace Jovanovich, 1988.

Stutmann, Robert M., and Richard Esposito. *Dead on Delivery: Inside the Drug Wars, Straight from the Street.* New York: Warner Books, 1992.

Szasz, Thomas. *The Therapeutic State: Psychiatry in the Mirror of Current Events.* Buffalo: Prometheus Books, 1984.

Taylor, John. "Econometric Models of Criminal Behavior: A Review." In *Economic Models of Criminal Behavior*, edited by J. M. Heineke, 35–82. Amsterdam: North Holland, 1978.

Thornton, Mark. *The Economics of Prohibition.* Salt Lake: University of Utah Press, 1991.

Toma, Mark, and Eugenia F. Toma. "Bureaucratic Responses to Tax Limitation Amendments." *Public Choice* 35 (1980):333–348.

Tonry, Michael. "Structuring Sentencing," In *Crime and Justice: A Review of Research*, edited by Michael Tonry and Norval Morris. Chicago: University of Chicago Press, 1988.

Trager, Kenneth, and Michael Clark. *Florida Drug Offender Profile.* Tallahassee: Florida Department of Law Enforcement, Statistical Analysis Center, February 1989.

Trumbull, William N. "Estimation of the Economic Model of Crime Using Aggregate and Individual Level Data." *Southern Economic Journal* (October 1989):423–439.

Tullock, Gordon. *The Politics of Bureaucracy.* Washington, D.C.: Public Affairs Press, 1965.

———. "Adam Smith and the Prisoners' Dilemma." *Quarterly Journal of Economics* 100 (1985):1073–1081.

U.S. Congress. *Comprehensive Drug Penalty Act. Hearings before the Subcommittee on Crime of the Committee on the Judiciary. House of Representatives, on H.R. 4901, 98th Congress, 2nd session, 1985.* Serial no. 136. Washington, D.C.: GPO, 1985.

———. *Federal Drug Forfeiture Activities. Hearings before the Subcommittee on Crime of the Committee on the Judiciary. House of Representatives, 101st Congress, 1st session, 1989.* Serial no. 55. Washington, D.C.: GPO, 1990.

U.S. Department of Health, Education, and Welfare Task Force. *Work in America.* Cambridge, Mass.: MIT Press, 1973.

U.S. Department of Justice. Bureau of Justice Statistics. *Crime in the United States.* Washington, D.C.: GPO, various years, a.

———. *Sourcebook of Criminal Justice Statistics.* Washington, D.C.: GPO, various years, b.

———. "Criminal Defense Systems". Washington, D.C.: GPO, 1984.

———. *Uniform Crime Reports.* Washington, D.C.: GPO, 1984/1989.

———. "Jail Inmates 1987". *Bureau of Justice Statistics Bulletin.* (1988).

———. "Prisoners in 1988." *Bureau of Justice Statistics Bulletin.* (1989).

———. *Criminal Victimization in the United States*. Washington, D.C.: GPO, various years.

———. *Census of State and Federal Correctional Facilities, 1990*. Washington, D.C.: GPO, May 1992.

U.S. Department of Justice. Office of the Attorney General. *Drug Trafficking: A Report to the President of the United States*. Washington, D.C.: GPO, 1989.

———. *Combating Violent Crime: 24 Recommendations to Strengthen Criminal Justice*. Washington, D.C.: GPO, July 1992.

Vaillant, George E. "The Natural History of Urban Narcotic Drug Addiction." In *The Scientific Basis of Drug Addiction*, edited by Hannah Steinberg. New York: Grune and Stratton, 1969.

Vandaele, Walter. "An Econometric Model of Auto Theft in the United States." In *Economic Models of Criminal Behavior*, edited by J. M. Heinke. New York: North Holland Publishing, 1978.

Viscusi, W.K. "The Risks and Rewards of Criminal Activity: A Comprehensive Test of Criminal Deterrence." *Journal of Labor Economics* (July 1986):317–340.

Waldorf, D. *Careers in Dope*. Englewood Cliffs, N.J.: Prentice-Hall, 1973.

Warburton, Clark. *The Economic Results of Prohibition*. New York: Columbia University Press, 1932.

Warren, R. S., Jr. "Bureaucratic Performance and Budgetary Reward." *Public Choice* 24 (Winter 1975):51–57.

Wassertrom, Silas J. "The Incredible Shrinking Fourth Amendment." *American Criminal Law Review* 21 (1983):257–402.

Weisheit, Ralph A. *Domestic Marijuana: A Neglected Industry*. New York: Greenwood Press, 1992.

Westley, William A. *Violence and the Police*. Cambridge, Mass.: MIT Press, 1970.

Wexler, H., G. Galkin, and D. Lipton. *Outcome Evaluation of a Prison Therapeutic Community for Substance-Abuse Treatment*. New York: Narcotic and Drug Research Inc., 1989.

White, Michael D., and William A. Luksetich. "Heroin: Price Elasticity and Enforcement Strategies." *Economic Inquiry* 21 (October 1983):557–564.

Williams, Gregory H. *The Law and Politics of Police Discretion*. Westport, Conn.: Greenwood Press, 1984.

Wilson, James Q. *The Politics of Regulation*. New York: Basic Books, 1980.

———. "Drugs and Crime." In *Drugs and Crime*, edited by Michael Tonry and James Q. Wilson. Chicago: University of Chicago Press, 1990a.

———. "Against the Legalization of Drugs." *Commentary* 89 (1990b):21–28.

Wilson, James Q., and Richard J. Herrnstein. *Crime and Human Nature: The Definitive Study of the Causes of Crime*. New York: Simon and Schuster, 1985.

Winick, C. "Physician Narcotic Addicts." *Social Problems* (Fall 1961).

Winston, Gordon. "Addiction and Backsliding: A Theory of Compulsive Consumption." *Journal of Economic Behavior and Organization* 1 (December

1980):295–324.

Wisotsky, Steven. "Crackdown: The Emerging 'Drug Exception' to the Bill of Rights." *Hastings Law Journal* 3F (1987):889–926.

———. *Beyond the War on Drugs*. Buffalo, N.Y.: Prometheus Books, 1990.

———. "Zero Tolerance/Zero Freedom." Paper presented at the Seventh Annual Critical Issues Symposium, Florida State University, Tallahassee, 1991.

———. "A Society of Suspects: The War on Drugs and Civil Liberties." Policy Analysis No. 180. Washington, D.C.: The Cato Institute, 1992.

Witte, Ann Dryden. "Estimating the Economic Model of Crime with Individual Data." *Quarterly Journal of Economics* 95 (1980):57–84.

———. "Estimating the Economic Model of Crime: Reply." *Quarterly Journal of Economics* 98 (1983):158–175.

Wold, John T., and Greg A. Caldeira. "Perceptions of 'Routine' Decision-Making in Five California Courts of Appeal." *Polity* 13 (1980):334–347.

Wyckoff, Paul Gary. "Bureaucracy and the 'Publicness' of Local Public Goods." *Public Choice* 56 (March 1988):271–284.

———. "Bureaucracy and the 'Publicness' of Local Public Goods: a Reply to Gonzalez, Folsom and Mehay." *Public Choice* 62 (July 1989):79–82.

———. "Bureaucracy, Inefficiency, and Time." *Public Choice* 67 (November 1990a):161–179.

———. "The Simple Analytics of Slack-Maximizing Bureaucracy." *Public Choice* 67 (October 1990b):35–47.

Zimring, Franklin E., and Gordon Hawkins. *The Scale of Imprisonment*. Chicago: The University of Chicago Press, 1991.

———. *The Search for Rational Drug Control*. Cambridge, Mass.: Cambridge University Press, 1992.

Index

About the Authors

Bruce L. Benson is Distinguished Research Professor of Economics at Florida State University. An internationally recognized expert in the law and economics field, Benson is the author of *The Enterprise of Law* (1990). He has also published widely in the fields of public finance, urban and regional economics, and the economics of crime.

David W. Rasmussen is Director of the Policy Sciences Center and Professor of Economics at Florida State University. He has published many articles on public policy questions in the areas of urban and regional economics, labor economics, and the economics of crime. Rasmussen has also served as a consultant to local, state, and federal agencies on urban and regional policy issues.

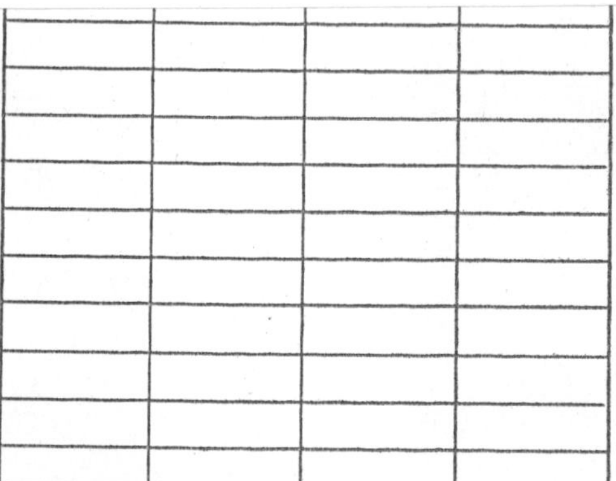